T0291262

The Economics of Accounting

The Economics of Accounting

RICHARD M. FRANKEL

S. P. KOTHARI

LUO ZUO

OXFORD

UNIVERSITY PRESS

OXFORD
UNIVERSITY PRESS

Oxford University Press is a department of the University of Oxford. It furthers
the University's objective of excellence in research, scholarship, and education
by publishing worldwide. Oxford is a registered trade mark of Oxford University
Press in the UK and certain other countries.

Published in the United States of America by Oxford University Press
198 Madison Avenue, New York, NY 10016, United States of America.

Library of Congress Cataloging-in-Publication Data
Names: Frankel, Richard (Richard Moses), author. |
Kothari, S. P., author. | Zuo, Luo, author.
Title: The economics of accounting / Richard M. Frankel,
S. P. Kothari, Luo Zuo.
Description: New York, NY : Oxford University Press, [2024] |
Includes bibliographical references and index.
Identifiers: LCCN 2023057236 (print) | LCCN 2023057237 (ebook) |
ISBN 9780197680766 (hardback) | ISBN 9780197680773 (epub)
Subjects: LCSH: Accounting. | Managerial accounting. | Economics.
Classification: LCC HF5636.F73 2024 (print) | LCC HF5636 (ebook) |
DDC 657—dc23/eng/20240119
LC record available at https://lccn.loc.gov/2023057236
LC ebook record available at https://lccn.loc.gov/2023057237

DOI: 10.1093/oso/9780197680766.001.0001

Printed by Integrated Books International, United States of America

To our families, the bedrock of our lives.
You give us joy, support, and humility.

The Economics of Accounting

"*The Economics of Accounting* is a refreshing and long overdue analysis of the role of accounting in the economy. The authors step back from the deluge of partial results in the literature—most of which is focused on the capital market—and provide the reader with a fine perspective on why accounting exists, what it affects, and in turn what affects the shape it takes. The book should be required reading for all doctoral students and, I suspect, many of their supervisors."

—RAY BALL, Sidney Davidson Distinguished Service Professor of Accounting, University of Chicago

"*The Economics of Accounting* provides an engaging and accessible analysis of the crucial significance of accounting in today's financial systems. It explores the integral role of accounting in producing information for firm valuation and managerial decision-making. Moreover, it demonstrates accounting's essential function in shaping and evaluating the agency relationship among shareholders, managers, and other stakeholders. Overall, this insightful work nicely illustrates the economic role of accounting."

—ANTOINETTE SCHOAR, Stewart C. Myers-Horn Family Professor of Finance and Entrepreneurship, Massachusetts Institute of Technology

Brief Contents

Contents

Preface

> A cloud of critics, of compilers, of commentators, darkened the face
> of learning, and the decline of genius was soon followed by the cor-
> ruption of taste.
>
> Edward Gibbon (1776)

Mindful of Gibbon's warning, this book tells a story and relates it to salient empirical phenomena. Why does accounting exist? Our answer is that accounting helps firms function efficiently. Firms gain efficiencies in many ways and contexts (e.g., investment decisions and capital allocation, corporate governance, managers' performance assessment, and contracts among various stakeholders). Shareholder value is our primary efficiency measure, and we also discuss regulatory, social, and contract efficiency.

This book has a point of view. Yet we select and discuss empirical research based on its relevance to the efficiency story, not on whether the evidence supports our view. We hope that greater clarity of the efficiency story will give future researchers a more visible target to attack. It also provides a truss for added structure, amendment, and alteration. In either case, we hope to spur and guide the collection of confirming and contradictory evidence, thereby developing a better understanding of the forces that explain observed phenomena and creating new pathways to enhance efficiency.

Is our story obvious? Yes and no. Accounting information has many uses—both within firms and outside of firms within an economy. A few examples of these activities are

- Governance, that is, evaluating firm and management performance
- Contracting among various stakeholders, that is, shareholders-managers, shareholders-debtors, shareholders-suppliers
- Internal corporate decisions, that is, evaluation of investment, financing, compensation, and product pricing
- Investors' decisions at the time of an initial public offering or seasoned equity offering, or when buying and selling securities traded on exchanges

- Price discovery in capital market exchange
- Arrangements made to settle disputes and determine fraud

Moreover, firms incur significant costs to produce accounting information, and its production engenders ancillary institutions such as audit verification and standard-setting regulation (Kothari, Zhang, and Zuo, 2023). A quick overview suggests that accounting has unique and material economic functions and is not solely a neutral mutation (to borrow a phrase Miller [1977] uses when explaining capital structure).

Does accounting matter? Competition among capital-market participants and their quest for gain imply that accounting would be unlikely to exist in its present form if it did not add shareholder value. Still, the effect of financial reporting on firm value "in equilibrium" might be difficult to discern. If high-quality financial reports were necessary to firm survival, we would be unlikely to observe firms without financial reports (Watts, 1977; Watts and Zimmerman, 1986). Moreover, we would expect to observe minimal variation in report quality; observable variation should be due to countervailing forces, and we might then, quite understandably, question empirical studies claiming that this variation produces first-order effects (Zimmerman, 2013). Thus, we distinguish between the importance of variation in financial reporting in equilibrium with liquid capital markets where firms (are required to) issue high-quality reports and the importance of high-quality financial reporting for maintaining this equilibrium.

Our efficiency story also embeds the stakeholder view of the firm recently advocated by the US Business Roundtable and the European Union. Given information asymmetry and agency conflicts, firms must consider the interests of their stakeholders (e.g., debtholders, customers, suppliers, workers, communities) to enhance efficiency. In a world where writing and enforcing contracts impose nontrivial costs, the winning contract structures often involve fixed promised payoffs to most stakeholders, with shareholders bearing the residual risk and getting most of the decision rights (Fama, 2021). Accounting facilitates firms' commitment to stakeholder protection through contract terms. Tying stakeholder protection (or ESG activities) to long-term shareholder value can discipline managerial actions and improve social welfare. In a sense, efficiency is the normative basis for evaluating various corporate policies toward stakeholders.

Perhaps our efficiency story is obvious. Yet we hope to show that it allows us to place research in a coherent framework. Moreover, accounting, more than economics and finance, is a field tied to specific institutional relations (e.g., debt contracts), actors (e.g., audit firms), regulations (e.g., the Sarbanes-Oxley Act), and legal structures (e.g., safe harbors for management-earnings forecasts). We connect specific accounting characteristics and empirical results to the efficiency story. Doing so allows us to recast essential research questions and reveal research avenues.

Who are the intended readers? Our audience is master's and PhD students, senior undergraduates, and researchers. These students need not be limited to those focusing on accounting but can also include economics and finance students seeking to understand the forces manifest in institutional relationships that create the data often employed in their studies. Without this knowledge, researchers are like chefs ignorant of the quality of their ingredients. Investment professionals seeking valuation guidance or trading strategies might be unwilling to put up with the abstraction required to follow our story. They might be uninterested in the interrelations between empirical studies. Still, they might find our discussion of corporate governance, valuation, and agency conflicts helpful.

What about human folly, non-Bayesian updating, learning, regulation, and externalities? An efficiency story seems to imply that these things do not exist or are unimportant. This conclusion is incorrect. *The hypothesis that accounting aids efficiency does not preclude the possibility that individuals can make common mistakes.* Human imperfection can blind actors to their mistakes, which often share a common thread, and a lack of competitive pressure can allow these correlated mistakes to persist and affect market outcomes. That is, if mistakes are pervasive and correlated and frictions stifle arbitrage, the effect of individual biases can persist and be measured. If most investors can be fooled most of the time, observed relations between financial information and market outcomes might be unrelated to shareholder value maximization. For example, managers might be able to manipulate share prices through accounting machinations, or managers might be "overpaid" beyond what we expect, given the costs of achieving full-information pay levels. We review the evidence in light of this alternative view. When the setting is not market outcomes, individual behavioral traits are more likely to play a role, for example, managers' effects on corporate policies, analysts' effects on their forecasts, and audit partners' effects on audit outcomes (Bertrand and Schoar, 2003; Hanlon, Yeung, and Zuo, 2022). We incorporate these behavioral aspects into our story.

In addition, *hypothesizing that accounting aids efficiency does not preclude learning or externalities.* For example, the hypothesis that vertical drilling aids oil exploration and extraction does not preclude the possibility of innovations, like those enabling directional drilling, that can improve the process. Nor does it imply that we need only consider the effects of drilling methods on the oil producer's investors and customers. Moreover, whether parties other than the firm are better suited to discovering value-added accounting innovations or counteracting investor foibles (and even whether such parties should be granted plenary power over accounting changes) depends on factors such as the incentives of these parties, potential externalities, and one's belief about the strength of market forces like competition and the quest for gain and the strength of attendant market frictions. As Leftwich (1980) notes, apparent market flaws should not be condemned until alternative arrangements can be shown to be superior. Whatever one's view, we might agree that regulations constrain financial reporting and auditing choices and that regulations and regulators can be decisive institutional features. To paraphrase Coase (1992), let us study the world of positive transaction costs and the actions of real rather than imaginary governments.

Finally, the efficiency story inevitably gets linked to the advocacy of free markets. This connection is logically incorrect. We raise this point so that the reader's views on politics and the best course in life do not overshadow our discussion of the role played by a commercial feature of our society. Answers to questions such as "What are the good, beauty, and truth?" and "What types of political institutions lead to a kinder, finer society?" are not found in our story. Our view is that these are not mere questions of efficiency.

References

Bertrand, M., Schoar, A., 2003. Managing with style: The effect of managers on firm policies. *Quarterly Journal of Economics* 118 (4), 1169–1208.

Coase, R. H., 1992. The institutional structure of production. *American Economic Review* 82 (4), 713–719.

Fama, E. F., 2021. Contract costs, stakeholder capitalism, and ESG. *European Financial Management* 27 (2), 189–195.

Gibbon, E., 1776. *The History of the Decline and Fall of the Roman Empire.* Strahan & Cadell, London, United Kingdom.

Hanlon, M., Yeung, K., Zuo, L., 2022. Behavioral economics of accounting: A review of archival research on individual decision makers. *Contemporary Accounting Research* 39 (2), 1150–1214.

Kothari, S. P., Zhang, L., Zuo, L., 2023. Disclosure regulation: Past, present, and future. In: Hilary G., McLean, R. D. (Eds.), *Handbook of Financial Decision Making*. Edward Elgar Publishing, Cheltenham, United Kingdom, 215–234.

Leftwich, R., 1980. Market failure fallacies and accounting information. *Journal of Accounting and Economics* 2 (3), 193–211.

Miller, M. H., 1977. Debt and taxes. *Journal of Finance* 32 (2), 261–275.

Watts, R. L., 1977. Corporate financial statements, a product of the market and political processes. *Australian Journal of Management* 2 (1), 53–75.

Watts, R. L., Zimmerman, J. L., 1986. *Positive Accounting Theory*. Prentice-Hall, Englewood Cliffs, New Jersey.

Zimmerman, J. L., 2013. Myth: External financial reporting quality has a first-order effect on firm value. *Accounting Horizons* 27 (4), 887–894.

Acknowledgements

We extend our deepest gratitude to the individuals whose invaluable contributions have shaped *The Economics of Accounting*. Their expertise, support, and dedication have been instrumental in bringing this book to fruition.

First and foremost, we express our heartfelt thanks to James Cook, Senior Acquisitions Editor, for his insightful comments and guidance during the developmental stages. Special appreciation goes to the three anonymous reviewers for their constructive feedback that significantly improved the content.

We are grateful to the following individuals for their helpful comments on earlier versions of the book: Paul Asquith, Ray Ball, Jeremy Bertomeu, Robert Bloomfield, Nicholas Gonedes, Andrew Karolyi, Xianwen Mao, Karthik Ramanna, Antoinette Schoar, Robert Swieringa, Ross Watts, Lawrence Weiss, and Jerold Zimmerman.

Our sincere thanks extend to Lacey Harvey, Project Editor, Lesle Johnson, Production Editor, Kalpana S, Senior Project Manager, and Nirenjena Joseph, Project Manager, for their indispensable assistance in the book production process. We also appreciate the meticulous copy editing provided by Timothy Gray, Bob Land, and Julie Steiff.

The excellent research assistance provided by Lingfeng Geng, Jiawen Yan, and Kelvin Yeung deserves special mention. Their dedication and contributions have significantly enriched the research behind this book.

Lastly, we thank our colleagues and students at Cornell University, Massachusetts Institute of Technology, National University of Singapore, and Washington University in Saint Louis, where the materials of this book have been used in our teaching. We are grateful for their feedback on various topics discussed, which has greatly contributed to the refinement of this work.

To everyone mentioned and those behind the scenes, thank you for being an integral part of this endeavor.

1

An Economic Framework of Accounting

1.1. Overview

Accounting is ubiquitous, arcane, and narcolepsy-inducing. Yet without accounting, the firms whose managers directly guide the bulk of our economy's resources could not exist, and meaningful capital-market exchanges would be rare. Accounting information is universally produced by corporations and used by parties inside and outside the corporation.[1] Absent observable market prices within firms for many production factors, parties use accounting and other information to track and govern resource exchanges within a firm, in evaluating employee performance, in various contracts, and in corporate decision-making. In the capital markets, accounting information and other information facilitate price discovery, that is, the process of determining the price of an asset, resource, or input in the marketplace through buyer-seller interactions. This book aims to aid our understanding of accounting's economic roles.[2]

In this chapter, we discuss accounting's economic functions, the logic of accounting, and the limitations of accounting information; we also outline the rest of the book. For the most part, we take the view that firms (managers) behave as if their goal is to increase long-term shareholder value (i.e., the present value of all future cash flows that a firm generates to its shareholders), subject to the constraints of competition, law, and ethics. These constraints are crucial. As we discuss in greater detail later, these guardrails blunt the

---

[1] This statement applies to any organization that requires outside funding or has sufficiently complex operations (e.g., sole proprietorships, charities, business schools, municipalities, and art museums). Perhaps the only organization that does not require accounting is a child's lemonade stand. We confine our discussion to limited-liability organizations formed to profit owners by providing goods or services (i.e., corporations), but the ideas discussed are applicable to other organizations as well (see, e.g., Zimmerman, 1977).

[2] Ball (2008, p. 428) elaborates on the importance of this analysis: "Financial reporting practice is influenced by the uses to which financial reporting is put, by managers' and auditors' incentives, and institutional variables such as regulation and litigation risk. So, to my mind, what firms actually do—not what they, their managers, their auditors or accounting standards say they do—is the more central issue in financial reporting."

The Economics of Accounting. Richard M. Frankel, S. P. Kothari, and Luo Zuo, Oxford University Press.
© Oxford University Press 2024. DOI: 10.1093/oso/9780197680766.003.0001

criticism that shareholder value maximization is exploitative or that it results in rampant wealth transfer to shareholders and management at the expense of other stakeholders like employees and consumers. Our explanations of accounting-related empirical phenomena begin with the premise that observed outcomes are consistent with the shareholder value maximization view. We also consider other explanations. In the Appendix, "The Shareholder Value Maximization Principle," we discuss the rationale for shareholder value maximization as the guiding principle for organizations.[3] It is worth emphasizing that shareholder value can increase if a firm takes actions (e.g., research and development) that reduce accounting earnings in the short term but increase them by more in the long term. We also note that shareholder value maximization and stakeholder protection are not at odds and that accounting information facilitates firms' commitment to stakeholder protection, which, in turn, leads to more value creation for shareholders.

1.2. Demand for Accounting in the Corporation

Corporations are legal creations comprising a web of exchange and contracting relations between individuals or with other firms (Jensen and Meckling, 1976; Watts and Zimmerman, 1978, 1986). The contracts might be formal or informal, written or unwritten. Rights and responsibilities might be specified in the contract or assumed from common law, regulation, or custom. It is self-evident that these relations are costly to arrange, facilitate, support, maintain, monitor, enforce, and so on, but we must unpack this assertion to understand its wide-ranging implications. To begin with our conclusion: accounting information's main functions are to (1) minimize these exchange and contracting costs, (2) foster a richer variety of exchange and contracting relations, and thereby (3) further the overarching objective of increasing shareholder value.[4]

The value and function of accounting are obscure because accounting is not a consumption good. Instead, like money, it facilitates the production

---

[3] The Appendix also elaborates on the concept of shareholder-value maximization, seeking to make it more palatable by reconciling it with social-welfare maximization, stakeholder theory, and behavioral economics.

[4] External financial reporting systems and internal management accounting systems both emphasize incentive alignment and value creation (Demski and Feltham, 1978; Johnson and Kaplan, 1991; Kothari, Ramanna, and Skinner, 2010).

of goods and services. Yet the obscure function of accounting belies its economic significance. Without the exchanges and contractual relations enabled by accounting information, many goods and services would be unavailable to us, or their cost would be so high that they would be available to only a wealthy few.

Take, for example, air travel. Publicly held corporations provide the majority of civilian air transportation. Transport requires the coordination of passengers, pilots, ground crews, flight crews, maintenance personnel, air-traffic control, reservation-system personnel, aircraft and equipment owners, airports, fuel suppliers, investors, and so on. These parties coordinate their activities subject to competition from other organizations. Competition implies that the organization must seek quality and cost improvements to survive because other airlines do likewise. In this context, the term *cost* captures the financial implications of a gamut of the firm's activities: innovation, research, development, marketing strategies, employee compensation and bonuses, production facilities, raw materials, offices, and so forth. Professional management administers the firm's activities under the weight of this competition. The managers' motivation is that superior performance will generate greater compensation and career advancement opportunities. It will also enhance shareholder value, which means that management and shareholder incentives are aligned.

However, human nature's quest for gain is (or should be) constrained by custom, virtue, ethics, laws, and regulations. Currently, these social institutions support private ownership of resources (i.e., property rights) and freedom to exchange. Without such structure, those possessing greater force would rule resources, and the objective would be the acquisition of force. Instead, to return to the airline example, customers and management can choose among various providers of air travel and employment, so airlines compete on quality and cost for customers and use pay, quality of life, and career-advancement opportunities to attract management talent. More generally, airlines, representing their owners, compete for labor, capital, and all scarce resources employed. Managers also compete to sell their services to airlines. Parties must expect gain to be enticed into exchanging their services or resources with the airline; so too, parties must convince the airline that their services are valuable.[5] The payments associated with these exchanges

---

[5] One exception is a resource that no individual or organization owns, such as the atmosphere surrounding the plane. It will be used for engine-exhaust disposal. The lack of "property rights" creates an "externality," because the community members who benefit from exhaust-free air cannot

and the rights and responsibilities enumerated in agreements reflect the opportunity costs of the exchanging parties.[6] That is, parties and a given airline agree to terms when the gain exceeds that available in other exchanges.

Managers choose how to allocate scarce resources among operational areas and strive against other firms to develop new and better products and services. Managers use accounting information to estimate, with varying degrees of precision, the costs of factors of production for use within the firm. Of course, other information is also compiled and used to guide operating decisions, for example, lost baggage percentages, on-time arrival percentages, airplane loading times, and customer satisfaction surveys. In addition, accounting information and other information facilitate exchanges with those outside the firm, for example, customers, suppliers, and tax authorities.

When shareholders hire professional managers to increase the value of their investment, shareholders require a means of assessing management performance. When product-market and resource-market competition is slow to reveal management incompetence or constrain management's self-serving behavior, investors need a more timely performance indicator to align management's incentives with their own. The market value of shareholder claims alone might not be a suitable indicator of a manager's contribution because the price might reflect results that the manager could not be expected to influence. The issue of responsibility is more salient for shareholders wishing to assess the contribution of executives below the CEO. Moreover, managers have yearly consumption needs, face liquidity constraints, and value the option to switch jobs or change careers. These factors create a demand for compensation contracts that pay managers each period, leading to a need for measures of a manager's contribution to shareholder value in each

---

voluntarily exchange the use of air without an institutional arrangement to facilitate the exchange of "community resources." The political or judicial system often controls these exchanges via regulation or common law. Establishing property rights is costly, but their decisiveness can be seen in the case of noise. Homeowners near an airport can be enticed to sell their homes or install soundproofing once common law or regulation decides their decibel-level property right. Airports can then weigh the costs of changing runway layouts or forcing changes to aircraft engines and capacities against the cost of satisfying homeowners.

[6] This assumes the absence of externalities and monopoly (or market power). To maximize surplus, monopolies and monopsonies restrain the quantity supplied so that price exceeds marginal cost. For example, airlines that dominate an isolated airport can earn monopoly profits, and their unionized labor can drive up wage rates. Under these conditions, laws and regulation are necessary to create a market structure that operates as if it is competitive.

period.[7] Shareholders rely on periodic accounting performance measures as one of the performance indicators in deciding how much to pay the manager and whether to allow the same manager to continue stewarding their investment in the company. In sum, accounting information serves as one input to measure the management's periodic performance.[8]

Naturally, managers recognize that the information they produce will be used to gauge their performance and set their compensation. This use of accounting information creates an incentive for them to influence the information produced. If owners recognize this possibility, then less credible managers will be less likely to be hired. Thus, labor-market competition and shareholders' desire to maximize firm value jointly impel managers to agree to incentive-aligning contracts that use accounting information. These, in turn, lead managers to enhance the information's credibility.

Firms might seek financing from lenders in addition to funds provided by owners. Loans require an agreement spelling out terms and conditions. Debt contracts control incentive conflicts between shareholders and debtholders, including differing preferences with regard to the return volatility of corporate investments and attempts by shareholders to subvert the primacy of debtholder claims (e.g., liquidating dividends).[9] For example, after borrowing, shareholders can transfer wealth from bondholders by investing the proceeds in risky projects because bondholders' claims might be impaired if these projects do not succeed, but if these projects succeed, bondholders do not participate in the upside. Absent covenants, bondholders anticipate incentive problems and incorporate the expected costs into the required rate of

---

[7] Yearly pay, in turn, creates demand for a measure that will limit the ex-post settling-up problem. Ex-post settling-up problems arise when payments made cannot be subsequently retrieved (e.g., when realizations are observable) because the payment receiver (e.g., the manager) has limited liability. Limited liability combined with managers' hidden actions creates the potential for wealth transfers from shareholders to managers. For example, managers might take actions that increase investor expectations and prices, knowing these effects are temporary. In such a case, compensation based on stock price could lead to overpayments to managers. Fama (1980) questions the existence of ex-post settling-up problems in efficient labor markets where managers have future salary concerns, that is, reputational concerns.

[8] For example, Singapore Airlines notes that the variable portion of senior management pay depends on a mix of performance measures including return on shareholder investment, operating profit margin, and passenger load factors. Economic-value added (EVA) also determines bonus pay. EVA is usually computed by subtracting an invested capital charge (e.g., weighted average cost of capital times the sum of debt and equity value) from net operating profit after tax (NOPAT). In the case of Singapore Airlines, the precise computation of the bonus is not disclosed. In 2016–2017, bonus and share payments represented 72 percent of CEO pay (Singapore Airlines, 2017).

[9] For example, Delta Air Lines' August 24, 2015, Credit and Guarantee Agreement (Delta Air Lines, 2015) requires the company to file financial statements with an unqualified audit opinion and prohibits Delta from merging with other firms or allowing its cash and investments and available revolving credit facilities to fall below $2 billion.

return (or decide not to lend). Therefore, shareholders consent to covenants. It follows that a manager acting on behalf of shareholders and therefore seeking to maximize shareholder value will devise methods to assure lenders that managers will not try to transfer wealth after contracting when such transfers are apt to destroy value.

The devices employed (debt covenants) will be imperfect. Shareholders, through management, retain postborrowing decision rights. Future events that can create opportunities to subvert lender rights are difficult to antici- pate or incorporate into contractual terms. In this sense, contracts are "in- complete." Shareholders look for contracting innovations to allay debtholder concerns because, as residual claimants, they bear these costs. For example, contracts might specify that lenders gain decision rights under certain conditions specified by accounting ratios.

The preceding discussion explained the demand for accounting infor- mation in contracts between shareholders and managers and between shareholders and debtholders; it also described the conflicts that arise be- tween the contracting parties due to their incentives to maximize their re- spective welfare. This discussion assumed, broadly speaking, that capital providers are debt and equity holders. But among equity claimants, large shareholders can often influence management, potentially harming the re- maining shareholders. In such circumstances, the remaining owners, labeled "minority shareholders," seek to protect their financial interests (cash-flow rights) from "tunneling" by majority shareholders, that is, diverting re- sources to themselves at the expense of minority shareholders.[10]

Armed with accounting information and a myriad of contractual arrangements, firms can serve the interests of various contracting parties, including capital providers, management, employees, customers, and regulators. But given all the hidden information problems and incentive conflicts, why do all of these parties coalesce into a firm rather than operating separately as independent providers of their services in the marketplace? That is, what explains the ubiquitous presence of modern corporations? Coase

---

[10] For example, Tamasek Holdings Limited holds 55.6 percent of Singapore Airlines, and the Singapore minister of finance holds one "special share" that allows it to veto certain board resolutions. Singapore Airlines' 2016/2017 annual report gives detailed information on the board structure, procedures, goals, and compensation policies (Singapore Airlines, 2017). The 2019 IPO prospectus of the state-controlled Saudi Arabian Oil Co. (commonly known as Aramco) notes that the Saudi government may direct Aramco "to undertake projects or provide assistance for initiatives outside the company's core business, which may not be consistent with the company's immediate commer- cial objectives or profit maximization" (Croft, 2019).

(1937) asks what determines a firm's boundaries and provides an approach to answering this question.[11] He surmises that firms arise because they are a more cost-effective way of coordinating relationships between parties than relying solely on market exchanges. And those arrangements that offer these products and services more cost-effectively thrive, whereas those that do not wither. He labels the costs incurred in coordinating relations within a firm as "contracting" costs and those arising in market exchanges as "transaction" costs. The boundaries of the firm are drawn to minimize these costs.[12]

The factors shaping the organizational limits appropriate for this cost-reduction problem vary by circumstance. For example, compare car transportation to air transportation. In contrast to air travel, most car travel occurs in cars owned or rented by the passenger. Perhaps the lower capital requirements of car ownership mean that it is inefficient to separate the benefits and risks of car ownership from control of the car's use. Ride-sharing firms like Uber and Lyft coordinate a far more limited set of activities than airlines. These firms provide a reservation, payment, pricing, and driver-passenger rating system. They do not offer maintenance or purchase equipment (for the most part), nor do they train employees, purchase fuel, or set the beginning and endpoints and times for each leg of transportation. The more limited investment required for automobiles; the car's alternative uses; the lack of coordination required among passengers; the deeper markets for drivers, auto fuel, parts, and maintenance; and the lack of preauthorized flight plans all suggest that capacity flexibility and market-provided equipment in automobile transportation outweigh the net benefits of the planned coordination we see in airline transportation. Substituting spot-market rental drivers and their cars for prepurchased auto fleets and long-term employment contracts with drivers allows the ride-sharing company to respond to last-minute contingencies by adding or reducing capacity. It also allows drivers to react to real-time changes in the opportunity cost of their time. In addition to these operating considerations, information quality and costs also determine the boundaries of the firms.

---

[11] Weisbach (2021) notes that Coase earned the 1991 Nobel Prize in economics largely because he asked such an important question that no one had asked before. More generally, Weisbach states in his insightful field guide to economics that at least half of the battle for an economist (versus a mathematician) is to come up with the right question to ask and the right way to ask it.

[12] Though the distinction between contracting and transaction costs is useful for conceptual understanding, Demsetz (1993) notes that firms incur a blend of transaction and contracting costs that is difficult to "unmix." Firms use inputs purchased from markets as well as from in-house production. Firms buy from separate firms across markets at prices that reflect the contracting costs incurred by these selling firms.

We have tried to show the role of financial accounting information within the firm in making contracts work better and aiding managerial decisions in the absence of prices. Airline corporations could not exist without accounting and other information because parties could not coordinate the exchange of resources via the contracts necessary to mediate this exchange within firms and between firms and customers or resource providers in markets. Airline transportation would be far more limited and costly.[13] The next section describes the role of accounting in market exchanges.

1.3. Demand for Accounting in Capital Market Exchanges

Capital-market exchanges permit specialization, the use of diffuse knowledge about ever-changing local facts and circumstances, and coordination between investors and firms seeking capital—all of which enable economic flourishing. Parties specialize in making goods and services because comparative advantage combined with exchange allows them to maximize consumption. In particular, investors wish to exchange current consumption for future consumption. Firms require capital today to produce goods and services, yielding future payoffs to their investors. However, exchanges of current consumption for future consumption funded by future payoffs require information that allows parties to assess a security's future cash flows and risks. The absence of reliable information available to buyers can cause sellers of high-quality securities to pull them from the market (Akerlof, 1970). Information collection and verification efforts are transaction costs that discourage trading.

In facilitating exchange, accounting information and money share a fundamental purpose. Adam Smith (1776, Chapter IV) recognized that "this power of exchanging must frequently have been very much clogged and embarrassed in its operations," and he noted the importance of economic institutions that exist only to minimize transaction costs. Chapter IV of his *Wealth of Nations* (Smith, 1776) chronicles the progression of commodities (from cattle to crude metals to stamped coins) employed by individuals, kings,

---

[13] This assertion has an empirical basis (e.g., Megginson and Netter, 2001), though the implications of efficient organizational structures on airline-travel efficiency are complex. For example, advancements in air-transportation technology depend on the knowledge gained through experimentation facilitated by the proliferation of air travel. Hayek (1960) elaborates on the advancement of knowledge with a subtlety we do not attempt to reproduce here.

and nations seeking to minimize the costs of storing, weighing, and assaying the medium of exchange.[14] Ensuring reliable coinage might seem a trivial task compared to accounting regulators' great intellectual burden of increasing the financial-reporting efficiency of public companies.[15] If so, one might be surprised that the Royal Mint employed the great Sir Isaac Newton for thirty-one years (1696–1727). Though Newton could have treated the appointment as a sinecure, he was industrious—interviewing witnesses and suspects, developing assay methods, and drafting hundreds of letters and reports. From coins to fiat money to Bitcoin, economic communities constantly refine their medium of exchange. These refinements include methods of more efficiently exchanging the medium of exchange![16] Similarly, we expect information-centered institutions, like financial reporting, to arise and evolve.

Once exchange advances beyond trading mink pelts for knives on a St. Lawrence River bank, traders need information to determine relative values and enforce responsibilities. Even at this primitive stage, parties might need more information to assess the quality of the knives and pelts than can be collected through visual inspection. The relevance of visual inspection is likely to be even more limited when an individual seeks to trade current consumption for future consumption, that is, to invest.

Prices of firm shares that are investment possibilities must be "discovered." Financial accounting information aids discovery by providing data helpful in assessing the amounts, timing, and uncertainty of future cash flows. Accounting information can also narrow the information gap between buyers and sellers. This gap causes less informed parties to reassess their expectations upon learning that a potentially more informed party is willing to sell. Thus, if a party suspected of having superior information wishes to sell, she must grant a price discount to mollify the suspicions of the less informed party. The probability of swapping with an informed counterparty (auspiciously set below 100 percent, thanks to the assumed participation of noise traders) and the information gap that will likely exist if one happens to trade with an informed party both increase transaction costs. The precise mechanism that contributes to the size of the transaction costs is the domain of the security microstructure literature, which is built on the foundation of studies

---

[14] Additional examples, including the "island of stone money," can be found in Friedman (1992).

[15] These organizations include the Financial Accounting Standards Board (FASB), the International Accounting Standards Board (IASB), and the Public Company Accounting Oversight Board (PCAOB).

[16] Examples include demand deposits, credit cards, public-key cryptography, and Apple Pay.

like Akerlof (1970), Grossman and Stiglitz (1980), and Kyle (1985). The size of the transaction costs is a function of the expected information advantage of an informed party and the prevalence of informed versus uninformed parties (labeled noise traders). The information difference between the informed and the uninformed, including the distribution of this gap among investors, is termed *information asymmetry*. At this stage, we merely assert that the wide availability of finer information to investors reduces information asymmetry and therefore reduces transaction costs. Lower transaction costs result in greater willingness to trade between the security owners. Accounting can ameliorate information asymmetry by serving as one source of information about a firm's cash-flow-generating ability, thereby enabling price discovery and reducing trading costs.

1.4. Double-Entry Bookkeeping

Double-entry bookkeeping converts economic events into income. Economic events include transactions, the passage of time, and market-price changes. Double entry is the process used by accountants to produce financial statements. We aim to help the uninitiated understand the thinking underlying the record-keeping system that produces revenues and expenses for a business over a period, typically one year.

Most of us are single-entry bookkeepers before our first accounting class. We open our wallets and see that our cash has declined by $30 and now stands at $70. We might ask for no additional information if we just want to make sure we can pay for lunch. Still, we might wonder about the cause of the $30 decline. At this point, we begin to see the usefulness of a double-entry system. By requiring a second entry that shows an account associated with the $30 cash decline, the double-entry system links the change in the cash balance to a cause.

In the case of a firm, the accountant must choose among six possible causes for a decline in cash and record a second entry reflecting this cause—the first being the entry to cash. These causes are (1) a purchase of another asset, (2) a payment to a lender, (3) a payment to a supplier, (4) a payment of an expense, (5) a payment of an expense previously recorded (e.g., last month's utility bill), or (6) a payment to the firm's owners (e.g., a dividend).[17]

---

[17] In the case of a cash increase, the six possible causes are (1) a sale of an asset, (2) a receipt from a lender, (3) a receipt from a customer related to a previous sale, (4) revenue from the sale of inventory

The economic cause of a cash decline might be unclear. Still, by requiring a second entry to accompany the cash payment, the double-entry system requires the accountant to attribute causality to each cash transaction as it occurs, rather than simply waiting until the end of the period to assess value changes and infer income. For example, if a firm spends $100 on research and development (R&D), one might argue that the second entry should be to an asset rather than an expense. The second entry does not affect the cash balance, but it will affect the amount of expenses recognized in a given period.[18]

Double entry forces causal attribution, so the verifiability of this attribution will be paramount due to potential incentive conflicts between the managers who record the entries and the owners and investors who rely on the output of the accounting system.[19] The accountant has no choice but to record an entry when cash is paid or received or when a physical asset (e.g., inventory or equipment) is obtained or destroyed. These events can be verified, and while we might question the appropriateness of the second entry (see the R&D example above), the scope for manipulation can be bounded.

The collection, categorization, and accumulation of a firm's transactions in a reliable way is *the* competitive advantage of the firm's accounting system over other information sources. To take two examples, analysts and the financial press do not have access to a firm's transaction-level data, though they might more reliably provide unverifiable opinions if they are not subject to the same incentive conflicts as managers. Given incentive conflicts, reliability is a necessary condition for financial reports to be relevant to users. In this sense, there is no trade-off between relevance and reliability. Irrelevant, verifiable information like the color of the CEO's shirt is not helpful to parties

or provision of a service, (5) a receipt in advance for a future delivery of a good or service, or (6) a receipt from owners. Moreover, once noncash assets and nondebt liabilities are permitted, these accounts can change with offsetting revenues and expenses. Our discussion focuses on expense recognition linked to cash payments and is not intended to be a comprehensive review of accrual and deferral accounting.

[18] This system need not be used to accumulate revenues and expenses for the computation of income during a period of time. During the fifteenth century, the main purpose of double-entry accounting was to allow merchants to know who their creditors were and how much they owed to each. For further reading, see Sangster (2016, 2018).

[19] Given incentive conflicts, reliability is a necessary condition for information to be relevant to users. In this sense, there is no trade-off between relevance and reliability as there is between a mechanical signal and noise. We might hypothesize that the accounting system used in sole proprietorships would be more likely to incorporate entries based solely on expectations. However, in a world with frictions, bagels do not slice themselves. Expectations must be formed, and this formation requires a costly record of realizations. Double entry, which is based on realized information, provides this record.

contracting with the firm. So too, information communicated by the firm that cannot be confirmed by evidence outside of the managers' minds (e.g., managers' opinions) is not useful to contracting parties either.

The centrality of reliability and a focus on financial accounting's competitive advantage seems to relegate financial reporting to a secondary role among information providers. However, in a world with information asymmetry between managers and outsiders, information intermediaries require a foundation of realized performance for their analysis. Double entry, which is based on realized information, provides this record. Financial reporting might not sufficiently ameliorate information asymmetry in high-growth firms, where the past is of limited relevance to predicting the future. However, this does not mean that other information sources (e.g., analysts and the financial press) can act as substitutes. They also lack information to assess performance. Instead, organization forms like private equity will substitute for that of a public company.

In addition, the full double-entry system incorporates transactions not triggered by cash payment. It includes promises to pay and receive cash as well as expenses associated with the reduction in asset values, such as depreciation. In the case of promises to receive cash, such as sales on credit, the accountant requires evidence of the promise and its collectability to record an asset and revenue entry. In the case of promises to pay cash, again, accountants require evidence of this promise and an estimate of the eventual cash sacrifice. The "matching principle" guides the recognition of asset-value reductions. Matching requires expense recognition to be linked to revenue recognition. As applied to long-lived assets, the original asset cost is allocated to each period based on the anticipated share of net benefits produced by the asset in the period. By incorporating estimates and anticipation, accountants seem to pull on the thread of verifiability. To prevent the garment from unraveling, they require evidence for assertions gleaned from transaction characteristics, apply criteria (i.e., bright lines), and require disclosure of key assumptions. Whether the cost of these measures exceeds the benefits of incorporating a given promise into the double-entry system is difficult to discern.

As we will discuss, the revenue recognition principle, the matching principle, and the real-time assignment of causality that characterize double entry provide the basis for income computation based on historical cost. Based on these principles, double entry produces the verifiable, cumulative record of outcomes that totals to the assets and liabilities on the balance sheet.

In a world with frictions, *earnings serve as an informational factor of pro-duction in the efficient functioning of a firm*; at the same time, competition pushes managers toward shareholder value maximization. These notions imply that managers will include less verifiable information in the earnings computation to the extent that the benefit to shareholders exceeds the cost. However, reporting requirements are often imposed on managers by a po-litical process that incorporates ends other than net shareholder benefits. Therefore, the logic of shareholder efficiency will not fully explain earnings properties.

Double entry is the mainstay of the current solution to the problem of producing a performance measure with sufficient verifiability to be rele-vant. It adds information by attributing causality to cash transactions. The verifiability of this information stems from the application of double entry to each transaction and its use of tangible characteristics when attributing cau-sality. Its mechanical grounding (e.g., R&D expensing or depreciation and matching) can limit the scope for manipulation and the necessity of costly devices seeking to limit manipulation (e.g., collection of additional evidence, bright-line rules, and disclosure of assumptions). Incorporating additional events, such as promises, often entails the application of less tangible transac-tion characteristics, such as expectations, to determine amount and causality. These events will be incorporated based on shareholder value maximization considerations, subject to regulatory mandates.

1.5. Accrual-Basis Accounting

Earnings differ from cash flows because earnings focus on the difference be-tween realized revenues and matched expenses, while cash flows focus on cash paid and cash received. The difference between earnings and cash flows is called *accruals*.[20] This definition of income casts net cash flows as its prin-cipal driver, with accruals introduced as temporary adjustments.

Accruals mitigate the timing and matching problems that arise from di-viding the firm's life into subperiods for measurement. Timing problems result when the fiscal period of a cash receipt (or payment) differs from

---

[20] A precise definition decomposes the cash flow/earnings difference into *accruals* and *deferrals*. The former results when items are recognized as revenue/expense *before* cash receipt/payment. The latter arises when items are recognized as revenue/expense *after* cash receipt/payment.

the fiscal period when it is earned (incurred). For example, customers pay in advance for air travel that will not occur until a subsequent fiscal period. Matching problems arise when cash inflows and outflows relating to the same operating transaction occur in different periods. For example, an airline pays vendors for pretzels and soft drinks consumed on a flight after passenger-ticket fees are collected and the flight is flown. Labeling particular cash-flow timing and matching characteristics as problems suggests that financial-reporting usefulness would be subverted if the accountant determined fiscal-period income solely by cash arrival and disbursement during the period. Thus, we have proposed that a goal of earnings is to measure the net benefits the airline earned from flying in a given fiscal period without regard to short-term cash flow timing discrepancies. As a general rule, accrual-basis accounting records revenue when earned and expenses when incurred, regardless of the timing of cash receipts and disbursements. In that sense, earnings are an accounting estimate of the value added by the firm in goods delivered or services performed to customers for a given reporting period.

1.6. Limitations of Accounting Information

This book begins with the assumption that shareholders seek to increase the value of their investment. They hire managers to do so, and additional contracting relations combine to form a firm. These contracting relations rely on information. For example, the employment of managers requires shareholders to design contracts and seek financial reports indicating whether managers' actions contribute to value. No information source is perfect (free from noise and sufficient for all contexts). The economy contains many potential producers of information with differing production functions (e.g., audit firms and buy-side analysts). It contains many potential information consumers with differing preferences (e.g., diversified mutual fund managers and activist investors). We would not expect financial reports produced by firms to be the most efficient way to satisfy all consumers. Instead, we might expect shareholders to require firms to produce accounting information where a comparative advantage for financial accounting information is present. We assume that consumers would recognize the imperfection and potential omissions of this information set. Consumers will supplement their accounting information set with other sources of information.

For example, earnings omit the economic value of R&D or advertising expenditures. While there is demand for information about R&D's economic value, corporate management faces the challenge of supplying such information reliably, without bias (optimism). An analogy is Akerlof's (1970) used-car problem, where sellers of good-quality cars withdraw from the market. The lack of car-quality information does not suggest that it is not demanded, just that it cannot be credibly conveyed. As a solution, sellers develop alternative means of communication (e.g., offering a warranty, building a reputation, installing an odometer, or collecting maintenance documents) to differentiate themselves from the rest. Though a tamper-resistant odometer is an imperfect quality measure, its reliability makes it a useful indicator of car quality (Cho, Frankel, and Martin, 2024).

Similarly, an accounting measure confined to capturing tamper-resistant data (e.g., past transactions) can convey firm-performance information to investors. Though this accounting measure omits the economic value of R&D or advertising, it might still be helpful. Moreover, the firm's accounting system might not be the most efficient way to convey this information. Instead, we might expect that alternative means of communicating or assessing the value of knowledge gained from R&D and the pricing power gained from advertising will develop (e.g., voluntary disclosures, news articles, or analyst reports).[21]

1.7. Structure of the Book

If we are to understand the role of accounting information, there must be objectives guiding its production. Two objectives come readily to mind: the stewardship and valuation roles of accounting information. The *steward-ship role* refers to "the role of the accounting system in ensuring that a firm's invested capital is maintained in such a way as to preserve the economic interests of stockholders and bondholders" (Kothari, Ramanna, and Skinner, 2010, p. 248). The *valuation role* refers to the role of the accounting system in

---

[21] Subtle differences in the supply of related products are difficult to discern. For example, Campbell's soup contains cooked carrots, and the company would seem well placed to supply fresh carrots and refrigerated juices to grocery stores. Campbell's paid $1.55 billion for Bolthouse Farms thinking it could do so. However, supply-chain differences between cooked and fresh produce were sufficient to make this acquisition a mistake (Gasparro and Lombardo, 2018). This and other failed acquisitions provide examples to ponder as we consider what types of information accountants ought to be able to supply in the financial statements.

providing information "that is helpful in assessing current cash flows and the amount, timing, and uncertainty of future cash flows, regardless of observed outputs and whether the management has already taken the actions necessary to generate those cash flows" (Kothari, Ramanna, and Skinner, 2010, p. 254). Throughout the book, we argue that the stewardship and valuation roles are largely coextensive. These complementary roles of accounting arise because (1) the relevance of accounting information for valuation presupposes (a degree of) reliability of the accounting information, notwithstanding the incentive conflicts influencing the preparers to distort it, and (2) shareholders demand valuation information in part to assess management and firm performance.

Chapters 2 and 3 examine the attributes of accounting earnings as produced and received in the market without delving into the preparers' incentives to influence the amount and nature of the information or considering how those incentives affect the information produced. These two chapters can be viewed as a reduced-form analysis of accounting earnings and their relation to other economic variables, for example, security prices. Security prices represent an observable, objective valuation of a firm's equity ownership. Absent prices for nonpublicly traded firms, we conjecture a relation between accounting and the valuation that might be observed if the firm were publicly listed. Such valuation is often referred to as fair value, although the latter term is also used for the valuation of individual assets and liabilities that are not traded in the marketplace.

Chapters 2 and 3 take the observed distribution of accounting information as an equilibrium outcome and provide its characteristics without analyzing the forces that shaped the outcome. In this sense, we provide a view of the visible features of the landscape without analyzing the underlying geological forces that produced it. This approach has been well-trodden in financial economics. For example, Fama and Miller (1972) begin their development of "the theory of finance" by assuming certainty before introducing the effects of uncertainty. The modeling of asset prices begins with the capital asset pricing model (CAPM) in an exchange setting before the effects of production and consumption on asset prices are introduced in more advanced models. Blanchard's (2017) book *Macroeconomics* introduces macroeconomic concepts and policy implications with a short-term focus that abstracts away from a more realistic macroeconomy with medium- and long-term effects of economic policies. In this vein, we too begin with an analysis in a reduced-form setting. For example, we describe the effect of earnings growth on security returns, but we remain silent on the influence of growth opportunities on the investment, financing, and reporting choices of various actors. However, growth opportunities facing a firm indicate disequilibrium: one firm's growth opportunities lead other firms in the industry to invest and vie for the promised gains. As firms raise funds for investments, they might be motivated to report an embellished view of the firm's prospects while simultaneously being disinclined to release bad news. In periods when a firm anticipates growth, investing activity might dominate, and the future might bring increased revenues for the firm. Thus, growth can limit the informativeness of accounting reports, which in turn could motivate the management to disclose soft or forward-looking information to fill in the gaps in the accounting reports. We omit discussion of these strategic or reactive effects in Chapters 2 and 3, and we develop them in Chapter 4.

Chapter 2 analyzes the relation between accounting earnings and stock prices. Earnings receive more attention than any other item in a firm's financial report. Earnings represent a summary measure of a firm's periodic performance and thus serve as a management-performance metric. Shareholders choose to hire a management team to increase the value of their shares. Therefore, intuition leads us to expect any good metric of the firm's performance or that of its management to be informative about firm value (its equity, to be more precise). Statistically speaking, we expect earnings to exhibit a positive co-movement with publicly listed firms' security prices. The modern literature in accounting began in the mid-1960s with Ball and Brown's (1968) seminal study documenting evidence on the earnings-price correlation.[22] This literature also marks the beginning of the reliance on positive science and efficient capital markets in accounting research testing hypotheses about the properties of financial accounting variables and their relations with other economic variables. In Chapter 2, we contrast the advent of positive science in accounting research with the state of accounting theory in the mid-1960s. We also explain how concurrent developments in economics and finance had an indelible influence on accounting research, including the framing of hypotheses, the research design, and the inferences drawn from the analyses. The newfound appreciation that security prices represent an objective measure of a firm's economic performance in an efficient market had the unintended consequence of advocating correlation or value

---

[22] Beaver (1968) documents increased return volatility and volume in the weeks around earnings announcements.

relevance to assay earnings' usefulness. Subsequent literature explicates the pitfalls of using value relevance as an acid test of usefulness or in choosing among alternative accounting standards. Interestingly, the intellectual antecedent of fair value accounting, which has many admirers today, is the "continuously contemporary accounting" scheme proposed by Chambers (1966).

Chapter 3 moves from providing evidence of the return-earnings relation's existence to exploring its extent and its determinants. Researchers conduct both association and event studies. The resulting earnings response coefficient (ERC) literature performs powerful tests of market efficiency and contracting theory, as well as tests of financial disclosures. Magnitude estimation distinguishes the ERC literature from a Ball-Brown type of association study. Studies of ERC use time-series properties of earnings and a valuation model. The predicted magnitude is a joint prediction about the time-series model and market valuation of earnings. Two prominent phenomena documented in the literature are as follows: (1) the estimated ERC is small relative to its predicted value, and (2) the earnings-return relation is stronger for negative stock returns than for positive stock returns. These two empirical patterns motivated researchers to advance several hypotheses and explanations. We emphasize that economic fundamentals and accounting practices jointly determine the observed earnings-return relation.

Chapter 4 presents a strategic analysis of accounting earnings. It recognizes that accounting information affects users' and producers' decisions, which, against the backdrop of self-interested behavior, influences the properties of the accounting information produced and affects how it is used in valuation (Kothari, 2001), in contracting (Armstrong, Guay, and Weber, 2010; Christensen, Nikolaev, and Wittenberg-Moerman, 2016), and in firms' investment decisions (Bushman and Smith, 2001; Roychowdhury, Shroff, and Verdi, 2019).[23] This chapter describes imperfect and incomplete markets as a prelude to understanding why firms arise and why the need for an earnings measure follows. Markets are imperfect and incomplete when transaction costs exist and certain goods or claims cannot be traded. The notion that earnings somehow enhance firms' efficiency because of imperfect and

---

[23] The knowledge that accounting information is produced and used by many self-interested parties influences standard setters, and many interested players seek to influence standard setters through lobbying. As a result, the properties of accounting standards (rules) governing the production of accounting information are affected, and this in turn has real effects (economic consequences). Ramanna (2015) discusses the political process of standard setting—standard setters, producers, users, and auditors are all actors in the political process. Kothari, Zhang, and Zuo (2023) provide an overview of the theories of disclosure regulation.

incomplete markets yields three implications for the nature of the earnings measure. First, the firm's value differs from the value of its separable assets and liabilities. Second, incentive conflicts inherent in imperfect and incomplete markets leave an indelible mark on the earnings report. Finally, the objective of accounting rules cannot be merely to measure the change in value or provide information to assess value. Accounting must have efficiency effects to be demanded and supplied. To make our discussion more concrete, we describe the income-statement and balance-sheet approaches to computing earnings to organize and highlight specific limitations and efficiency considerations that arise in the earnings computation. Our thesis is that earnings and other outputs of accounting help firms function more efficiently.

References

Akerlof, G. A., 1970. The market for "lemons": Quality uncertainty and the market mechanism. *Quarterly Journal of Economics* 84 (3), 235–251.

Armstrong, C. S., Guay, W. R., Weber, J. P., 2010. The role of information and financial reporting in corporate governance and debt contracting. *Journal of Accounting and Economics* 50 (2–3), 179–234.

Ball, R., 2008. What is the actual economic role of financial reporting? *Accounting Horizons* 22 (4), 427–432.

Ball, R., Brown, P., 1968. An empirical evaluation of accounting income numbers. *Journal of Accounting Research* 6 (2), 159–178.

Beaver, W. H., 1968. The information content of annual earnings announcements. *Journal of Accounting Research* 6, 67–92.

Blanchard, O., 2017. *Macroeconomics*, 7th ed. Pearson Prentice Hall, Upper Saddle River, New Jersey.

Bushman, R. M., Smith, A. J., 2001. Financial accounting information and corporate governance. *Journal of Accounting and Economics* 32 (1–3), 237–333.

Chambers, R. J., 1966. *Accounting Evaluation and Economic Behavior*, Prentice Hall, Englewood Cliffs, New Jersey.

Cho, C., Frankel, R., Martin, X., 2024. Information reliability and market outcomes. *Management Science*, forthcoming.

Christensen, H. B., Nikolaev, V. V., Wittenberg-Moerman, R., 2016. Accounting information in financial contracting: The incomplete contract theory perspective. *Journal of Accounting Research* 54 (2), 397–435.

Coase, R. H., 1937. The nature of the firm. *Economica* 4 (16), 386–405.

Croft, A., 2019. Meddling monarchs, terrorism and climate change—Bankers would like investors to ignore these concerns looming over Saudi Aramco IPO. *Fortune*. November 11. Retrieved from https://fortune.com/2019/11/11/saudi-aramco-ipo-meddling-monarchs-terrorism-climate-change/.

Delta Air Lines, 2015. Credit and Guaranty Agreement. Retrieved from https://www.sec. gov/Archives/edgar/data/27904/000002790415000013/dal9302015ex101.htm.

Demsetz, H., 1993. George J. Stigler: Midcentury neoclassicalist with a passion to quantify. *Journal of Political Economy* 101 (5), 793–808.

Demski, J. S., Feltham, G. A., 1978. Economic incentives in budgetary control systems. *The Accounting Review* 53 (2), 334–347.

Fama, E. F., 1980. Agency problems and the theory of the firm. *Journal of Political Economy* 88 (2), 288–307.

Fama, E. F., Miller, M. H., 1972. *The Theory of Finance*. Dryden Press, Hinsdale, Illinois.

Friedman, M., 1992. *Money Mischief: Episodes in Monetary History*. Harcourt Brace & Company, New York, New York.

Gasparro, A., Lombardo, C., 2018. Family members of Campbell Soup founder bank board in Daniel Loeb's proxy fight. Market Watch. October 17. Retrieved from https:// www.marketwatch.com/story/family-members-of-campbell-soup-founder-back-board-in-daniel-loebs-proxy-fight-2018-10-17?siteid=rss&rss=1.

Grossman, S. J., Stiglitz, J. E., 1980. On the impossibility of informationally efficient markets. *American Economic Review* 70 (3), 393–408.

Hayek, F. A., 1960. *The Constitution of Liberty*. University of Chicago Press, Chicago, Illinois.

Jensen, M. C., Meckling, W. H., 1976. Theory of the firm: Managerial behavior, agency costs, and ownership structure. *Journal of Financial Economics* 3 (4), 305–360.

Johnson, H. T., Kaplan, R. S., 1991. *Relevance Lost: The Rise and Fall of Management Accounting*. Harvard Business School Press, Boston, Massachusetts.

Kothari, S. P., 2001. Capital markets research in accounting. *Journal of Accounting and Economics* 31 (1–3), 105–231.

Kothari, S. P., Ramanna, K., Skinner, D. J., 2010. Implications for GAAP from an analysis of positive research in accounting. *Journal of Accounting and Economics* 50 (2–3), 246–286.

Kothari, S. P., Zhang, L., Zuo, L., 2023. Disclosure regulation: Past, present, and future. In: Hilary G., McLean, R. D. (Eds.), *Handbook of Financial Decision Making*. Edward Elgar Publishing, Cheltenham, United Kingdom, 215–234.

Kyle, A. S., 1985. Continuous auctions and insider trading. *Econometrica: Journal of the Econometric Society* 53 (6), 1315–1335.

Megginson, W. L., Netter, J. M., 2001. From state to market: A survey of empirical studies on privatization. *Journal of Economic Literature* 39 (2), 321–389.

Ramanna, K., 2015. *Political Standards: Corporate Interest, Ideology, and Leadership in the Shaping of Accounting Rules for the Market Economy*. University of Chicago Press, Chicago, Illinois.

Roychowdhury, S., Shroff, N., Verdi, R., 2019. The effects of financial reporting and disclosure on corporate investment: A review. *Journal of Accounting and Economics* 68 (2–3), 101246.

Sangster, A., 2016. The genesis of double entry bookkeeping. *The Accounting Review* 91 (1), 299–315.

Sangster, A., 2018. Pacioli's lens: God, humanism, Euclid, and the rhetoric of double entry. *The Accounting Review* 93 (2), 299–314.

Singapore Airlines, 2017. Annual Report FY2016/17. Retrieved from https://www.singa poreair.com/saar5/pdf/Investor-Relations/Annual-Report/annualreport1617.pdf.

Smith, A., 1776. *An Inquiry into the Nature and Causes of the Wealth of Nations*. Retrieved from http://name.umdl.umich.edu/004861571.0001.001.

Watts, R. L., Zimmerman, J., 1978. Towards a positive theory of the determination of accounting standards. *The Accounting Review* 53 (1), 112–134.

Watts, R. L., Zimmerman, J. L., 1986. *Positive Accounting Theory*. Prentice-Hall, Englewood Cliffs, New Jersey.

Weisbach, M. S., 2021. *The Economist's Craft: An Introduction to Research, Publishing, and Professional Development*. Princeton University Press, Princeton, New Jersey.

Zimmerman, J. L., 1977. The municipal accounting maze: An analysis of political incentives. *Journal of Accounting Research* 15, 107–144.

2
Accounting Earnings and Stock Prices

2.1. Overview

As discussed in Chapter 1, earnings and other financial accounting outputs help firms function more efficiently. For earnings to be useful as an input to decisions and contracts, earnings must bear some relation to firm value. For decades, this idea, combined with the efficient market hypothesis (EMH) and valuation theory, has prompted accounting researchers to examine the relation between earnings and security prices. Market efficiency and valuation theory permit a mathematical formulation equating prices to the present value of expected future dividends. The relation between earnings and prices derives from a hypothesized (deterministic) relation between earnings and dividends. We amend this hypothesized relation to explain data given that earnings are a noisy and untimely indicator of the change in the marginal investor's future cash flow (i.e., dividend) expectations. These earnings-return properties challenge any story proposed to explain the "role of accounting" or the "usefulness" of earnings (e.g., the efficiency-grounded story). We summarize the salient findings from the research on the relation between earnings and security prices.

We hope to leave the reader with a sense of unease, the sense that the story linking the efficiency thesis of our book and the earnings-return evidence is tentative and is a work in progress. For example, we might accept the view that earnings will have a nonzero correlation with returns if we posit that earnings enhance firm efficiency by measuring performance so shareholders can incentivize managers and make appropriate retention decisions. However, this logic implies that we would observe some correlation; it does not allow us to predict its magnitude and need not imply that a higher correlation is better. To obtain a higher correlation beyond a certain point would necessitate that earnings contain unverifiable expectations. We find that a simple performance-measurement story requires further elaboration. At this stage, it does not allow us to generate predictions

The Economics of Accounting. Richard M. Frankel, S. P. Kothari, and Luo Zuo, Oxford University Press.

of sufficient refinement to satisfy our demand for completeness or, at minimum, comfortable coherence.[1]

We also note that the researcher's maintained hypotheses are critical. Interpretation of earnings-return correlations follows from the maintained hypothesis of market efficiency. Still, even granting market efficiency, the low correlation between contemporaneous earnings and returns presses us to delve more deeply into the nature of the underlying game that produces this outcome. We do not explore the equilibrium and incentive forces that might (one day) address our unease.

Our *reduced-form analysis* takes earnings as given. We do not inject cost/benefit or incentive/efficiency views into our explanation of these regularities. Instead, we discuss how far a discounted cash flow–based valuation framework, asset pricing theory, and the EMH can take us in formulating research designs and explaining results. We bridge the gap between earnings and cash flows using proportions, time-series analysis, noise, and/or lags. This formulation is consistent with our reduced-form analysis.

To understand the benefits/costs of our current empirical-research path, we contrast the present, positive-research approach to the a priori theorizing about the preferred income model that governed research before Ball and Brown (1968).[2] As noted, the "maintained hypothesis" of market efficiency aids interpretation of results. Our approach does not advocate a market efficiency view. Instead, our objective is to raise questions calling for further exploration by highlighting simplified logic, anomalies, and features that warrant explanations.

Of course, the notion of market efficiency is apt to raise the temperature of many academic discussions.[3] The intensity is understandable because truth, prestige, wealth, and honor—or at least a top journal publication—seem to require winning converts. We ask readers to indulge our use of market efficiency as the maintained hypothesis to simplify interpretation. Give us a little time. We consider other maintained hypotheses and provide alternative interpretations in light of these. However, we ground our analysis in

---

[1] Comfortable coherence is an imprecise, subjective state that changes with the depth of our understanding, but Gödel's theorem tells us that a complete logical system (i.e., a system that does not generate internally contradictory statements) is impossible.

[2] Detailed reviews of the impact of Ball and Brown (1968) are provided by Watts and Zimmerman (1986); Kothari (2001); Ball and Brown (2014, 2019); Dechow, Sloan, and Zha (2014); Clinch, Lyon, and Pinnuck (2019); Kothari (2019); and Kothari and Wasley (2019).

[3] Weitzman (2016) facilitates a thought-provoking conversation on this subject featuring Eugene Fama and Richard Thaler.

firm-value maximization, incentives, and competition, so our analysis shares an affinity for some form of market efficiency.

Despite its shortcomings, a reduced-form analysis offers several advantages as a starting point. First, reduced-form analysis provides a valuation-driven explanation for empirical regularities. Equilibrium-based stories should be consistent with these empirical relations. Second, an understanding of the valuation effects is central to a vast body of financial accounting research. Implicitly or explicitly, researchers account for these valuation effects in formulating research designs that attempt to test conjectures or theories about accounting's role, incentives, and other effects, including biases or irrational effects. Third, managers might find it helpful to understand how reported accounting numbers link to stock prices because their compensation often depends on reported accounting numbers and stock prices, and managers often use accounting as a guide to value maximization.[4]

Our discussion proceeds as follows. We begin by discussing the limits of a priori theorizing and explaining the notions of normative science (concerning what ought to be) and positive science (concerning what is). We then discuss the essentials of market efficiency, asset pricing, and valuation theory to formulate a relation between earnings and returns. We next summarize the evidence of the earnings-return relation and discuss its interpretations and misinterpretations. Finally, we offer some concluding remarks.

2.2. Developments That Laid the Foundation for Studying the Earnings-Return Relation

The correlation between earnings and returns is the most salient and robust empirical regularity in accounting research. The implications that researchers draw—or believe they can draw—from this correlation provide a window into their view of the function of accounting. Therefore, the quest to uncover the factors governing the earnings-return relation shaped the course of research for at least thirty years after Ball and Brown's publication of the first paper documenting this relation in 1968.

[4] The majority of management compensation likely rewards skill and performance. Evidence that managers manipulate earnings only proves that managers are mindful of the effects of this performance measure on their welfare and that shareholders use earnings to assess management performance. In the battle between speed guns and radar detectors, the police might find that the benefit of adopting more sophisticated methods to catch speeders does not offset the cost. Similarly, eliminating all earnings management is unlikely to be cost effective.

Those outside the field of accounting research can get a sense of the centrality of this correlation if they equate it to market-efficiency theory (Fama, 1970, 1991), the Modigliani-Miller theorem (Modigliani and Miller, 1958), behavioral theory (Tversky and Kahneman, 1974), and Coase's economic-efficiency theorem (Coase, 1960) in the fields of finance and economics. Comparing *correlation* to *theory* might strike the reader as inconsistent. It is. Yet this correlation shaped research and thought in accounting as much as theory shaped research and thought in other fields.[5]

We have journeyed far enough from Ball and Brown (1968) to see by a backward glance that serendipitous factors and path dependence—rather than foresight—shaped the route. These factors include (1) the state of accounting theory in the 1950s, 1960s, and early 1970s; (2) the rise of positive economics, especially at the University of Chicago; and (3) the influence of market efficiency and asset pricing theory. These factors continue to direct researchers' views and thus the questions they ask, the data they gather, and the conclusions they draw. In reexamining these factors, we aim to make this view explicit so that we can reexamine it and view not only Ball and Brown but also current research with new eyes. The circuitous route of accounting research is not unusual in scientific inquiry because the mind cannot foresee its own advancement (Popper, 1959; Hayek, 1960; Kuhn, 1962).

2.2.1. The Limits of A Priori Theorizing

Our discussion begins with historical context to understand what insight was thought at the time to be gained by examining the correlation between earnings and returns. Before Ball and Brown (1968) and Beaver (1968), research published in *The Accounting Review* and the *Journal of Accounting Research* tended to be a priori theorizing.[6] Accounting theory developed based on the objectives assumed by a researcher, and it was evaluated with logic and deductive reasoning (instead of empirical testing). For example, accounting theory proposed methods to produce an earnings measure more closely approximating the economic-income concept. Several developments

---

[5] We might wonder at the lack of theoretical influence at the start of modern accounting research. Recall that accounting's function relates to information asymmetry, moral hazard, and adverse selection—forces originally demoted to the status of "frictions" in neoclassical economics (e.g., see Hart, 1989). The information and agency theories were largely undeveloped when Ball and Brown (1968) and Beaver (1968) were published.

[6] The first volume of the *Journal of Accounting and Economics* was published in March 1979.

deflected this tendency toward the direction of "positive" empirical re-search. First, researchers began to realize that the proper accounting number depended on the decision that the number would guide. Different decisions required different concepts to be measured. For example, if managers contemplated an asset sale, the "exit value" of the asset and its "value-in-use" were relevant to the decision. The different concepts were not prob-lematic if they all pointed to the same number, but the researcher also saw that in markets with frictions (e.g., transaction costs and contracting costs), attempts to measure these concepts generally produced different results. Only a finer measure that could yield each of these concepts was unambigu-ously preferred by all decision-makers (ignoring production and processing costs).[7]

One conclusion that emerged from research on differing income models (e.g., historical cost, current cost, and replacement costs) was that using a mixture of these models to calculate income would produce balderdash. It would be like baking chocolate-chip cookies using a recipe that employed both English and metric units and omitted certain ingredients. A mixture of flour, butter, sugar, salt, baking soda, and vanilla will not produce a de-licious cookie unless their amounts are determined in appropriate relative proportions by measuring them along the same scale. Likewise, the cookie will not turn out as it should if the chef omits key ingredients like chips. The resulting concoction would more aptly be called a "baked mass" rather than a "chocolate-chip cookie." So, too, it seemed that the accountant could not pro-duce a useful or intelligible "income" measure when, for example, sales were measured at current values, inventory costs were measured at historical costs, and economically relevant events (e.g., changes in the value of land owned by the firm) were ignored. Ray Chambers (1976), a premier accounting theorist of that era, expressed these views vividly in his 1976 Saxe Lecture:

> Only a system of accounting which makes use of one valuation method will yield intelligible figures for assets and income, and figures which are con-sistent with one another; and that only if the valuation method is "dated value in exchange" or "dated money equivalent" will the balance sheet be serviceable as indicating "financial position" and the income account be

---

[7] Beaver (1998) labeled this change in belief the "accounting revolution." Financial accounting's role was no longer deemed to be the measurement of net asset value. Instead, researchers (and then regulators) shifted to the belief that accounting should provide useful information.

serviceable as indicating a genuine increment in net wealth or general capacity to pay dividends, make new investments, repay debts and make other such financial arrangements.

Ball and Brown (1968) use a quotation by Canning (1929) that expresses a similar sentiment to motivate their examination of the relation between earnings and returns. According to Canning, the mixture of income concepts results in a number with no intuitive meaning beyond a number that the accountant produces. The inscrutability of income and the seeming impossibility of constructing an argument for the best valuation basis led to the conclusion that a priori theorizing had limited use in guiding what accountants should do or interpreting the earnings number that accountants produced.

2.2.2. Positive Economic Theory

A second development that pulled research in an empirical testing direction was Friedman's (1953) and Popper's (1959) idea that science advances by testing falsifiable predictions. Positive economics (Friedman, 1953) equates understanding with prediction. There is no knowledge other than what one can obtain from falsifiable predictions, and predictions not yet falsified are in limbo awaiting rejection. According to Popper (1959), falsifiability distinguishes science from nonscience.

A belief (hypothesis) underlying positive research is that a limited number of forces predict accounting-related phenomena and, by implication, that others are of second-order importance. According to Friedman (1953, p. 33),

> A fundamental hypothesis of science is that appearances are deceptive and that there is a way of looking at or interpreting or organizing the evidence that will reveal superficially disconnected and diverse phenomena to be manifestations of a more fundamental and relatively simple structure.

According to the positive scientist, our current inability to isolate the key forces that enable prediction from the myriad of facts and circumstances indicates the meagerness of our current knowledge. It should therefore prompt further thought and encourage researchers to search for these forces, rather than abandoning the positive approach.

Prediction, the objective of positive economics, differs from interpretation or causation. A maintained hypothesis is necessary to interpret results or attach a causal story to an observed relation and isolate the factors useful for prediction. A maintained hypothesis is an assumption regarding the unobserved conditions underlying the world that lead to the observed relations. Friedman's essay provides an excellent elaboration of this concept and its subtlety. He uses the example of an object falling under the force of gravity. He notes that, in many instances, an equation describing objects falling in a vacuum can predict any object's velocity. Rather than describing the equation as "assuming" a vacuum, Friedman frames the velocity equation as predicting that, under a wide range of circumstances, an object falls "as if" it were in a vacuum. His "as if" formulation conveys his point that we should use the prediction-accuracy standard to judge the aptness of a maintained hypothesis. Assumptions simplify reality to enable prediction. They are literally false. It is fruitless to argue about the validity of assumptions in isolation. We can only assess the importance of their violation by comparing predictions of the equation to observed results.[8] If the object we study is a bowling ball, predictions assuming a vacuum might offer a useful degree of accuracy. However, neither a bowling ball at terminal velocity nor a feather falls "as if" it is in a vacuum. The predictions of the basic velocity/time equation will be useless in these contexts, and researchers must use more complex equations that incorporate the force of air on the object's surface as it falls.[9] Positive science advances by explaining a broader class of observed results with a more limited set of factors.

Any story formed from maintained hypotheses, while not scientific, might not be meaningless. The story can be useful to positive economics if it offers a means to refine predictions. For example, the story might suggest the existence of other observable relations not yet examined. The story might imply additional forces and interactions between forces that allow predictions under a greater variety of circumstances. The story might suggest outcomes when data are sparse and statistical power is limited. Data might become

---

[8] An old joke shows the mischief caused by misunderstanding the role of assumptions. "To open a can of corn found in a desert, an economist only needs to assume that he has a can opener." An economist acting within the guidelines of positive theory would do no such thing, because it would lead to incorrect predictions. The economist in the joke does not open the can, so he does not behave "as if" he has a can opener.

[9] More complex equations continue to fall short in some contexts. Despite advances in computational fluid dynamics and computer modeling, aeronautical engineers continue to use wind tunnels to test their designs.

available or creative means might one day be devised to test the story's implications.

Still, overemphasis on stories is troublesome when it elevates conjectures in unobserved or untestable areas to the level of testable predictions. Few economists confine their assertions to cases where their predictions have been tested or are testable. They are tempted to generalize empirical results or make statements about concepts that are difficult to quantify, like social welfare. A maintained hypothesis and the story engendered by it provide the basis for such statements. Such statements degenerate into pseudoscientific knowledge when the economist contorts the story to accommodate contradictory observations so that the original statements cannot be rejected.

An important criticism of positive science is that an investigative process based on positive science and falsifiability lacks direction. Its best route cannot be grounded in deduction (Hume, 1748; Popper, 1959). The scientific method offers insufficient guidance for assessing what predictions and relations should be tested. Tests are seldom definitive, and the scientist must decide whether to retest or formulate a new hypothesis.[10] In short, we use intuition and stories based on maintained hypotheses to suggest which relations are important and warrant investigation. Unscientific concepts like *values* (i.e., axioms for assessing the relative merits of unresolved questions) and *intuition* guide the course of positive science. Therefore, positive science is not a product of pure observation. Friedman (1953) also notes that positive science does not guide us in choosing among the infinite number of hypotheses consistent with observations. He concedes, "The choice among alternative hypotheses equally consistent with available evidence must to some extent be arbitrary, though there is general agreement that relevant considerations are suggested by the criteria 'simplicity' and 'fruitfulness,' themselves notions that defy completely objective specification" (p. 10). We can understand the severity of this defect if we omit the words "to some extent" and "completely" from Friedman's statement.[11]

---

[10] There is some debate on the extent of capriciousness inherent in scientific inquiry. Popper (1959) quotes Einstein: " 'Search for those highly universal laws . . . from which a picture of the world can be obtained by pure deduction. There is no logical path,' he says, 'leading to these . . . laws. They can only be reached by intuition, based upon something like an intellectual love ("Einffihlung") of the objects of experience' " (p. 31). Simon (1973) suggests that some search paths can be shown to be more efficient, at least when scientists are engaged in the process of what Kuhn (1962) calls "ordinary science."

[11] A different view is that scientific knowledge is not the only form of knowledge. See Strauss (1989), who reasserts the role of political "philosophy" in contrast to political "science" as a way to understand regimes and statesmanship. Such arguments are beyond the scope of our discussion. Our goal is to aid readers in applying the positive science method to accounting research. However, some

Still, we agree with Friedman (1953, p. 34): "A theory is the way we perceive 'facts' and we cannot perceive 'facts' without a theory." Ball and Brown (2014, p. 21) make the same point in discussing Ball and Brown (1968): "In that sense, the modern 'positivist' literature allows arm-chair theorizing to be replaced with theorizing based on systematic observation." Since the seminal work of Friedman, mainstream research methodology in economics, finance, and accounting has been positive rather than normative. Watts and Zimmerman (1986, p. 2) state, "The objective of accounting theory is to *explain* and *predict* accounting practice." Yet positive accounting research has normative implications, and normative reasoning can guide empirical tests (Watts, 1977; Ball, 2008; Kothari, Ramanna, and Skinner, 2010; Ball and Brown, 2014; Leuz and Wysocki, 2016). As noted in Watts (1977, p. 54),

The development of prescriptions and the development of theory are not incompatible. The development of prescriptions which are likely to achieve their objectives requires an underlying theory which explains observed phenomena: which predicts the effects of particular prescriptions.

2.2.3. Finance Theory: The Efficient Market Hypothesis, Asset Pricing, and Equity Valuation

Theories (stories) developed in finance are the third component of the foundation used to support the study of the earnings-return relation. Some form of the EMH and capital asset pricing model are the maintained assumptions in research examining the relation between earnings and returns. What follows is a brief overview of efficient market theory, asset pricing theory, and valuation theory that underlies studies of the relation between earnings and returns. Our discussion here draws heavily from Watts and Zimmerman (1986).

2.2.3.1. The Efficient Market Hypothesis
Fama (1965) developed the EMH by combining economics with earlier work on the statistical properties of stock prices (Bachelier, 1900). Efficient markets are a natural consequence of zero economic profits in competitive

awareness of the world next door can help us understand the limits and advantages of the path we choose.

markets. Economic profits are the surplus left after deducting the cost of the capital invested. Securities markets (e.g., the market for The Home Depot Inc. shares on the New York Stock Exchange) are highly competitive. Fama (1965, p. 4) describes them as characterized by a "large number of rational, profit maximizers actively competing, with each trying to predict future market values of individual securities, and where important current information is almost freely available to all participants." Under these conditions, the EMH predicts that "security markets fully reflect all available information" (Fama, 1991, p. 1575). Jensen (1978, p. 96) provides an operational definition of an efficient market as a market that is "efficient with respect to information set θ_t if it is impossible to make economic profits by trading on the basis of information set θ_t."

Jensen's definition has two components that warrant further explanation. These are "economic profits" and "information set." To begin with the latter, efficiency is defined with respect to an information set. The set could include past prices, past insider trades, or past Super Bowl winners, though sensible information sets include data helpful in assessing the value of securities. This logic leads to the prediction that if earnings intersect with the set of data useful for assessing the value of securities, earnings will correlate with stock prices.

As noted above, economic profit is the return earned in excess of the cost of capital. In the case of stock investments, economic profit is a return that differs from the return required by investors, given the security's risk. A security of a given risk is expected to earn a "required" or "normal return" in a competitive market because if investors believe its return exceeds the required return, they will buy the security, increasing its price and reducing its expected return to where it equates to its normal return. The idea that firms and individuals will adjust investment based on the difference between expected and required rates of returns is the central prediction of microeconomics (Stigler, 1963; Modigliani and Miller, 1966).[12]

We might better understand the limits and importance of this zero-economic-profit prediction if we liken it to the prediction that water seeks its level in hydrology. The "water seeks its level" theory might lead us to believe

[12] "There is no more important proposition in economic theory than that, under competition, the rate of return on investment tends toward equality in all industries" (Stigler, 1963, p. 54). "The central normative proposition of the micro theory of capital is that the firm should adjust its capital stock until the marginal rate of return on further investment (or disinvestment) is equal to the cost of capital" (Modigliani and Miller, 1966, p. 333).

that all the water on earth will be at sea level, in the oceans. According to estimates, approximately 97 percent of the earth's water is contained in the oceans (Gleick, 1993), so the theory seems to result in a prediction consistent with the data. Yet, to us, the 0.0001 percent of the earth's water contained in biological organisms is paramount. We would not be reading this discussion without this unpredicted water. This analogy gives us insight into the problem of assessing the descriptive validity of any prediction, including the predictive validity of the central microeconomic prediction that underlies market efficiency. For the most part, we might expect it to be descriptively valid. Still, we might also wonder whether prediction errors are critical in some contexts.[13]

The development of the EMH spawned an industry of empirical research in accounting, finance, and economics. This research tries to refute the null hypothesis of market efficiency by examining whether, on average, nonzero economic profits can be earned by trading on particular information sets. Since economic profits are net of the cost of capital, their calculation from a trading strategy entails cost-of-capital estimates. For publicly traded stocks, total profit is measured as the stock return, R_t, from t−1 to t. R_t is computed as $(P_t + D_t)/P_{t-1}$, where P_t is the stock price at time t, and D_t is the dividend paid on the security between time t−1 and t. Computation of an abnormal return requires a normal return or cost of equity capital to be deducted from R_t. Another term for the cost of capital is the expected rate of return, $E(R)$. Presumably, this expected return varies with the riskiness of the underlying security. So an asset pricing model is needed to convert risk to a normal return or a certainty equivalent that can be used to test stock-price observations for abnormal returns.[14] An overview of the underlying theory and methods of estimating the cost of capital for stocks appears in the Supplement of this chapter.

If the cost of obtaining an information set is zero, then the abnormal return from trading on the information set in an efficient market is also expected to be zero. Information sets that are costly to acquire have the potential to generate positive abnormal trading profits. The fact that a particular information

---

[13] The hydrology example illustrates the incoherence of the "Do you believe in market efficiency?" question. A more lucid question is, "To what extent should market efficiency influence our decisions or predictions in this context?" or "Under what conditions do asset prices behave as if the markets were efficient?"

[14] See, for example, Modigliani and Miller (1958, p. 262): "Investment decisions are then supposed to be based on a comparison of this 'risk adjusted' or 'certainty equivalent' yield with the market rate of interest. No satisfactory explanation has yet been provided, however, as to what determines the size of the risk discount and how it varies in response to changes in other variables."

set is costly for an investor to acquire does not imply that she would earn positive abnormal returns by trading on that information set. For example, if multiple individuals incur costs to obtain the same information set and they compete in trading against each other, some of them may not make any trading profits to cover their information costs. Moreover, the cost of acquiring and processing an information set varies across investors, in which case the high-cost acquirers might not be able to recoup their costs (and therefore might not survive in the long run or will learn and refrain from incurring the costs).[15] Competition and the resulting innovation it engenders reduce information-collection costs and imply that price can also reflect information that is difficult to acquire. Indeed, competitive forces extend the bounds of the information set reflected in price; consider, for example, firms' extensive investments in communication infrastructure that equates prices across geographically distinct exchanges (Onstad, 2013). Thus, cost is not a static barrier. The evolving cost of efficient information producers continually resets the limit of the information set in a competitive environment.[16]

Researchers have crafted tests of the EMH based on variations in the nature of the information set, θ_t, that is assumed to be available to implement a trading strategy. Fama (1970) places these tests in three categories: In the *weak* form tests, θ_t is only historical prices or returns. In the *semi-strong* form tests, θ_t expands to include all publicly available information at time t (e.g., earnings announcements or stock splits). In the *strong* form tests, θ_t includes any information at time t that is relevant for price formation (i.e., public and private information).

Early evidence from the tests of market efficiency was generally consistent with the weak and semi-strong forms of the EMH. Tests of the strong form of the EMH produced systematic abnormal returns, but the evidence was restricted to corporate insiders and specialists on security exchanges with monopolistic access to information.[17] As a result of the supportive evidence, the

---

[15] The implication is that SEC filings should be designed to be most interpretable by professional analysts rather than average retail investors (Loughran and McDonald, 2020).

[16] Bloomfield (2002) makes a similar argument that statistics that are more costly to extract from public data are less completely revealed by market prices. It is worth noting that incomplete revelation does not necessarily mean market underreaction. For example, the market can overreact to accruals in annual earnings when it fails to fully reflect information about future earnings contained in the accrual and cash flow components of current earnings (Sloan, 1996).

[17] Grossman and Stiglitz (1980, p. 405) note that the market cannot be strong-form efficient (i.e., fully revealing traders' private information) "since if it [were], those who spent resources to obtain [information] would receive no compensation." In their noisy rational expectations model, incomplete revelation is not caused by irrational investors' information-processing bias (a behavioral explanation) but rather by rational investors' information costs (an economic explanation). See

EMH gained wide acceptance among academics as descriptive (see Fama, 1976, Ch. 5). This, however, did not last. In the 1980s and 1990s, researchers produced evidence suggesting that capital markets might not be informationally efficient. Before getting to this evidence, we describe the EMH's role in the breakthrough developments in empirical accounting research in the 1960s and its continued importance as a maintained hypothesis in theoretical and empirical research in accounting and financial economics.

Under a maintained hypothesis of market efficiency, researchers can specify the relation between accounting information and stock prices under the null hypothesis. For example, a positive relation between accounting earnings and stock returns constitutes evidence that earnings information overlaps with the information used by investors to price securities. Market efficiency suggests that investors price securities based on underlying economic reality. Therefore, the maintained hypothesis of market efficiency combined with the empirical evidence of a positive earnings-return correlation implies that earnings contain value-relevant information. Absent market efficiency, a positive earnings-return correlation could imply that earnings contain misleading information or that earnings mislead investors (i.e., investors fixate on earnings).[18] In addition, if the maintained hypothesis is market efficiency, neither systematic positive nor negative abnormal returns in the periods following earnings announcements are predicted.[19] Post-earnings announcement drifts (i.e., systematic abnormal returns after earnings announcements predicted based on the earnings surprise) would constitute evidence that the market is not efficient in the Fama (1970) sense.[20]

A maintained hypothesis of market inefficiency permits a wide range of possible relations between value-relevant (or value-irrelevant) information and returns depending on the type of information-processing bias assumed

---

also Verrecchia (1982) and Admati and Pfleiderer (1988). See Lee and So (2015) and Blankespoor, deHann, and Marinovic (2020) for comprehensive reviews of the literature on disclosure processing costs.

[18] An equilibrium can exist where firms manage earnings and investors correctly discount these earnings numbers for valuation purposes (Stein, 1989).

[19] See also Kormendi and Lipe (1987), who find no evidence that the reactions of stock returns to unexpected earnings are excessively volatile.

[20] Ng, Rusticus, and Verdi (2008) provide evidence that transaction costs constrain the informed trades that are necessary to incorporate earnings information into price and lead to the existence and persistence of post-earnings announcement drifts. Thus, the market is still efficient in the Jensen (1978) sense in that investors cannot earn profits based on this information.

to be reflected in prices.[21] The three conditions for market inefficiency are (a) investors' information-processing biases that result in market over- and underreaction, (b) correlation of biases across investors, and (c) limited arbitrage (i.e., the existence of rational investors who understand that their corrective actions should not be sufficient to make markets efficient). Without additional assumptions about which processing bias is dominant and applicable to earnings and other available information, researchers cannot specify the earnings-return relation when earnings reflect (or do not reflect) value-relevant information (Fama, 1998). Investors might overreact or underreact to value-relevant news in earnings, depending on the information-processing bias and specific facts and circumstances. For example, investors might overreact (underreact) to positive (negative) earnings news that is consistent (inconsistent) with a string of past positive earnings news. Therefore, predictions require behavioral theories of inefficient markets to specify these relations with the maintained hypothesis of limited arbitrage (e.g., Bernard and Thomas, 1990; Chan, Frankel, and Kothari, 2004).

An alternative way to assess market efficiency is to examine whether time-series or cross-sectional variation in stock returns is explained by economic fundamentals (Fama, 1990). In this analysis, the maintained hypothesis is that explanatory variables like industrial production are real, economic, fundamental variables measured with reasonable accuracy.

2.2.3.2. The Relation between Earnings, Dividends, and Prices

According to Williams (1938, p. 56), financial economics defines a security's value as the discounted present value of expected dividends, that is, future cash flows, from the security.[22] Formally, assuming a constant expected rate of return, E(R), equal to r for discounting expected dividends, the market value, or the price, of a security at time t is

$$P_t = \Sigma_{k = 1 \text{ to } \infty} E_t\left(D_{t+k}\right) / \left(1 + r\right)^k \qquad (2.1)$$

---

[21] Information is value relevant if it correlates with the information rational investors use to value the firm's stock. Such information includes information helpful for assessing the amount, timing, and riskiness of the firm's future cash flows, including the value of investment options available to the firm.

[22] See Hirshleifer (1958), Fama and Miller (1972), or Brealey et al. (2023, Ch. 4).

where $E_t(D_{t+k})$ represents the market's expectation of dividends to be paid in period $t + k$.[23] The price of a stock is based on the market's expectation of dividends from owning the stock and the expected rate of return the market requires for the risk of those cash flows. We call the present value, P_t, in equation (2.1) the market value. It is the value of the claims on the firm in the capital market.

Equation (2.1) shows a relation between security prices and expected dividends and discount rates. Empirically, accounting earnings can be associated with a firm's current and future dividends. This association is more intuitively understood from the relation between a firm's cash flows, dividends, investments, and earnings. Corporations generate cash flows from operating activities that they either pay out as dividends or reinvest in the firm's operations. Reinvestments increase future cash flows. If earnings and cash flows are associated, then a firm's accounting earnings for the current period can provide information on the firm's current cash flows (i.e., dividends and investments). In addition, if current cash flows provide information about future cash flows, then earnings would be informative about expected future cash flows. This information about cash flows, in turn, conveys information about dividends and affects firm value according to equation (2.1).

We use a simple example to illustrate the relation between accounting earnings and stock prices. At time t, assume that investors expect the firm to generate cash flow (CF) in each future period and reinvest \$I in the firm's operations each period. The remaining cash flow is paid out as dividends, that is, dividends are the difference between a firm's cash flows from its operating activities, CF, and the investment, I, in a period:[24]

$$D = CF - I \qquad (2.2)$$

[23] If the expected rate of return is not constant over time, then the valuation equation (2.1) is modified as

$$P_t = \Sigma_{k=1\,to\,\infty} E_t\left(D_{t+k}\right) / \Pi_{k=1\,to\,\infty}[1 + E\left(r_{t+k}\right)]$$

where $E(r_{t+k})$ is the expected rate of return for period $t + k$. This standard valuation model assumes that real options (Dixit and Pindyck, 1994) have zero value.

[24] Dividends here should be interpreted broadly as free cash flows to equity holders. We assume that all these free cash flows are distributed to shareholders. This assumption does not affect equity valuation as long as the cost of equity equals the return generated from reinvesting these free cash flows. Value is created by beating the competitive return, i.e., the cost of equity. Merely paying more or fewer dividends will not alter value.

Finally, assume that the only accounting accrual is depreciation, and it is expected to remain level at Depr. Accounting earnings in a period, X, are

$$X = CF - Depr$$

$$= D + I - Depr, \tag{2.3}$$

or

$$D = X + Depr - I. \tag{2.4}$$

For simplicity, assume that depreciation equals the investment each year. Hence, $D = X$. Since we assume that the market expects the firm to generate a constant stream of cash flows, earnings, and dividends, we can represent these expectations as

$$E_t(X_{t+k}) = X_t \tag{2.5}$$

and

$$E_t(D_{t+k}) = D_t. \tag{2.6}$$

Price at time t, P_t, using equation (2.1) and the above assumptions about earnings and dividends, can be expressed as

$$P_t = \Sigma_{k=1\,to\,\infty}\, E_t\left(D_{t+k}\right)/\left(1 + r\right)^k$$

$$= \Sigma_{k=1\,to\,\infty}\, E_t\left(X_{t+k}\right)/\left(1 + r\right)^k$$

$$= \Sigma_{k=1\,to\,\infty}\, X_t\,/\left(1 + r\right)^k$$

$$= X_t\,/\,r. \tag{2.7}$$

This is the P-E multiple valuation of a stock in which price is a multiple of earnings with no growth.[25]

[25] Because we do not observe negative prices, if the simple price-earnings multiple model is descriptive, earnings must be positive.

This simple example illustrates that accounting earnings are related to stock prices if earnings contain information on expected cash flows. We also expect accounting numbers to provide information on the expected rate of return used in calculating the present value of expected dividends in equation (2.1). The expected rate of return reflects the riskiness of the expected dividend stream. Risky firms' cash flows are likely to be more volatile than less risky firms' cash flows. Because earnings and cash flows might be positively associated, realized earnings are likely to reflect the riskiness of the cash flows in their volatility over time.

Another reason to expect earnings to convey information about the expected rate of return is that dividends and earnings include the expected (i.e., normal) rate of return on the firm's investments.[26] Consider a $1,000 investment. If the expected rate of return is 12 percent, then we expect a dividend and earnings stream of $120 in perpetuity so that the value of the investment, according to equations (2.1) or (2.7), will be $1,000. If the risk of the investment goes up such that the expected rate of return becomes 14 percent and if the firm can pass on the increased cost of the capital to its customers, then we expect the dividend stream to rise to $140 per period. Because the cost of the (equity) capital invested is not deducted in determining earnings, earnings can convey information about the expected rate of return used in calculating firm value according to equation (2.1).[27] This is also seen from differences in the price-earnings multiples that arise from differences in the expected rates of return.[28] In the simple example with a $1,000 investment, the price-earnings multiple is 8.3 (= $1,000/$120) when the expected rate of return is 12 percent, whereas it falls to 7.1 (= $1,000/$140) when the expected rate of return rises to 14 percent.

2.2.3.3. The Relation between Changes in Earnings and Changes in Stock Prices

While an empirical test based on the valuation equation (2.7) is intuitive, factors that affect current and expected future cash flows and earnings would confound this straightforward test. These factors influence the estimated

---

[26] See Ball, Kothari, and Watts (1993) and Ohlson (1995).

[27] Kothari, Lewellen, and Warner (2006) find that aggregate returns and contemporaneous earnings growth are *negatively* correlated partly because good earnings are associated with higher discount rates. They argue that aggregate earnings fluctuate with discount rates because both are tied to macroeconomic conditions, while firm earnings primarily reflect idiosyncratic cash-flow news.

[28] See Beaver and Morse (1978).

statistical relation between prices and earnings and create the potential for observing a spurious relation between the levels of earnings and stock prices. For example, large firms often generate more earnings and have higher stock prices than small firms. This cross-sectional scale difference among sample firms can result in an observed positive relation between share prices and earnings even when these variables are independent of current-period earnings for a given firm. In addition, growth firms may have lower current-period earnings and higher stock prices than mature firms, resulting in a downward bias in the estimated correlation between share prices and earnings.[29]

Instead of correlating the levels of prices and earnings as in Ball and Brown (1968), accounting researchers estimate the relation between *changes* in earnings and *changes* in stock prices using annual or quarterly data. Researchers can also examine the relation between earnings changes and price changes over a narrow window of a day or two around earnings announcement dates. Valuation equations (2.1) and (2.7) allow us to show that changes in accounting earnings *are* related to the *realized* rate of return on the firm. The larger the sample of firm-year earnings announcements pooled over time, and the narrower the measurement window, the more likely it is that other random factors affecting future cash flows and the level of stock prices average out to zero. This approach enables researchers to more definitively conclude that the estimated relation indicates that earnings convey information about current and future cash flows.

To see these properties of the earnings change/return formulation more clearly, we derive the relation between changes in accounting earnings (a surrogate for changes in cash flows) and rates of return. Assume that the firm has a constant expected rate of return and a constant stream of expected earnings, X_t, at time t. The valuation is according to equations (2.1) and (2.7). Suppose that at time t + 1, the firm announces earnings X_{t+1}. Because the market's expectation at time t is $E_t(X_{t+1}) = X_t$, the unexpected earnings are the change in earnings from X_t to X_{t+1}, or ΔX_{t+1}. Whether the earnings surprise influences the market's expectation of future periods' earnings depends on the process that generates earnings. If the process is a martingale or random walk, then expected earnings for *all* future periods would be revised to the

---

[29] Holthausen and Watts (2001) point out that the extent to which current earnings capture future cash flows is likely to be smaller for riskier and higher-growth firms.

most recent earnings observation, that is, $E_{t+1}(X_{t+k}) = X_{t+1}$. If expected future earnings are a constant regardless of current earnings realizations, that is, $E_{t+1}(X_{t+k}) = X$, current unexpected earnings do not affect the expectation of future earnings. This means the change in expected earnings for all future periods is zero.

We begin by assuming that the earnings announcement causes the market to revise its earnings expectations for all future periods to be X_{t+1}. That is, for all k,

$$E_{t+1}(X_{t+k}) = X_{t+1}. \tag{2.8}$$

Substituting this expectation into equation (2.7) to value the stock at time t + 1, we obtain

$$P_{t+1} = X_{t+1}/r. \tag{2.9}$$

Assuming that dividends equal earnings in each period, dividends and capital appreciation for the stock from time t to t + 1 are

$$\Delta P_{t+1} + D_{t+1} = (X_{t+1}/r) - (X_t/r) + X_{t+1}$$

$$= (\Delta X_{t+1}/r) + X_{t+1}. \tag{2.10}$$

Adding and subtracting X_t from the right-hand side of equation (2.10), we obtain

$$\Delta P_{t+1} + D_{t+1} = (\Delta X_{t+1}/r) + \Delta X_{t+1} + X_t \tag{2.11}$$

which can be rewritten as

$$\Delta P_{t+1} + D_{t+1} = (1 + 1/r)\Delta X_{t+1} + E_t(X_{t+1}). \tag{2.12}$$

Dividing both sides by P_t expresses equation (2.12) in the rate of return form as

$$R_{t+1} = (1 + 1/r)\Delta X_{t+1}/P_t + E_t(X_{t+1})/P_t. \tag{2.13}$$

Since at time t, the stock is expected to pay a perpetuity of $D_t = X_t = E_t(X_{t+1})$, the expected return on the stock is

$$E_t(R_{t+1}) = r = E_t(X_{t+1})/P_t \qquad (2.14)$$

so equation (2.13) can be rearranged as

$$R_{t+1} - E_t(R_{t+1}) = (1 + 1/r)\Delta X_{t+1}/P_t \qquad (2.15)$$

or

$$R_{t+1} - E_t(R_{t+1}) = (1 + 1/r)[X_{t+1} - E_t(X_{t+1})]/P_t. \qquad (2.16)$$

Equation (2.16) shows that earnings surprises (i.e., unexpected earnings) would be positively associated with the realized rates of return in excess of the expected rate of return on a stock. That is, the larger the unexpected earnings in a period, the larger the abnormal rate of return for the period. Equation (2.16) also shows that much of the impact of the earnings surprise on the realized rate of return comes from the (assumed) permanent revision in expectation of future earnings that is implied by the earnings surprise. More generally, the greater the revision in future earnings (i.e., persistence of earnings), the greater the price reaction to a unit surprise in earnings. The coefficient relating the current earnings surprise to current returns embeds revisions in future earnings expectations.

Equation (2.16) explains why researchers estimate the relation between *changes* in earnings and *changes* in stock prices. The estimation removes the potentially confounding effect of expected rates of return. The abnormal rate of return for period t, $R_{t+1} - E_t(R_{t+1})$, is the unexpected *change* in the firm's stock price for period t, adjusted for dividends, relative to the firm's stock price at the beginning of period t. The term in parentheses on the right-hand side of equation (2.16) is the *unexpected change* in the firm's earnings in period t. Recall that the preceding analysis assumes earnings are a perfect surrogate for cash flows. However, even if accounting earnings are an imperfect surrogate for cash flows, unexpected accounting earnings are likely to be correlated with unexpected cash flows and hence with the realized rates of return in excess of the expected rate of return on a stock.

To empirically test the relation between unexpected earnings and abnormal returns, researchers must estimate expected earnings and normal rates of returns.[30] Expected earnings are often derived from time series models (e.g., the random walk model in our simple example) or analysts' forecasts. The deterministic earnings-return relation in Equation (2.16) is derived under the assumption that earnings are the only source of information that affects stock prices. Under this assumption, the market's expectation of future earnings is based purely on the information in the past time series of earnings. However, prices reflect a richer information set than the past time series of earnings (Beaver, Lambert, and Morse, 1980) and even beyond managers' information set (Zuo, 2016; Goldstein, 2023). If prices lead earnings (i.e., prices reflect information about future earnings that the past earnings time series does not contain), then the market's and the time-series expectations of earnings differ, and an accurate proxy for the market-unexpected earnings is needed.[31] Normal rates of return are based on theories and empirical research in finance on expected rates of return. In particular, researchers typically employ the capital asset pricing model (CAPM) and its extensions to determine the normal rate of return. We briefly discuss the asset pricing models in the Supplement of this chapter.

2.3. Evidence of the Earnings-Return Relation

To determine the usefulness of accounting earnings in assessing current and expected cash flows, researchers empirically test the relation between unexpected earnings and abnormal returns. There are two types of studies. Association studies test the relation between accounting earnings

---

[30] Some researchers directly use unadjusted realized rates of return as the dependent variable (e.g., Collins et al., 1994). They rely on the argument that only a small fraction of the variation in annual returns in the time series or cross-section is accounted for by the variation in expected rates of return (e.g., Black, 1993). However, Ball, Kothari, and Nikolaev (2013) show, both analytically and empirically, that failing to control for expected returns and expected earnings leads to biased estimators of the relation between the unexpected "news" components of earnings and returns (e.g., the conventional Basu [1997] regression coefficients).

[31] Under the assumption that prices do not lead earnings, the earnings-level-deflated-by-price and earnings-change-deflated-by-price specifications yield identical slope coefficients. When prices lead earnings, the specification using the earnings-level-deflated-by-price variable outperforms the specification using the earnings-change-deflated-by-price variable. The specification with an accurate proxy for the market-unexpected earnings performs the best. See Kothari (1992) for detailed derivations of these conclusions.

and security price performance contemporaneously measured over a long window (e.g., one or more years). In contrast, event studies typically rely on short windows (e.g., two to three days) surrounding an accounting information event (e.g., an earnings announcement) to test whether the market price reacts to the event.[32] The maintained hypothesis underlying the studies on the earnings-return relation is that the stock market quickly reflects all public information and is efficient in the semi-strong form. This section briefly summarizes the empirical results and discusses their interpretations and misinterpretations.

The two seminal papers in this area are Ball and Brown (1968) and Beaver (1968). Ball and Brown document a significantly positive association between the sign of the unexpected change in annual earnings and the sign of the abnormal return in each of the twelve months preceding the annual report announcement. Their calculation suggests that accounting earnings capture one-half or more of all the information reflected in contemporaneous stock returns.[33] Thus, the information content of accounting earnings is considerable in that a significant portion of the information used by investors to assess cash flows to equity investors and value them overlaps with the change in earnings. This analysis does not assume that accounting earnings are the only source of information available to investors, and the correlation does not allow us to infer a causal connection between earnings and returns—in the sense that prices respond to earnings releases. Investors might obtain information from more timely or readily available sources than earnings reports. In their event study (around the earnings announcement month), Ball and Brown's calculation shows that the market anticipates more than 85 percent of the information in the annual earnings number before the earnings announcement event. This evidence suggests that information sources (e.g., quarterly reports, macroeconomic data, private information gathering) preempt the annual report.

[32] Fama et al. (1969) published the first event study in financial economics. They align sample firm return windows in the stock-split event time and study their stock returns before, during, and after this event. In short-horizon event studies, risk adjustment is typically unimportant (given daily expected returns of about 0.05 percent); in multiyear, long-horizon event studies, appropriate adjustment for risk is critical in calculating abnormal returns. See Kothari and Warner (2007) for a thorough discussion of the econometrics of event studies.

[33] Ball and Brown (1968) estimate the value of information contained in the annual income number using the returns of the two portfolios constructed from (buying or selling short) all firms and years as classified by the sign of the unexpected change in annual earnings.

Beaver (1968) uses a shorter-window, event-study method and examines the variability of stock returns and trading volume in the weeks surrounding the annual earnings announcement date. An advantage of this approach is that he does not need to specify an earnings expectation model (as in Ball and Brown). Beaver documents significantly larger price and volume spikes around earnings announcements than at other times. These results suggest that earnings announcements alter investors' expectations and induce trading, and through investor trading, prices incorporate information conveyed by earnings announcements.[34] As conclusions from event studies critically depend on whether the events are dispersed in calendar time and whether there are concurrent confounding events (e.g., dividend or stock-split announcements), Beaver's sample comprises firms listed on the New York Stock Exchange (NYSE) with fiscal-year-ends other than December 31, and featuring fewer than twenty news items in the *Wall Street Journal*. In his discussion of Beaver (1968), Davidson (1968, p. 97) carefully notes, "Any inferences that can be drawn from the study apply only to this particular subpopulation."[35] Bamber, Christensen, and Gaver (2000) investigate the generalizability of Beaver's results and show that most individual earnings announcements do not generate unusual market reactions, including announcements by Fortune 200 firms. Recently, Beaver, McNichols, and Wang (2020) find that management guidance, analyst forecasts, and disaggregated financial statement line items are more frequently bundled with earnings announcements from 2001 to 2016, and these concurrent information releases explain a substantial fraction of the increase in market response to earnings announcements since 2001.

The evidence of Ball and Brown and Beaver rejects the criticism that accounting numbers produced by the accounting system are meaningless and do not capture economic fundamentals (i.e., the null hypothesis is that the reaction/correlation will be insignificant). While Beaver's evidence suggests that earnings announcements are an important information event, Ball

[34] The famous no-trade theorem of Milgrom and Stokey (1982) states that if there is common knowledge about the structure of a market, rational expectations of all agents will lead to no trade. The intuition is that any attempt an agent makes to initiate a trade will reveal the agent's private information, and no other agents will agree to trade. Verrecchia (2001) discusses various models that relax the assumptions in Milgrom and Stokey and predict investor trading following informative public disclosure.

[35] Davidson (1968, p. 99) also says, "As a CPA, my first reaction to Mr. Beaver's excellent paper is to feel like a bumblebee confronted by an aeronautical engineer. The engineer has just proved to the bumblebee that the bumblebee can fly. The bumblebee's outraged: he knew he could fly all the time. But he's also glad: now he may learn to straighten out and fly right...."

and Brown's evidence shows that earnings announcements are not a timely source of information to investors. Later research provides more systematic evidence that quantifies the relative importance of earnings announcements in providing new information to the stock market. Ball and Shivakumar (2008) find that the adjusted R^2 in a regression of annual stock returns on the firms' four quarterly earnings-announcement returns averages approximately 5 percent to 9 percent. Using this R^2 as a measure of the proportion of total information incorporated in stock prices annually that is associated with earnings announcements, they conclude that the average quarterly earnings announcement provides modest incremental information (i.e., 1 percent to 2 percent of total annual information) to the market. They find that management forecasts and analyst forecast revisions before earnings announcements provide substantial information to investors, but earnings announcements per se are not associated with abnormal information arrival. Together, the empirical evidence suggests that the primary economic function of accounting is not to provide timely information to the stock market at earnings announcements.[36] Yet independently verified accounting information can discipline alternative disclosures made by managers or other parties. Thus, the information role of accounting cannot be evaluated solely based on the magnitude of market reactions around announcement periods (Ball, Jayaraman, and Shivakumar, 2012). *How* accounting matters is an enduring question (Ball, 2024) that we explore in this book.

Motivated by Ball and Brown and Beaver, earnings response coefficients (ERC) research examines the magnitude of the relation between accounting earnings and stock returns. Assuming that annual earnings follow a random walk, equation (2.16) shows that the expected magnitude of the earnings response coefficient is $(1 + 1/r)$. The ERC of a firm with a discount rate of 10 percent should be about 11. However, empirical estimates of the earnings response coefficient are between 1 and 3 (Kothari, 2001), much lower than its theoretical value. A vast literature has developed to understand the economic determinants and properties of ERCs (e.g., Beaver, Clarke, and Wright, 1979; Kormendi and Lipe, 1987; Easton and Zmijewski, 1989; Collins and Kothari, 1989; Kothari and Sloan, 1992). For example, using a

---

[36] Shao, Stoumbos, and Zhang (2021) document that earnings announcement returns explain roughly 20 percent of the annual return in the years after 2003—almost twice as much as they did before. This finding suggests that fundamental information has become more important in explaining stock returns.

simple discounted dividends valuation model, Collins and Kothari (1989) show that the earnings response coefficient varies negatively with the risk-free interest rate and systematic risk and positively with growth prospects and earnings persistence.

Researchers attempt to draw support for accounting standards from the earnings-return relation. For example, Beaver (1972, p. 428) states in the *Report of the American Accounting Association Committee on Research Methodology in Accounting* that the "method which is more highly associated with security prices . . . ought to be the method reported in the financial statements." Similarly, Lev (1989) advocates changes in financial accounting standards to improve the correlation between accounting earnings and stock returns. However, economic demand for accounting requires objective, verifiable information that summarizes the effects of actual, rather than expected, transactions. Our analysis leads us to expect the reported earnings to have *some* correlation with returns, but changes in expected future profitability also drive stock returns. Therefore, a low earnings-return correlation is expected (Kothari, 1992). Note that the earnings-return correlation does not measure the social value of earnings or even the private value to the shareholders of the firm, since the evidence is based on investors being informed in the first place and takes the welfare effects of information on shareholders as given (Ball and Brown, 2019).

In addition, the interpretation of the earnings-return relation hinges critically on the maintained hypothesis of market efficiency. The informational efficiency of capital markets has long been debated. John Maynard Keynes (1936) used the term "animal spirits" to describe the psychological biases that affect investor behavior. He used the following example in his book *General Theory of Employment, Interest, and Money* to illustrate this point:

> Day-to-day fluctuations in the profits of existing investments, which are obviously of an ephemeral and non-significant character, tend to have an altogether excessive, and even an absurd, influence on the market. It is said, for example, that the shares of American companies which manufacture ice tend to sell at a higher price in summer when their profits are seasonally high than in winter when no one wants ice.

Chambers (1974) challenges Ball and Brown's maintained hypothesis of market efficiency and argues that their findings are consistent with investors' naïve functional fixation. Specifically, Chambers (1974, pp. 49–50) notes,

"The test of a pharmaceutical preparation does not lie in the number of consumers who can be induced to believe in its efficacy. But that is just the kind of inquiry which the Ball and Brown paper reports. That the paper supports the efficient market hypothesis is not contested."

Later research uses the relation between changes in accounting procedures and stock price changes to discriminate between the EMH and the functional fixation hypothesis. Assume zero transaction, information, and contracting costs and no taxes. Under that assumption, the EMH predicts that a pure change in accounting procedures (e.g., accounting for lease obligations) has no effects on stock prices, while the functional fixation hypothesis predicts a mechanical relation between accounting earnings and stock prices (i.e., a change to accounting procedures that produce higher earnings numbers is associated with a positive stock market reaction). However, this line of research faces several methodological challenges. Accounting procedure choices matter (i.e., they have implications for contracts or other real effects), and managers who are aware of these effects select procedures to enhance firm value. Therefore, firms that change accounting procedures are likely different from firms that do not make the change, which leads to a selection bias. Researchers gradually developed more powerful tests to better discriminate between the EMH and the functional fixation hypothesis (e.g., Sunder, 1973, 1975; Ricks, 1982; Biddle and Lindahl, 1982).[37]

A related question raised by this line of research is why managers care about the earnings number if the market is informationally efficient and can see through different accounting procedures. This question led researchers to reconsider the assumption of zero transaction, information, and contracting costs, and to use those costs to explain the observed accounting phenomena.

2.4. Concluding Remarks

Early research suggested that drawing conclusions on the role of accounting from earnings-return analysis could be problematic (e.g., Paton and Littleton, 1940; Demski, 1973; Beaver and Demski, 1974; Gonedes and Dopuch, 1974; Watts, 1977), but we have little basis for concluding that researchers' efforts could have been fruitfully redirected. Knowledge accumulates by trial and

---

[37] See Watts and Zimmerman (1986) for a detailed discussion of this early research evolution.

error because, again, the mind cannot foresee its own advancement (Hayek, 1960). Edison is said to have supervised tests of over six thousand filament materials before concluding that carbonized bamboo was the most durable and inexpensive (Latson, 2014). In addition, more data and improved techniques have facilitated theoretical developments and widened our views.

More importantly, thoughtful consideration of the empirical relations unearthed by the earnings response coefficient literature remains essential to current and aspiring researchers. These relations serve as either the *foundation*, supporting current beliefs about what questions and methods are appropriate, or as a *foil* to criticize these same beliefs and methods. If one is willing to posit that stock prices behave *as if* they incorporate information in earnings and other sources, the relation between earnings and returns provides insight into the nature of information in financial accounting (e.g., its timeliness and error) and the valuation implications of earnings. These empirical results can be used to build hypotheses about the role of accounting, just as anthropologists draw inferences about the use of prehistoric artifacts from their physical characteristics and surroundings. Understanding the relation between earnings and firm value is also useful to managers employing earnings to assess the efficiency of their use of their firm's resources.

Finally, questions such as, "What is the role of financial accounting?" or "What should regulators do?" are intractable. Researchers in the 1950s and 1960s believed these questions could be addressed by a priori normative arguments. Similarly, a belief that a better understanding of the empirical properties of the price-earnings relation could answer these questions propelled empirical research on the earnings-return relation. A sober approach need not imply that the problems are too refractory or logically irreducible to attempt a solution. Rather, it requires us to recognize that the idea that a limited number of forces are important for predicting accounting-related phenomena, and by implication, that others are of second-order importance, is itself a hypothesis subject to empirical testing. The assertion that this hypothesis should be rejected is, at bottom, an assertion of the meagerness of our current knowledge that should prompt further thought and investigation.

In addition, prudence suggests that we consider the precision of understanding *possible* in social science in general and in accounting phenomena in particular. As Aristotle noted in Book I, chapter 3 of *The Nicomachean Ethics* in 340 BCE (Ross and Brown, 2009):

Our discussion will be adequate if it has as much clearness as the subject-matter admits of, for precision is not to be sought for alike in all discussions, any more than in all the products of the crafts. . . . It is evidently equally foolish to accept probable reasoning from a mathematician and to demand from a rhetorician demonstrative proofs.

The realization that phenomena arising from human social interactions have contingent rather than deterministic outcomes is *not* inconsistent with the belief that a few underlying factors can largely predict these outcomes. Instead, it requires us to understand that the prediction of these outcomes will not be as clear as those involving inanimate objects, like electrons. We set our expectations accordingly.

Supplement: Asset Pricing Models

The capital asset pricing model (CAPM) is a model of the expected return on a security. Its genesis is in the modern portfolio theory developed in Markowitz (1952). We therefore first summarize portfolio theory and then describe the CAPM.[38] We also give an overview of multi-factor models developed in the recent finance literature.

S1. Portfolio Theory

Economic analysis typically assumes that individuals are rational, risk-averse utility maximizers. A risk-averse investor's utility increases in the expected return (i.e., mean return) on a portfolio and decreases in the variance of return (i.e., total risk) on the portfolio. Assuming a mean-variance setting (i.e., stock return distributions are characterized by only the first two moments, mean and variance), Markowitz (1952) developed a theory for optimal portfolio construction. For any set of risky stocks, Markowitz's portfolio theory derives compositions of the portfolios that yield the highest expected return for each given level of portfolio return variance. He labeled such portfolios as efficient. The entire set of efficient portfolios is called the efficient frontier. Figure 2.1 graphs an efficient frontier. As the figure shows, portfolios on the efficient frontier dominate those to the right and below the frontier; that is,

---

[38] For a good introduction to portfolio theory, see Bodie, Kane, and Marcus (2021, Chs. 5–8).

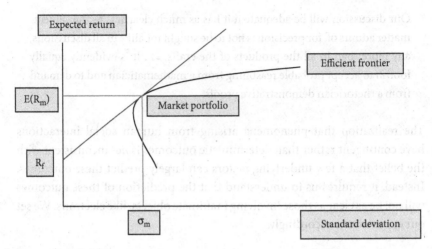

Figure 2.1 The Efficient Frontier

frontier portfolios have higher expected returns for a given level of standard deviation of return.

To mathematically derive the composition of an efficient portfolio using portfolio theory requires the knowledge of each security's expected return and standard deviation of return as well as each security's covariance with every other security's return (i.e., pairwise covariances).[39] This means that efficient portfolio construction using N risky stocks requires estimates of N expected returns, N standard deviations, and N × (N − 1)/2 pairwise covariances as inputs into the optimization algorithm. As N grows, the number of return-distribution parameters (i.e., means, standard deviations, and covariances) to be estimated in constructing efficient portfolios grows rapidly. The explosion in the number of terms is due largely to the pairwise covariances. The main insight from portfolio theory is that the pairwise covariances are primarily responsible for a portfolio's risk. Why do covariances among the securities' returns, rather than individual security return variances, drive portfolio risk? Assume that an individual holds a portfolio of N assets with proportion x_i invested in asset i. The variance of the rate of return on the portfolio, $\sigma^2(r_p)$, is

$$\sigma^2\left(r_p\right) = \Sigma_{i\,=\,1\,to\,N}\Sigma_{j\,=\,1\,to\,N}x_i x_j Cov\left(r_i,\,r_j\right). \qquad (2.17)$$

[39] For the derivation, see Bodie, Kane, and Marcus (2021, Chs. 5–8).

Since equation (2.17) contains many more pairwise covariance terms than variance terms, they collectively contribute most to a typical portfolio's variance (risk).[40]

S2. The Capital Asset Pricing Model

Sharpe (1964) and Lintner (1965) developed the CAPM by extending portfolio theory.[41] It is a model of the expected rate of return on a security as a function of the (covariance) risk of the security. The CAPM is derived by adding a few simplifying assumptions that dramatically reduce the parameter space from $N \times (N - 1)$ pairwise covariance terms to N relative risk parameters necessary for optimal portfolio construction. The CAPM is a single-period model in which investments are made at the beginning of a period and cash flow is realized at the end of the single period. Investors seek to maximize the expected cash flow per dollar of initial investment, that is, expected returns, for a given level of risk, that is, the standard deviation of return. The CAPM maintains the mean-variance setting for return distributions, and it additionally assumes that investors have homogeneous expectations. With the latter assumption, there is no disagreement among investors about the efficient portfolio at any given level of risk. Therefore, all investors agree upon the same efficient frontier.[42]

The CAPM further simplifies investors' optimal portfolio decision with the assumption that the investor can borrow or lend a risk-free asset at the same rate of interest in a perfect capital market. The risk-free asset enables investors to hold combinations of the portfolios on the efficient frontier of risky securities and the risk-free asset such that they can be to the left of and above the efficient frontier in Figure 2.1. The resulting portfolios earn the weighted average return on the risk-free security and a portfolio of risky securities on the efficient frontier. In fact, the most desirable of such portfolios (i.e., portfolios that yield the highest expected return for a given level of risk)

---

[40] The contribution of the covariance terms depends on the signs of the covariances and the proportion of the portfolio invested in individual securities, i.e., the x_i weights. However, in the case of typical mutual fund portfolios consisting of thirty or more stocks, with no stock constituting a disproportionate fraction of the total portfolio investment, the vast majority of the contribution to risk is attributable to the pairwise covariances.

[41] For a detailed discussion of the CAPM, see Bodie, Kane, and Marcus (2021, Ch. 9).

[42] If the market participants had heterogeneous expectations, each would have a unique efficient frontier derived on the basis of the individual's estimates of mean, standard deviation, and pairwise covariances of returns for the securities available in the market.

lie on a straight line (called the capital market line) that is tangent to the efficient frontier as depicted in Figure 2.1. Thus, all investors hold combinations of the tangency portfolio of risky securities and the risk-free asset. In equilibrium, the market-clearing condition requires the unique tangency portfolio of risky securities to be the market portfolio of risky securities. That is, the market portfolio is the entire collection of the risky securities available in the economy.

How does the fact that all investors hold combinations of the risk-free asset and the market portfolio of risky assets in a CAPM world help us derive the expected rate of return on a security? Consider an investor moving from holding only the risk-free asset to holding only the market portfolio. The risk of her portfolio has risen from zero to the risk of the market portfolio, that is, the variance of the return on the market portfolio, $\sigma^2(R_m)$. If the expected return on the market portfolio is $E(R_m)$, then the price (i.e., the expected return or the reward) per unit of the market portfolio's risk is

$$\text{Price of risk} = \left[E(R_m) - R_f \right] / \sigma^2(R_m) \qquad (2.18)$$

where R_f is the one-period risk-free rate of return (e.g., the yield on a one-month US Treasury bill). The intuition for the price of risk in equation (2.18) is that the increase in the expected return as an investor moves from an all risk-free asset portfolio to the market portfolio is $[E(R_m) - R_f]$, and the extra risk the investor bears is $\sigma^2(R_m)$. Recall that the risk-free asset has zero variance of return in the one-period CAPM model. $[E(R_m) - R_f]$ is referred to as the market risk premium.

Now consider an individual security i for which we wish to know the expected rate of return. If we knew the risk of such a security, we would be able to use the price per unit of risk we established above to determine the expected return on the security. So—what is the risk of the security? Because all risky securities are included in the market portfolio, each security's contribution to the market portfolio's risk is the relevant measure of each security's risk. This means that the sum of the risks of all the individual securities is the risk of the market portfolio. Recall that a portfolio's risk is due mostly to the pairwise covariances of the securities in a portfolio. Therefore, any one security's contribution to the risk of the market portfolio is its covariance with all the securities in the market portfolio. However, all the securities in the market portfolio themselves constitute the market portfolio. Therefore, it follows that security i's contribution to the market portfolio's risk is its co-variance of return with the market portfolio, $\text{Cov}(R_i, R_m)$. This dramatically simplifies the risk-estimation problem. Instead of estimating N pairwise covariances, we need only estimate the covariance of a firm's returns with the return on the market portfolio.

To arrive at the CAPM relation for the expected return on security i, we begin by denoting the expected return on security i as $E(R_i)$. Note that security i earns a return of R_f simply because the risk-free rate is R_f. Therefore, only the expected return in excess of R_f, that is, $E(R_i) - R_f$, must be the in-cremental amount of the expected return as compensation to i's owners for bearing its risk, $\text{Cov}(R_i, R_m)$. Security i's risk and equation (2.18) for the market price per unit of risk together yield a measure of the expected excess return for security i as

$$E(R_i) - R_f = \left(\text{Price per unit of risk}\right) \times \left(\text{Quantity of i's risk}\right)$$

$$= \left[E(R_m) - R_f\right] / \sigma^2(R_m) \times \text{Cov}(R_i, R_m). \qquad (2.19)$$

The CAPM relation for the expected excess return on a security is obtained by rearranging equation (2.19):

$$E(R_i) - R_f = \text{Cov}(R_i, R_m) / \sigma^2(R_m) \times \left[E(R_m) - R_f\right]$$

$$= \beta_i \left[E(R_m) - R_f\right] \qquad (2.20)$$

where β_i is a measure of i's risk expressed as a multiple of the risk of the market portfolio. Therefore, β_i is also referred to as a security's relative risk. β_i is estimated as the slope coefficient from a regression of (monthly or daily) ex-cess returns for a security on the excess returns on a market portfolio of stocks (e.g., all stocks listed on the New York and American Stock Exchanges). The CAPM states that a security's expected rate of return increases linearly in its beta, as shown in Figure 2.2. The slope of the line (called the security market line) is the risk premium, $[E(R_m) - R_f]$.

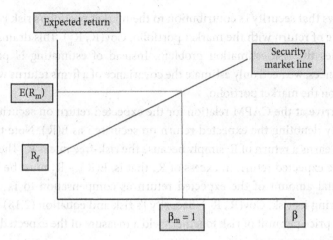

Figure 2.2 The Capital Asset Pricing Model

S3. Multi-Factor Models

Despite its appealing theoretical foundation, the Sharpe-Lintner CAPM fails to explain the average return of stocks observed in the data (Fama and French, 1996). The average-return anomalies of the CAPM have led researchers to develop multi-factor models to better describe average returns. These asset pricing models are motivated by Merton's (1973) intertemporal CAPM and Ross's (1976) arbitrage pricing theory.[43] As in the CAPM, investors are rewarded only for risk that is conditional on diversified security holdings. However, multi-factor models adopt a view that systematic risk (i.e., risk conditional on diversification) is multifaceted, that is, there are common risk factors beyond the market return. Thus, a security's expected rate of return is determined by its exposure to multiple risk sources, each with a risk premium.

Researchers generally employ one of three approaches to determine common risk factors: factor analysis (or principal component analysis), use of macroeconomic variables (e.g., GDP growth, inflation), or use of firm-specific variables (e.g., firm size, book-to-market equity). The first approach, factor analysis, is a purely statistical exercise, and researchers often cannot associate the common factors extracted with economically meaningful risks that investors might seek to avoid. The second and third approaches focus on economic variables. These variables can provide the basis for intuitive

---

[43] For a detailed discussion of the multi-factor models, see Bodie, Kane, and Marcus (2021, Ch. 10).

risk-based explanations of their observed correlations with realized returns. As pioneered by Fama and French (1993), the use of firm-specific variables has become a popular approach. However, some researchers claim that this approach leads to empirical data-dredging models or that these factors based on firm-specific variables pick up mispricing rather than risk attributes (e.g., Lakonishok, Shleifer, and Vishny, 1994). We briefly discuss these standard multi-factor models here.

Fama and French (1993) develop a three-factor model that includes an overall market factor (the sole factor in the CAPM) and factors related to firm size and book-to-market equity. The Fama-French three-factor model's superiority over CAPM in explaining average returns leads to the adoption of the three-factor model as the standard empirical asset pricing model. Researchers often augment the three-factor model with the momentum factor of Carhart (1997) and/or the liquidity factor of Pástor and Stambaugh (2003). More recently, Fama and French (2015) advance a five-factor model that adds profitability and investment factors to their three-factor model. Fama and French (2016) show that the list of return anomalies shrinks when the five-factor model is used.[44] Some variant of the Fama-French five-factor model (possibly augmented with the momentum or liquidity factor) is likely to be the empirical model researchers use when computing abnormal returns.[45] The Fama-French five-factor model is

$$R_{it} - R_{Ft} = a_i + b_i \left(R_{Mt} - R_{Ft} \right) + s_i SMB_t$$
$$+ h_i HML_t + r_i RMW_t + c_i CMA_t + e_{it} \quad (2.21)$$

where R_{it} is the return on security or portfolio i for period t, R_{Ft} is the risk-free return, R_{Mt} is the return on the value-weighted market portfolio, SMB_t is the return on a diversified portfolio of small stocks minus the return on a diversified portfolio of big stocks, HML_t is the difference between the returns on diversified portfolios of high and low book-to-market stocks, RMW_t is the difference between the returns on diversified portfolios of stocks with robust

[44] The accrual and momentum anomalies remain even with the use of the five-factor model. Hou, Xue, and Zhang (2020) compile an extensive data library with 452 anomaly variables and show that most anomalies fail to hold up to currently acceptable standards for empirical finance.

[45] Fama and French (2018) add the momentum factor to their five-factor model. Fama and French (2020) show that time-series models that use only cross-section factors provide better descriptions of average returns than time-series models that use time-series factors.

and weak profitability, and CMA_t is the difference between the returns on diversified portfolios of low and high investment stocks.[46] The intercept a_i is expected to be zero for all securities and portfolios i if the sensitivities to the five factors, b_i, s_i, h_i, r_i, and c_i, capture all variation in expected returns. A nonzero a_i reflects omitted risk factors in the model or systematic mispricing. Estimates of these parameters (a_i, b_i, s_i, h_i, r_i, and c_i) are often obtained using return data over a window prior to the period for which abnormal rates of return, e_{it}, need to be calculated.

References

Admati, A. R., Pfleiderer, P., 1988. Selling and trading on information in financial markets. *American Economic Review* 78 (2), 96–103.

Bachelier, L., 1900. Theory of speculation, translation from doctoral thesis at the Academy of Paris, in Cootner (1964), 17–78.

Ball, R., 2008. What is the actual economic role of financial reporting? *Accounting Horizons* 22 (4), 427–432.

Ball, R., 2024. By what criteria do we evaluate accounting? Some thoughts on economic welfare and the archival literature. *Journal of Accounting Research*, 62 (1), 7–54.

Ball, R., Brown, P. R., 1968. An empirical evaluation of accounting income numbers. *Journal of Accounting Research* 6 (2), 159–178.

Ball, R., Brown, P. R., 2014. Ball and Brown (1968): A retrospective. *The Accounting Review* 89 (1), 1–26.

Ball, R., Brown, P. R., 2019. Ball and Brown (1968) after fifty years. *Pacific-Basin Finance Journal* 53, 410–431.

Ball, R., Jayaraman, S., Shivakumar, L., 2012. Audited financial reporting and voluntary disclosure as complements: A test of the confirmation hypothesis. *Journal of Accounting and Economics* 53 (1–2), 136–166.

Ball, R., Kothari, S. P., Nikolaev, V. A., 2013. On estimating conditional conservatism. *The Accounting Review* 88 (3), 755–787.

Ball, R., Kothari, S. P., Watts, R. L., 1993. Economic determinants of the relation between earnings changes and stock returns. *The Accounting Review* 68 (3), 622–638.

Ball, R., Shivakumar, L., 2008. How much new information is there in earnings? *Journal of Accounting Research* 25 (2), 103–129.

Bamber, L. S., Christensen, T. E., Gaver, K. M., 2000. Do we really "know" what we think we know? A case study of seminal research and its subsequent overgeneralization. *Accounting, Organizations and Society* 25 (2), 103–129.

Basu, S., 1997. The conservatism principle and the asymmetric timeliness of earnings. *Journal of Accounting and Economics* 24 (1), 3–37.

---

[46] Data on all these factors can be obtained from Kenneth French's website, https://mba.tuck.dartmouth.edu/pages/faculty/ken.french/data_library.html, and Wharton Research Data Services, https://wrds-www.wharton.upenn.edu/.

Beaver, W. H., 1968. The information content of annual earnings announcements. *Journal of Accounting Research* 6, 67–92.

Beaver, W. H., 1972. Report of the committee on research methodology in accounting. *The Accounting Review* 47, 399–520.

Beaver, W. H., 1998. *Financial Reporting: An Accounting Revolution*. Prentice Hall, Upper Saddle River, New Jersey.

Beaver, W. H., Clarke, R., Wright, W. F., 1979. The association between unsystematic security returns and the magnitude of earnings forecast errors. *Journal of Accounting Research* 17 (2), 316–340.

Beaver, W. H., Demski, J. S., 1974. The nature of financial accounting objectives: A summary and synthesis. *Journal of Accounting Research* 12, 170–187.

Beaver, W. H., Lambert, R. A., Morse, D., 1980. The information content of security prices. *Journal of Accounting and Economics* 2 (1), 3–28.

Beaver, W. H., McNichols, M. F., Wang, Z. Z., 2020. Increased market response to earnings announcements in the 21st century: An empirical investigation. *Journal of Accounting and Economics* 69 (1), 101244.

Beaver, W. H., Morse, D., 1978. What determines price-earnings ratios? *Financial Analysts Journal* 34 (4), 65–76.

Bernard, V. L., Thomas, J. K., 1990. Evidence that stock prices do not fully reflect the implications of current earnings for future earnings. *Journal of Accounting and Economics* 13 (4), 305–340.

Biddle, G. C., Lindahl, F. W., 1982. Stock price reactions to LIFO adoptions: The association between excess returns and LIFO tax savings. *Journal of Accounting Research* 20 (2), 551–588.

Black, F., 1993. Choosing accounting rules. *Accounting Horizons* 7 (4), 1–17.

Blankespoor, E., deHann, E., Marinovic, I., 2020. Disclosure processing costs, investors' information choice, and equity market outcomes: A review. *Journal of Accounting and Economics* 70 (2–3), 101344.

Bloomfield, R. J., 2002. The "Incomplete Revelation Hypothesis" and financial reporting. *Accounting Horizons* 16 (3), 233–243.

Bodie, Z., Kane, A., Marcus, A. J., 2021. *Investments*, 12th ed. McGraw-Hill, New York City, New York.

Brealey, R. A., Myers, S. C., Allen, F., Edmans, A., 2023. *Principles of Corporate Finance*, 14th ed. McGraw Hill, New York City, New York.

Canning, J. B., 1929. *The Economics of Accountancy: A Critical Analysis of Accounting Theory*. Ronald Press Company, New York City, New York.

Carhart, M. M., 1997. On persistence in mutual fund performance. *Journal of Finance* 52 (1), 57–82.

Chambers, R. J., 1974. Stock market prices and accounting research. *Abacus* 10 (1), 39–54.

Chambers, R. J., 1976. *Fair Financial Reporting in Law and Practice*. Saxe Lecture in Accounting, Baruch College–CUNY. Retrieved from https://academicworks.cuny.edu/cgi/viewcontent.cgi?article=2093&context=bb_pubs.

Chan, W. S., Frankel, R., Kothari, S. P., 2004. Testing behavioral finance theories using trends and consistency in financial performance. *Journal of Accounting and Economics* 38, 3–50.

Clinch, G., Lyon, J. D., Pinnuck, M., 2019. A review of the impact of Ball and Brown (1968) on research in the Asia-Pacific Basin. *Pacific-Basin Finance Journal* 53, 268–277.

Coase, R. H., 1960. The problem of social cost. *Journal of Law and Economics* 3, 1–44.

Collins, D. W., Kothari, S. P., 1989. An analysis of intertemporal and cross-sectional determinants of earnings response coefficients. *Journal of Accounting and Economics* 11 (2–3), 143–181.

Collins, D. W., Kothari, S. P., Shanken, J., Sloan, R. G., 1994. Lack of timeliness and noise as explanations for the low contemporaneous return-earnings association. *Journal of Accounting and Economics* 18 (3), 289–324.

Cootner, P., ed., 1964. *The Random Character of Stock Market Prices*. MIT Press, Cambridge, Massachusetts.

Davidson, H. J., 1968. Discussion of the information content of annual earnings announcements. *Journal of Accounting Research* 6, 96–100.

Dechow, P. M., Sloan, R. G., Zha, J., 2014. Stock prices and earnings: A history of research. *Annual Review of Financial Economics* 6, 343–363.

Demski, J. S., 1973. The general impossibility of normative accounting standards. *The Accounting Review* 40 (4), 718–723.

Dixit, A. K., Pindyck, R. S., 1994. *Investment under Uncertainty*. Princeton University Press, Princeton, New Jersey.

Easton, P. D., Zmijewski, M. E., 1989. Cross-sectional variation in the stock market response to accounting earnings announcements. *Journal of Accounting and Economics* 11 (2–3), 117–141.

Fama, E. F., 1965. Random walks in stock market prices. *Financial Analysts Journal* 21 (5), 3–7.

Fama, E. F., 1970. Efficient capital markets: A review of theory and empirical work. *Journal of Finance* 25 (2), 383–417.

Fama, E. F., 1976. *Foundations of Finance*. Basic Books, New York City, New York.

Fama, E. F., 1990. Stock returns, expected returns, and real activity. *Journal of Finance* 45 (4), 1089–1108.

Fama, E. F., 1991. Efficient capital markets: II. *Journal of Finance* 46 (5), 1575–1617.

Fama, E. F., 1998. Market efficiency, long-term returns, and behavioral finance. *Journal of Financial Economics* 49 (3), 283–306.

Fama, E. F., Fisher, L., Jensen, M. C., Roll, R., 1969. The adjustment of stock prices to new information. *International Economic Review* 10 (1), 1–21.

Fama, E. F., French, K. R., 1993. Common risk factors in the returns on stocks and bonds. *Journal of Financial Economics* 33 (1), 3–56.

Fama, E. F., French, K. R., 1996. Multifactor explanations of asset pricing anomalies. *Journal of Finance* 51 (1), 55–84.

Fama, E. F., French, K. R., 2015. A five-factor asset pricing model. *Journal of Financial Economics* 116 (1), 1–22.

Fama, E. F., French, K. R., 2016. Dissecting anomalies with a five-factor model. *Review of Financial Studies* 29 (1), 69–103.

Fama, E. F., French, K. R., 2018. Choosing factors. *Journal of Financial Economics* 128 (2), 234–252.

Fama, E. F., French, K. R., 2020. Comparing cross-section and time-series factor models. *Review of Financial Studies* 33 (5), 1891–1926.

Fama, E. F., Miller, M. H., 1972. *The Theory of Finance*. Dryden Press, Hinsdale, Illinois.

Friedman, M., 1953. *Essays in Positive Economics*. University of Chicago Press, Chicago, Illinois.

Gleick, P. H., 1993. Water and conflict: Fresh water resources and international security. *International Security* 18 (1), 79–112.

Goldstein, I., 2023. Information in financial markets and its real effects. *Review of Finance* 27 (1), 1–32.

Gonedes, N. J., Dopuch, N., 1974. Capital market equilibrium, information production, and selecting accounting techniques: Theoretical framework and review of empirical work. *Journal of Accounting Research* 12, 48–129.

Grossman, S. J, Stiglitz, J. E., 1980. On the impossibility of efficient markets. *American Economic Review* 70 (3), 393–408.

Hart, O., 1989. An economist's perspective on the theory of the firm. *Columbia Law Review* 89 (7), 1757–1774.

Hayek, F. A.,1960. *The Constitution of Liberty*. University of Chicago Press, Chicago, Illinois.

Hirshleifer, J., 1958. On the theory of optimal investment decision. *Journal of Political Economy* 66 (4), 329–352.

Holthausen, R. W., Watts, R. L., 2001. The relevance of the value-relevance literature for financial accounting standard setting. *Journal of Accounting and Economics* 31 (1–3), 3–75.

Hou, K., Xue, C., Zhang, L., 2020. Replicating anomalies. *Review of Financial Studies* 33 (5), 2019–2133.

Hume, D., 1748. *An Enquiry concerning Human Understanding*. Oxford University Press, Oxford, United Kingdom.

Jensen, M. C., 1978. Some anomalous evidence regarding market efficiency. *Journal of Financial Economics* 6 (2–3), 95–101.

Keynes, J. M., 1936. *General Theory of Employment, Interest, and Money*. Palgrave Macmillan, London, United Kingdom.

Kormendi, R., Lipe, R., 1987. Earnings innovations, earnings persistence, and stock returns. *Journal of Business* 60 (3), 323–345.

Kothari, S. P., 1992. Price-earnings regressions in the presence of prices leading earnings. *Journal of Accounting and Economics* 15 (2–3), 173–202.

Kothari, S. P., 2001. Capital markets research in accounting. *Journal of Accounting and Economics* 31 (1–3), 105–231.

Kothari, S. P., 2019. Accounting information in corporate governance: Implications for standard setting. *The Accounting Review* 94 (2), 357–361.

Kothari, S. P., Lewellen, J., Warner, J. B., 2006. Stock returns, aggregate earnings surprises, and behavioral finance. *Journal of Financial Economics* 79 (3), 537–568.

Kothari, S. P., Ramanna, K., Skinner, D. J., 2010. Implications for GAAP from an analysis of positive research in accounting. *Journal of Accounting and Economics* 50 (2–3), 246–286.

Kothari, S. P., Sloan, R. G., 1992. Information in prices about future earnings. *Journal of Accounting and Economics* 15 (2–3), 143–171.

Kothari, S. P., Warner, J. B., 2007. Econometrics of event studies. In: Eckbo, B. E. (Ed.), *Handbook of Corporate Finance: Empirical Corporate Finance*. Elsevier, North Holland, Amsterdam, 3–36.

Kothari, S. P., Wasley, C. E., 2019. Commemorating the fifty-year anniversary of Ball and Brown (1968): The evolution of capital market research over the past fifty years. *Journal of Accounting Research* 57 (5), 1117–1159.

Kuhn, T. S., 1962. *The Structure of Scientific Revolutions*. University of Chicago Press, Chicago, Illinois.

Lakonishok, J., Shleifer, A., Vishny, R. W., 1994. Contrarian investment, extrapolation, and risk. *Journal of Finance* 49 (5), 1541–1578.

Latson, J., 2014. How Edison invented the light bulb—And lots of myths about himself. *Time*. October 21. Retrieved from http://time.com/3517011/thomas-edison/.

Lee, C. M., So, E. C., 2015. Alphanomics: The informational underpinnings of market efficiency. *Foundations and Trends° in Accounting* 9 (2–3), 59–258.

Leuz, C., Wysocki, P. D., 2016. The economics of disclosure and financial reporting regulation: Evidence and suggestions for future research. *Journal of Accounting Research* 54 (2), 525–622.

Lev, B., 1989. On the usefulness of earnings and earnings research: Lessons and directions from two decades of empirical research. *Journal of Accounting Research* 27, 153–192.

Lintner, J., 1965. The valuation of risk assets and the selection of risky investments in stock portfolios and capital budgets. *Review of Economics and Statistics* 47 (1), 13–37.

Loughran, T., McDonald, B., 2020. Textual analysis in finance. *Annual Review of Financial Economics* 12, 357–375.

Markowitz, H., 1952. Portfolio selection. *Journal of Finance* 7 (1), 77–91.

Merton, R. C., 1973. An intertemporal capital asset pricing model. *Econometrica* 41 (5), 867–887.

Milgrom, P., Stokey, N., 1982. Information, trade and common knowledge. *Journal of Economic Theory* 26 (1), 17–27.

Modigliani, F., Miller, M. H., 1958. The cost of capital, corporation finance and the theory of investment. *American Economic Review* 48 (3), 261–297.

Modigliani, F., Miller, M. H., 1966. Some estimates of the cost of capital to the electric utility industry. *American Economic Review* 56 (3), 333–391.

Ng, J., Rusticus, T. O., Verdi, R. S., 2008. Implications of transaction costs for the post-earnings announcement drift. *Journal of Accounting Research* 46 (3), 661–696.

Ohlson, J. A., 1995. Earnings, book values, and dividends in security valuation. *Contemporary Accounting Research* 11 (2), 661–687.

Onstad, E., 2013. Lasers, microwave deployed in high-speed trading arms race. *Reuters*. May 1. Retrieved from https://www.reuters.com/article/us-highfrequency-microw ave/lasers-microwave-deployed-in-high-speed-trading-arms-race-idUSBRE9400L92 0130501.

Pástor, L., Stambaugh, R. F., 2003. Liquidity risk and expected stock returns. *Journal of Political Economy* 111 (3), 642–685.

Paton, W. A., Littleton, A. C., 1940. *An Introduction to Corporate Accounting Standards*, Monograph No. 3. American Accounting Association, Chicago, Illinois.

Popper, K., 1959. *The Logic of Scientific Discovery*. Routledge Classics, London, United Kingdom.

Ricks, W. E., 1982. The market's response to the 1974 LIFO adoptions. *Journal of Accounting Research* 20 (2), 367–387.

Ross, S. A., 1976. The arbitrage theory of capital asset pricing. *Journal of Economic Theory* 13 (3), 341–360.

Ross, W. D., Brown, L., 2009. *Aristotle: The Nicomachean Ethics*. Oxford University Press, Oxford, United Kingdom.

Shao, S., Stoumbos, R., Zhang, X. F., 2021. The power of firm fundamental information in explaining stock returns. *Review of Accounting Studies* 26, 1249–1289.

Sharpe, W. F., 1964. Capital asset prices: A theory of market equilibrium under conditions of risk. *Journal of Finance* 19 (3), 425–442.

Simon, H. A., 1973. Applying information technology to organization design. *Public Administration Review* 106, 467–482.

Sloan, R. G., 1996. Do stock prices fully reflect information in accruals and cash flows about future earnings? *The Accounting Review* 71 (3), 289–315.

Stein, J. C., 1989. Efficient capital markets, inefficient firms: A model of myopic corporate behavior. *Quarterly Journal of Economics* 104 (4), 655–669.

Stigler, G. J., 1963. *Capital and Rates of Return in Manufacturing Industries.* Princeton University Press, Princeton, New Jersey.

Strauss, L., 1989. *The Rebirth of Classical Political Rationalism.* University of Chicago Press, Chicago, Illinois.

Sunder, S., 1973. Relationship between accounting changes and stock prices: Problems of measurement and some empirical evidence. *Journal of Accounting Research* 11, 1–45.

Sunder, S., 1975. Stock price and risk related to accounting changes in inventory valuation. *Accounting Review* 50 (2), 305–315.

Tversky, A., Kahneman, D., 1974. Judgment under uncertainty: Heuristics and biases. *Science* 185 (4157), 1124–1131.

Verrecchia, R. E., 1982. Information acquisition in a noisy rational expectations economy. *Econometrica* 50 (6), 1415–1430.

Verrecchia, R. E., 2001. Essays on disclosure. *Journal of Accounting and Economics* 32 (1–3), 97–180.

Watts, R. L., 1977. Corporate financial statements, a product of the market and political processes. *Australian Journal of Management* 2 (1), 53–75.

Watts, R. L., Zimmerman, J. L., 1986. *Positive Accounting Theory.* Prentice-Hall, Englewood Cliffs, New Jersey.

Weitzman, H., 2016. Are markets efficient? Chicago Booth Review. June 30. Retrieved from https://www.chicagobooth.edu/review/are-markets-efficient.

Williams, J. B., 1938. *The Theory of Investment Value.* Harvard University Press, Cambridge, Massachusetts.

Zuo, L., 2016. The informational feedback effect of stock prices on management forecasts. *Journal of Accounting and Economics* 61 (2–3), 391–413.

3

The Earnings-Return Relation

3.1. Overview

This chapter examines research on the earnings-return relation. Simply put, this research studies the magnitude and determinants of the relation between stock returns and accounting earnings, that is, the earnings response coefficient (ERC). The mention of ERC seems to provoke antipathy among researchers who know of the topic and angst among those who did the studies. Once popular between 1970 and 2000, research on the factors that determine ERC has waned. However, understanding the earnings-return relation from a reduced-form perspective remains an intellectual prerequisite in our quest for the role of financial accounting in a strategic setting. Unpacking this relation yields insights into valuation, earnings timeliness and noise in earnings, the implications of the maintained hypothesis of market efficiency and tests of market efficiency, tests of contracting and disclosure theory, and regression econometrics. The purpose of this chapter is to discuss these insights.

First, valuation theory links a firm's stock returns to expected cash-flow shocks, time-varying expected returns, and shocks to expected returns (Fama, 1990). These relations require us to predict how the current earnings surprise causes investors to revise their earnings expectations and, in turn, how these future earnings-expectation revisions relate to cash flow–expectation revisions. Following this logic, researchers began to consider what the time-series process believed to generate earnings implies about the relation between the current earnings surprise and the revision of future earnings expectations (Kormendi and Lipe, 1987; Collins and Kothari, 1989). The composition of the current earnings surprise (i.e., transitory and persistent components) might also provide insight into the time-series characteristics of the firm's earnings. For example, cash flow and accrual components might differ in persistence (Sloan, 1996). Therefore, investors can use this composition and other firm characteristics (size, market-to-book, gross-profit

The Economics of Accounting. Richard M. Frankel, S. P. Kothari, and Luo Zuo, Oxford University Press. © Oxford University Press 2024. DOI: 10.1093/oso/9780197680766.003.0003

margin) to forecast future earnings. In this chapter, we give the details of these earnings-based valuation relations.

Second, under the maintained hypothesis of market efficiency, we can use the earnings-return relation to infer earnings characteristics. Subsequent tests might produce inferences about the role of earnings from these characteristics.[1] For example, current prices or returns can predict earnings (e.g., Beaver, Lambert, and Morse, 1980). Subsequent research suggests that accounting measurement rules are such that earnings are slow to reflect information impounded in price (Collins et al., 1994). One inference from this lack of timeliness (under the maintained hypotheses of market efficiency and shareholder value maximization) is that the role of earnings is not simply to provide the most timely information to investors to aid valuation. Perhaps financial reports are not the most efficient means to convey timely information. Perhaps financial reports enhance firm value by confirming more timely information from other sources. To take another example, the correlation between share prices and unrealized gains on available-for-sale securities can allow us to infer whether such gains correlate with unexpected cash flows. In this way, we can further our understanding of how investors use accounting information, how their use of accounting information varies across contexts (i.e., rich information environments vs. poor ones), or what factors are associated with variation in the overlap between information in earnings and the information used by investors to price stock.

Third, the earnings-based valuation relations under the maintained hypothesis of market efficiency are the source of predictions or null hypotheses useful for testing market efficiency. For example, if firms with more persistent earnings should show larger valuation consequences for a given earnings surprise, one can use this prediction along with an asset pricing model to formulate a test using ERCs (e.g., Kormendi and Lipe, 1987). In addition, researchers can use realized returns to see whether the market overreacts or underreacts to future earnings implications of current earnings. For example, we can address whether more transitory (persistent) income components seem to receive appropriately lower (higher) valuations or whether more transitory (persistent) income components are associated

---

[1] If we wish to draw inferences on the role of earnings in aiding the firm's efficiency, we add the maintained hypothesis that earnings characteristics are the outcome of management choices seeking to enhance shareholder value. Under the maintained hypothesis of management opportunism, we might infer that earnings characteristics result from managers' attempts to transfer wealth from shareholders.

with lower (higher) future returns. We can ask whether analyst-forecast revisions reflect predictable variation in persistence.

Fourth, researchers use ERC-based designs to address questions on the role of financial accounting. For example, Ball, Kothari, and Robin (2000) show that differences in the demand for accounting earnings in different institutional contexts predictably affect how accounting earnings incorporate economic shocks over time. They find that accounting earnings are significantly timelier in common-law countries than in code-law countries due to the quicker incorporation of economic losses. These results suggest that information asymmetry is more likely to be resolved in code-law countries by private communication with major stakeholders rather than timely and conservative public disclosure (see Lennox and Wu [2022] for a thorough review of China-related accounting research). As another example, studies can use unexpected earnings as a control variable in return regressions. The market reaction associated with a firm's announcement of an accounting-policy change can be a means to infer the firm-value consequences of accounting methods. Revsine et al. (1999) note that on March 18, 1992, Chambers Development Co.'s stock price dropped 63 percent when the company announced it would expense development costs instead of capitalizing them. To interpret the market's reaction to accounting-method changes, one must model changes in cash-flow expectations concurrent with the accounting-method change and other cash-flow effects arising from contracting, tax, and/or regulatory considerations. If poorly performing firms are likely to make a change, including the current earnings surprise (calculated as if no accounting-method change had been made) as an independent variable in the return regression can be a means to control for this selection effect and thereby isolate the expected consequences of the accounting change. Below, we elaborate on this use of the ERC method using the example of LIFO-adoption studies.

Though appreciative of these benefits, researchers immediately saw limits to the inferences they could draw about the efficiency role of earnings from the earnings-return correlation. Perhaps researchers also feared that incorrect inferences from the return-earnings correlation might sway policymakers and regulators. Inferential limits result from the efficiency considerations and logical ambiguities to be described here.

Stripped of embellishment, a correlation merely implies that earnings and prices map intersecting sets of events (Gonedes, 1975; Beaver, Clarke, and Wright, 1979). Under the maintained hypothesis of market efficiency, the correlation implies that earnings offer a measure of equity value. In this way, evidence of correlation supports the idea that the potential roles of earnings include performance measurement and equity valuation. Correlations of returns and earnings surrounding earnings announcements suggest that earnings alter investors' views on the equity value, and earnings aid investors' asset-allocation decisions.

However, it is problematic to reach beyond these confines to infer that a higher earnings-return correlation enhances firm or societal efficiency.[2] Even if a higher correlation brings benefits (which is doubtful), this inference ignores the forces leading to the present correlation. At the firm level, it assumes that participants cannot assess the costs and benefits of higher correlation or have no incentive to implement an improvement. At the societal level, steps to increase the correlation by regulation assume that costs are negligible or that any costs are less than the societal gain. One must also consider regulator motives and the costs required to collect information. The regulator might not have a cost advantage in determining more efficient accounting policies, or the regulator might not have sufficient incentive to implement such policies. In short, the costs of enhancing this correlation might exceed the benefits.

In addition, we encounter ambiguity in ranking alternative accounting measures by the criterion of earnings-price correlation when we examine the logical implications of altering our assumption that earnings reporting choices affect equity price (Sunder, 2017). If *the earnings reports affect prices*, different financial reporting systems lead to different prices. Consider two potential accounting systems (A and B) that a regulator might impose on publicly owned firms. Assume that earnings reports from accounting system A, $R_{A,i}$, lead to $Price_{A,i}$ (i.e., prices for firm i conditional on firm i's use of accounting system A) and earnings reports from accounting system B, $R_{B,i}$, lead to $Price_{B,i}$. The implications of differing correlations are unclear because, as Kanodia (1980) shows, in an economy with rational agents, different accounting systems lead to different production/investment decisions by firms, but prices under both accounting systems are efficient with respect to the firms' production-investment policies. The efficiency of prices under both accounting systems is an important insight because price efficiency implies that the economy's savings are allocated appropriately to firms based on the

[2] Brown, Lo, and Lys (1999) note that researchers who perform analyses using per-share or firm-level data should be cautious in interpreting the levels of R^2 because they are generally higher when scale effects are present.

expected payoffs and riskiness of their projects. The relative welfare of the firm's investors (and society) under these two accounting systems rests in the relative efficiency of production/investment decisions the accounting system generates. Unfortunately, this relative efficiency cannot be discerned from the earnings-return correlation.

On the other hand, if we assume that *reports do not affect prices and, therefore, production investment decisions,* an analysis of how different financial reporting systems affect investors or social welfare requires us to make further stipulations. For example, we might venture into the realm of price formation to understand the costs and benefits of different accounting systems. Beaver and Dukes (1972) argue for using the accounting method "most consistent with information impounded in an efficient determination of security prices. Since the market will incur nonzero costs in adjusting from any other method to the preferred one, failing to report the method preferred forces the market to incur excessive costs of data processing" (p. 331). However, Beaver and Dukes (1972) qualify this position by noting that a "complete analysis" would require specification of alternative sources of information and the cost of these alternatives relative to providing information in financial statements (p. 321).

Arguments for the superiority of one accounting system over another based on the strength of the earnings-return correlation seem easier to make if we assume that earnings reports mislead a sufficient number of investors so that society's savings are misallocated. When investors respond naively to an accounting report, one can argue that changing the reporting system can aid naïve investors. The trouble with this line of reasoning occurs in the next steps: (1) demonstrating that naïve investors are harmed and (2) explaining how changing the correlation between earnings and prices reduces this harm. If naïve investors do not determine prices, then naïve investors are protected because they trade at the same prices as sophisticated investors. Again, we are forced to make stipulations about price formation if we wish to proceed with this argument.

The inferential limits arising from unknown net benefits and ambiguities produce discontent with ERC research. Yet we do not discard the hammer because it cannot cut a joist; we recognize that tools are valuable when used according to their purpose. The same principle applies to ERC research. This chapter describes the logic behind two empirical regularities in the ERC literature and offers interpretations. The first is that empirical estimates of ERC(s) are smaller than expected based on earnings-valuation analysis.

The second is that the incremental slope on negative returns is positive in a piecewise-linear regression of earnings on returns.

3.2. ERC Described and Valuation-Based Determinants

3.2.1. ERC Described

We organize our discussion of the relation between earnings and returns around the following equation:

$$UR_{it} = \gamma_0 + \gamma_1 UX_{it} + \varepsilon_{it}, \tag{3.1}$$

where UR_{it} is the realized stock return minus the expected return for firm i measured over period t; UX_{it} is the reported earnings minus a proxy for market expectations of earnings at the beginning of period t, scaled by price at the beginning of period t; γ_0 is the intercept; γ_1 is the earnings response coefficient; and ε_{it} is a disturbance term.[3] Researchers estimated this model via linear regression in pooled, cross-sectional samples, seeking insight into earnings characteristics from estimates of γ_1 and the model's explanatory power (R-squared). In association studies, researchers use yearly and quarterly return measurement periods. In event studies, researchers use short (e.g., daily or hourly) windows around the earnings announcement date. Event studies test the causal relation between earnings announcements and returns.

3.2.2. ERC Intuition

To understand the insights one might draw from equation (3.1) estimates, we begin by considering why we might expect some overlap between earnings and returns from an intuitive, nonmathematical point of view. Begin by assuming that a firm's share price at the beginning of the fiscal period reflects the broad set of information available to market participants. During this period, the firm engages in a series of activities,

---

[3] "X" is used to designate earnings rather than "E," to avoid confusing earnings with the expectations operator, E[.].

encountering obstacles and opportunities. For example, it sells products, buys materials to produce its products, encounters changes in the labor market affecting product costs, and so on. Some of these events are surprises. Some are anticipated. For example, the firm's sales are $100 million during the fiscal period. Investors and managers had expected sales of $90 million, but an unexpectedly robust economy and an unlikely change in customer taste led to higher demand. Some of these activities and encounters affect earnings, and some affect prices. Earnings tend to reflect outcomes, so the entire $100 million of sales would be included in earnings. Prices anticipate the future effects of outcomes, so only the $10 million sales surprise causes a price change. Prices would also reflect the anticipated effects of current surprises. In the case of the $10 million sales surprise, investors use available information to understand whether this sales shock will recur in subsequent years. Investors will examine the firm's competitive position in its product market and assess the likely growth of the product market overall. In this way, the price change also includes the anticipated effect of the $10 million on future performance. Earnings will not record these anticipated sales changes until they are realized in subsequent periods.

Yet we expect some overlap between current earnings and prices in the surprise portion of current earnings. At a minimum, earnings and returns both reflect the $10 million sales surprise. The example illustrates why we use the unexpected portion of earnings to assess the correlation between earnings and returns. Assuming that price anticipates some events that will affect the firm, only the unanticipated events will affect price, so only the unanticipated portion of earnings would overlap with returns. This conclusion points to the importance of accurately measuring unexpected earnings and implies that failure to incorporate earnings expectations that are already incorporated into price at the start of the return measurement period will reduce the estimated correlation between UR_{it} and UX_{it}.

Moreover, the example suggests that price changes reflect the anticipated effect of current surprises on future performance (i.e., revision in expectations of future output). These newly anticipated effects are unlikely to be fully reflected in current earnings. In particular, these anticipated effects are unlikely to be proportional to the current surprise, for example, the $10 million current sales shock does not imply the same amount of cumulative additional future sales for all firms in all circumstances! As noted earlier, this neat, proportional relation between surprise and future effects is unlikely because many factors (e.g., product-market competition, rate of innovation, alteration of consumer tastes) differ across firms and industries. Investors in competitive capital markets will use all available information to estimate these effects and not simply rely on the current earnings surprise. For example, investors might study whether the change in customer tastes is a fad or due to lasting changes in customer characteristics like demographic shifts or leisure-time changes. Investors might also check competitors' ability to react to customer-taste changes. These are only examples; one could extend the list of important factors affecting the relation between the current surprise and its anticipated future effects. Each surprise will likely differ and scatter investors in various directions in search of information. Thus, revisions in investor expectations related to anticipated effects can attenuate the correlation between UR_{it} and UX_{it}.

3.2.3. Relating Unexpected Earnings to Unexpected Price Changes

To analyze the pricing of the anticipated effects of current surprises, researchers (e.g., Beaver, Lambert, and Morse, 1980; Kormendi and Lipe, 1987; Beaver, Lambert, and Ryan, 1987; Collins and Kothari, 1989) modeled (1) the relation between unexpected earnings and changes in future earnings expectations and (2) the relation between future earnings expectations and current security prices. In formalizing the relations, they pull back from considering the industry- and firm-specific factors described earlier. Researchers aim to formulate a relation between earnings surprises and price changes for a generic firm. Their competitive advantage resides in building abstract mathematical relations with intuitive appeal using statistical and valuation models. For example, they are not experts in assessing whether a given advance in semiconductor architecture—for example, ARM design—will produce lasting competitive advantage for a firm or what the size and growth of its market will be. Each firm has distinctive strengths and weaknesses and faces varying opportunities and threats. In fairness to accounting researchers, few can adequately analyze the forces and characteristics that link earnings to returns for a single company, let alone the large panels of data used to estimate the coefficient on unexpected earnings. Given the expansive dimensions of the relation, its compression to a formulation with sufficient formality to guide econometric estimation of the empirical regularity first revealed by Ball and Brown (1968) is impressive. But we recognize that readers will vary in their taste for abstraction.[4]

3.2.3.1. Time Series Models: The Relation between Current Unexpected Earnings and Revisions in Future Earnings Expectations

To see how the relation between unexpected earnings and changes in future earnings expectations can be modeled, consider a firm that realizes earnings per share of $0.48, including an unexpected earnings realization of $0.08. The relation between current and future earnings can be modeled by assuming that the firm's earnings follow a particular time-series process. This process allows us to infer the persistence of earnings and future earnings expectations with mathematical precision. We can place the persistence of earnings on a continuum between two extremes. At one end, earnings follow a random walk and are persistent—that is, $X_{t+1} = X_t + \varepsilon_{t+1}$, where ε is an independent and identically distributed mean-zero-shock term. In the present example, $\varepsilon_{t+1} = \$0.08$ and $X_{t+1} = \$0.48$. A random-walk earnings price implies that our expectation of $X_{t+1+\tau}$ at time $t+1$ is 0.48 for all $\tau > 0$. In short, with a random walk, investors anticipate that the effect of the current $0.08 shock will be $0.08 for all future periods.

We might wonder whether assuming that earnings follows a random-walk process makes economic sense. Would earnings follow a random-walk process in a competitive environment? Take the case of a farmer who discovers a new technology that enables him to grow 20 percent more corn on his acreage. The increased crop yield will last indefinitely, but as this innovation spreads, corn supply will increase, and the future price of corn might drop along with a portion of the earnings produced by this innovation. Even in the case of earnings produced by unanticipated drug patents, we might be reluctant to assume a perpetual profit increase because future innovations by competitors might diminish profits, and patents have a finite life.

The autoregressive time-series model accommodates this potential lack of persistence in the earnings series. In an autoregressive model of order one,

---

[4] Coase (1992, p. 714) called the "system which lives in the minds of economists but not on earth" *blackboard economics*. Yet all generalizations require some degree of abstraction. The issue is whether the omission is substantive in the sense that it impairs prediction or omits factors essential for intuitive understanding of significant empirical facts. George Eliot (1871–1872) was not optimistic about our ability to avoid the pitfalls of abstraction, "for all of us, grave or light, get our thoughts entangled in metaphors, and act fatally on the strength of them."

$$X_{t+1} = \phi X_t + \varepsilon_{t+1}, \tag{3.2}$$

where $\phi < 1$. Our intuition about the expected life of an earnings surprise depends in part on the assumption that competition tends to drive *rates of return* toward the required rate of return, but we are trying to apply this intuition to the persistence of an *earnings level*, earnings per share. An increase in earnings per share will tend to persist if it results from new investment or increased risk of current investment.

At the other end of the earnings-shock persistence continuum, we assume that earnings shocks lack persistence. That is, $X_{t+1} = \mu + \varepsilon_{t+1}$, where ε is an independent and identically distributed mean-zero-shock term and μ is the mean of the earnings series. In this formulation, $E_{t+1}[X_{t+1+\tau}] = \mu$, where $E_{t+1}[.]$ is the expectations operator at period $t + 1$, and the anticipated effect of current unexpected earnings on future earnings is zero. Miller and Rock (1985) popularized this formulation, noting that expected earnings depend on the investment base and investment risk. Miller and Rock (1985) use a slightly more elaborate time-series process. They allow for the possibility that the earnings shock persists ($\gamma > 0$) or reverses ($\gamma < 0$). The formulation is

$$X_{t+1} = \mu + \varepsilon_{t+1} + \gamma \varepsilon_t. \tag{3.3}$$

This formulation is called a moving average process of order one. If $\gamma = 0$, the formulation reduces to a process without persistence and is labeled a white-noise process.

To gain intuition on the applicability of the moving average (MA) and autoregressive (AR) models to the earnings of an actual firm, first note the differences between the models. The MA series models the persistence of the earnings shocks, while the AR series models the persistence of total earnings, that is, the shock and the existing core earnings. Core earnings are set to μ in the MA formulation (equation 3.3). To return to our farm example, many factors associated with time (e.g., technological innovation, changing tastes, demographics, government policy) could erode the earnings produced by growing corn on farmland. Of course, the farmer might also find a more valuable use for his land (e.g., suburban housing). The AR formulation allows us to incorporate factors we believe will affect the persistence in the time-series model of core earnings.

On the other hand, if earnings are higher than expected this year because of abundant rains during the growing season and dry fields for planting and harvest, we expect this year's shock to be less persistent than core earnings. The MA model allows us to adjust for shock persistence without affecting core earnings' persistence. As the weather example shows, shocks and core earnings can have differential persistence. Autoregressive moving average (ARMA) models can accommodate this differential persistence. They combine the attributes of the AR and MA processes. When we must difference a time series for it to be stationary, we can measure earnings persistence by estimating an autoregressive integrated moving average (ARIMA) model.[5]

3.2.3.2. Relating Earnings Expectations to the Current Price

Assuming that shocks to earnings follow a time-series process allows a parsimonious formulation of the valuation consequences of the current earnings shock. The formulation describes the periods expected to be affected by the current earnings innovation and the expected amount of each effect. This specificity and regularity permit computation of the present value of a current earnings innovation by applying a rate to these expected earnings changes and by using mathematical techniques to determine the sum and limit of an infinite series.

Discounting earnings assumes that earnings are equivalent to payoffs to the owners. To relate future earnings to current security prices, we must convert earnings to payoffs (i.e., cash flows that can be distributed or reinvested at zero net present value).[6] The relation between earnings and payoffs defies the mathematical compactness necessary for modeling. For example, the relation between the cash paid to purchase equipment and its earnings effect depends on the depreciation method used and the assumed useful life and salvage value. Thus, the accounting-method choice and its attendant

[5] An ARIMA model is characterized by three terms: p (the order of the AR term), d (the number of differencing transformations required to make the time series stationary), and q (the order of the MA term). The statistical properties (mean, variance, correlation, etc.) of a stationary series are constant through time. The random-walk model is nonstationary. Its variance increases over time. The series of first differences of random-walk-model realizations $(X_t - X_{t-1})$ is stationary, so a random walk is said to be integrated of order one. An AR(1) model is stationary when $|\phi| < 1$, and an MA(1) model is always stationary. Stationarity is critical for statistical inference, because it permits the derivation of distributions of estimated means and variances. See Greene (2012), Chapters 20 and 21.

[6] Pricing is grounded in payoffs to the investors, because pricing relies on the assumption of no arbitrage (Ross, 2005). The no-arbitrage theorem prohibits an equilibrium from arising when an existing investment strategy provides a guaranteed *payoff* in some state with zero initial investment. The no-arbitrage (linear) pricing rule relates payoffs, not earnings, to price. We also assume that discounting payoffs at a risk-adjusted discount rate yields an approximation of value (rather than converting payoffs to a certainty equivalent and discounting this certainty equivalent at the risk-free rate).

assumptions affect the relation between cash flows and earnings in discontinuous, nonlinear ways.

Furthermore, the choice of accounting method is interdependent with expected cash flows. The choice affects cash flows—if accounting has an economic role—and conversely, expected cash flows affect the accounting choice.[7] Rather than untangle this Gordian knot, one can assume that cash flows are proportional to earnings. An alternative is to assume that unexpected returns are a linear function of unexpected earnings and other information variables, where the coefficients on earnings and the other information variables are a function of risk and time-series parameters. In some unspecified way, these time-series parameters relate the information variables to future information variables and future dividends (Garman and Ohlson, 1980; Beaver, Lambert, and Morse, 1980). In short, the relation between future earnings and future payoffs is unspecified or abridged. Researchers incorporated the valuation complexities due to accounting methods into a factor called earnings capitalization rate (see, e.g., Beaver, Lambert, and Morse, 1980). They understood that by generalizing and abstracting from messy details, ERC analysis lost a potentially significant portion of its accounting content, and ERC analysis transformed into a valuation problem.[8]

With this background, we can describe the equations that express the relation between (1) unexpected earnings and changes in future earnings expectations and (2) future earnings expectations and current security prices. We model relation (1) by assuming that earnings follow a random-walk process, and we model relation (2) by assuming that earnings are equivalent to payoffs and by discounting these payoffs to the present. The formula for the present-value factor for a perpetuity is $(1 + 1/r)$, where r is the expected rate of return on the security, and the perpetuity includes an immediate payoff plus the same payoff assumed to be received each year, forever. Thus, the present value of an \$0.08 earnings innovation is \$0.08 + \$0.08/r.[9] This present value will decline as the persistence of earnings surprise declines. For

---

[7] For example, the tax effects of LIFO-adoption choice imply that the choice relates to firm performance. We discuss this example in detail later.

[8] We follow this proportionality assumption in the reduced-form exposition. The mapping of earnings to payoffs can be complicated by management-reporting incentives, the information in accounting choices, or nonlinearities in the mapping of depreciated book values to economic asset values.

[9] Table 1 in Collins and Kothari (1989) provides present-value factors for a variety of plausible earnings time-series processes.

example, Beaver, Lambert, and Morse (1980) assume that the earnings time-series process is as follows:

$$X_{t+1} = X_t + \varepsilon_{t+1} - \gamma \varepsilon_t, \tag{3.4}$$

where $0 < \gamma < 1$. In this formulation, only $(1-\gamma)$ of the current earnings surprise, ε_{t+1}, persists into subsequent periods.[10] Thus, the present value of an $0.08 year t earnings innovation is $0.08(1-\gamma)/r + $0.08. As γ approaches 1, the persistence of the shock declines, as does its present value. As γ approaches 0, the model approaches the random-walk formulation. The present-value formulation for the random walk provides a basis for relating UR_{it} to UX_{it}. Researchers used this time-series formulation because prior research suggested that the random walk was a reasonable approximation of the annual earnings process (e.g., Ball and Watts, 1972). Assuming a random walk,

$$UR_{t+1} = (1/r + 1)UX_{t+1}/P_t \tag{3.5}$$

3.3. Issues in ERC Empirical Estimation and Key Empirical Features

3.3.1. Low ERCs

Assuming a discount rate of about 10 percent, the expected magnitude of the ERC based on equation (3.5) is about 11. However, estimated ERCs are too small, ranging from 1 to 3 (e.g., Kormendi and Lipe, 1987; Easton and Zmijewski, 1989). Four issues arise in cross-sectional estimation of equation (3.5): (1) cross-sectional variation in earnings capitalization rates, (2) mismeasurement of unexpected earnings, (3) returns reflecting information about future cash flows beyond that contained in unexpected earnings (including prices leading earnings), and (4) behavioral biases.

---

[10] This formulation shows the variety of processes that can be produced by one time-series model through the use of differencing transformations. This process is a moving-average process in first differences of earnings: $X_{t+1} - X_t = \varepsilon_{t+1} - \gamma \varepsilon_t$. It also becomes a random walk when $\gamma = 0$.

3.3.1.1. Cross-Sectional Variation in Earnings Capitalization Rates

First, this formulation omits the firm's earnings capitalization rate discussed earlier. To use the notation of Beaver, Lambert, and Morse (1980), $P_{it} = \rho_i E(X_{it+k})$, where ρ_i is the earnings capitalization rate for firm i, and $E(X_{it+k})$ is the expected future (permanent) earnings of the firm. This rate incorporates earnings-valuation differences across firms that arise from cross-sectional differences in accounting method, risk, dividend payout rates, earnings persistence, earnings growth, and discount rates.[11] Thus, for example, the coefficient on UX/P in equation (3.5) will vary with investor beliefs that the firm's time-series process differs from a random walk. As noted earlier, the coefficient will decline as earnings persistence declines (γ increases). Higher expected earnings growth also implies a higher coefficient because the current surprise adds to the growing earnings base. "Growth" refers to opportunities for and expectations of growth in earnings that become apparent upon realization of earnings, which differs from growth that comes simply as a result of earnings retention and as captured in earnings persistence. Growth from the retention of earnings invested at the required rate of return does not increase today's price. Imagine a corporation comprising a farmer with land and a savings account. If today, the farmer retains the net proceeds from selling his crops today and places them in a savings account, future earnings will grow by the interest on these saved proceeds. However, today's price will not change because the farmer's decision to save does not add value. If, instead, we observe earnings growth via enhanced production efficiency, today's price will increase, and the increase will be determined by whether we believe the current innovation bodes well for future innovation. In addition, the coefficient will be decreasing in the risk-free interest rate and risk—these factors imply a lower capitalization rate.

Research provides empirical support for these cross-sectional relations. For example, Kormendi and Lipe (1987) estimate an individual firm's earnings persistence by regressing its current earnings change on two lagged earnings changes. They find a positive relation between this earnings-persistence measure and the coefficient on unexpected earnings in a regression of returns on unexpected earnings (i.e., the earnings response coefficient or ERC).

---

[11] ρ_i likely varies across firms. However, if we assume that it is constant over time, it will cancel out in equation (3.5) if we scale the right-hand side by X_t rather than P_t. $P_{it} = \rho_i E(X_{it+k})$ and $\Delta P_{it} = \rho_i \Delta E(X_{it+k})$, so $\Delta P_{it}/P_{it-1} = \Delta E(X_{it+k})/E(X_{it+k})$. However, this capitalization rate represents a reduced-form combination of nonlinear, discontinuous relations, so it is unlikely to be constant for one firm over time.

Easton and Zmijewski (1989) estimate earnings persistence by examining revisions in Value Line analyst earnings forecasts surrounding the earnings release. They find a significant, positive correlation between the sensitivity of these forecast revisions to unexpected earnings and the sensitivity of returns to unexpected earnings (i.e., the ERC). Collins and Kothari (1989) estimate the γ coefficient from equation (3.4) and find that ERC is increasing in earnings persistence (i.e., decreasing in γ). They also find that the ERC is increasing in growth, measured by market-to-book (a higher market-to-book implies more expected growth). In addition, Easton and Zmijewski (1989) and Collins and Kothari (1989) find that the ERC is declining in discount rates (risk-free interest rates and risk). These results support the joint hypothesis that (1) stock prices relate to the present value of expected future shareholder benefits, and (2) the present value of revisions in expected future earnings approximates the present value of the revisions in these expected future benefits (Kormendi and Lipe, 1987).

However, they also suggest that cross-sectional estimations will be misspecified if they fail to account for these differences in earnings capitalization rates across observations. The estimated ERC will be a cross-sectional average ERC that gives greater weight to larger prediction errors (the regression minimizes the sum of squared residuals). It need not apply to any one firm-year observation, and it is likely to differ from an ERC derived from the earnings time-series process most representative of the population. The failure to incorporate the earnings-capitalization rate differences does not imply that the ERC will be greater or less than that implied by a random-walk model, so it does not necessarily explain why estimated ERCs are lower than 10. However, omitting these observation-level capitalization-rate determinants from the estimation will reduce the model's explanatory power.

3.3.1.2. Earnings Prediction and Measurement of Unexpected Earnings

The second issue arising in empirical estimation of the ERC is that UX is likely to be measured with error. Measuring unexpected earnings requires a proxy for the earnings expectation of the marginal investors before the earnings announcement. To forecast earnings, investors likely use information beyond prior earnings realizations. Market participants compete to find information relevant for pricing securities; therefore, earnings expectations built into price likely reflect a broad set of information and forecasts based on prior earnings, and time-series models are imperfect proxies of earnings expectations.[12] Stated differently, random-walk models will not match earnings expectations that investors formed with information beyond prior earnings realizations.

Additional information is available to aid investors' earnings predictions. Earnings realizations reflect value-relevant events with a lag (Ball and Brown, 1968), which suggests that investors use information in addition to financial statements (e.g., factory visits, aerial photos of store parking lots) to predict earnings. This lag occurs because earnings are reported periodically (Ball and Shivakumar, 2008) and because accountants require evidence (such as a transaction with a customer) to record a sale, while investors anticipate the realization of this evidence. An example of investor anticipation can be seen in stock-price reactions to potential trade agreements with China or the lack thereof. Investors anticipate the earnings effects of such agreements and update prices.[13]

Research finds that analyst forecasts are more accurate than time-series models (e.g., Brown and Rozeff, 1978; O'Brien, 1988), though research also documents bias in analyst forecasts that may result from analyst incentives other than maximizing accuracy (e.g., Abarbanell, 1991; McNichols and O'Brien, 1997; Frankel and Lee, 1998; Lin and McNichols, 1998; Dechow, Hutton, and Sloan, 2000; Bradshaw, 2004; Groysberg, Healy, and Maber, 2011). An important realization that drove earnings-expectation research beyond the use of time-series estimates and analyst forecasts was the finding that firm characteristics (e.g., market-to-book, size, accrual-based earnings) could be associated with expected future earnings (e.g., Ou and Penman, 1989a, b; Sloan, 1996). Research also examines price-based earnings forecasts on the premise that prices reflect a richer information set than the past time series of earnings (e.g., Beaver, Lambert, and Morse, 1980; Beaver, Lambert, and Ryan, 1987; Kothari and Sloan, 1992; Beaver, McAnally, and Stinson, 1997; Zuo, 2016).

---

[12] Hayek (1945, p. 521) notes that markets aggregate the unique knowledge of "particular circumstances of time and place" dispersed among individuals. No single mind knows all the facts. Yet the market's production of prices helps society adapt to changes in circumstances and coordinate use of resources. Prices guide individual participants to take appropriate actions in response to these changing circumstances, though these individuals have no understanding of the effects of their actions beyond their immediate aim.

[13] Additional information can arrive during the return-measurement window. If so, even an accurate measure of unexpected earnings will not fully explain returns. To the extent that this additional information is uncorrelated with unexpected earnings, it will not bias the estimated earnings response coefficient, but it will reduce the regression's R^2.

The effect of the misestimation of unexpected earnings on empirical estimates of γ_1 in equation (3.1) can be seen with statistics and algebra. Recall that the linear regression defines γ_1 as follows:

$$\gamma_1 = \text{Cov}(\text{UX, R}) / \sigma^2(\text{UX}). \qquad (3.6)$$

However, we do not observe UX. Instead, we use $\text{UX}_{it} + u_{it}$ in our regression estimate, where u_{it} is an independent identically distributed error with variance $\sigma^2(u)$ (i.e., it is uncorrelated with UX, R, or any other realization of u). We observe unexpected earnings combined with our estimation error and use this noisy measure of unexpected earnings to estimate ERC. Our regression thus produces the following estimate of γ_1:

$$\begin{aligned}
\check{\gamma}_1 &= \text{Cov}(\text{UX}_{it} + u_{it}, \text{R}) / \sigma^2(\text{UX}_{it} + u_{it}) \\
&= \text{Cov}(\text{UX}_{it}, \text{R}) / [\sigma^2(\text{UX}_{it}) + \sigma^2(u_{it})] \qquad (3.7)
\end{aligned}$$

Because $\sigma^2(u_{it}) > 0$, our estimated ERC will understate the underlying ERC, i.e., $\check{\gamma}_1 < \gamma_1$.

3.3.1.3. Returns Reflecting Future Cash-Flow Information beyond That in Unexpected Earnings

If investors can predict earnings better than time-series models, and if earnings contain transitory elements recognized by investors, estimated ERCs will be lower than a random-walk model would predict. For example, consider a large gain (loss) recognized from the sale (disposal) of a business unit above (below) its book value. Unlike value-irrelevant noise, this gain (loss) is associated with an increase (decrease) in shareholder value. If the event causing the gain (loss) occurs in the present period, it will be reflected in current-period returns.[14] Generally, we might expect earnings to be a mixture of persistent and transitory components. If investors can distinguish these components, the ERC will reflect this mixture, and we would expect ERC estimates to be less than implied by a random-walk earnings process. If we posit that large earnings changes are more likely to contain these

---

[14] If the event occurred in a prior period and was known to investors at the time, the event will be reflected in prior-period returns. Current-period returns will be unaffected when the gain (loss) is reported in current-period earnings. This leads to a downward bias in the ERC.

transitory elements, we expect the cross-sectional relation between earnings changes and returns to be S-shaped. That is, observed price changes will be proportionally larger for smaller, more persistent earnings changes and proportionally smaller for larger, less persistent earnings changes (see, e.g., Freeman and Tse, 1992).

The issue of transitory items can also arise when current earnings contain errors that investors anticipate will be corrected in future earnings. For example, if managers overestimate future write-offs of accounts receivable and record excess bad-debt expense, and investors detect this overestimate, they will not react to the current earnings decline. The overstated bad-debt expense is "value-irrelevant noise" (Collins et al., 1994). It is not only transitory; it also reverses. A $0.02 per-share excess in bad-debt expenses in period t leads to a $0.02 lower EPS in period t and a $0.02 higher cumulative EPS in periods t + 1 and beyond, depending on the time required to correct this overestimate. The period t overestimate is an earnings component uncorrelated with investor payouts and does not affect investors' reaction to earnings.[15] In sum, measurement error in the independent variable and value-irrelevant noise in earnings will reduce the coefficient on the unexpected earnings proxy (or earnings response coefficient) in regressions of returns on unexpected earnings.[16]

Note that the issue of transitory items differs from the mismeasurement of unexpected earnings. In the case of transitory items, we fail to distinguish the differing future earnings implications of some surprises, even though the earnings surprise might be correctly measured. The earnings surprise is more transitory and thus less valuable than predicted by a random-walk model. The ERC estimates are not a biased measure of the population ERC. Instead, the population ERC reflects the transitory nature of some earnings surprises.

[15] The existence of unpriced earnings components raises questions. For example, Why do investors have more insight into bad-debt estimates than managers? If managers' misestimation is not a mistake, why might managers knowingly overestimate bad-debt expense? Might the overestimate result in a wealth transfer from investors to managers that was unanticipated by investors, leading to price effects? The last two questions concern the topic of earnings management, which we discuss in Chapter 4.

[16] Researchers (e.g., Beaver, Lambert, and Ryan, 1987; Collins and Kothari, 1989) use a reverse regression to overcome the coefficient bias stemming from random mismeasurement of the independent variable UX. The assumption is that the UR is properly measured. Noise in the dependent variable UX does not lead to biased estimates of the coefficient on UR, assuming that measurement error in UX is independent of UR. If so, the regression estimation correctly forces the error term to be orthogonal to UR, and the error term correctly reflects this measurement error. In the example above, returns are independent of the overestimate of bad debt expense.

3.3.1.3.1. Prices Leading Earnings

Extending Fama's (1990) analysis, Kothari (2001) provides an analytical framework that illustrates the implications of delayed earnings recognition on the earnings-return relation. To spotlight the effect of untimely earnings, Kothari (2001) models the relation between returns and earnings growth rates (i.e., $\Delta E_{t+1}/E_t$) and constrains earnings to be positive. We also assume that all earnings changes and returns are permanent. These assumptions permit a one-to-one relation between returns (i.e., growth in shareholder value) and earnings growth when both are equally timely.[17]

Denote period t earnings (returns) as X_t (R_t) and assume

$$X_t = x_t + y_{t-1}, \tag{3.8}$$

where x_t is the portion of period t earnings that is news to the market, and y_{t-1} is the portion of current-period earnings that is already known to the market. Assume that x_t and y_t are independent and identically distributed processes with variance $\sigma^2(x) = \sigma^2(y) = \sigma^2$. Prices lead earnings by one period. They contain growth-rate information not yet recognized in earnings, y_t, and respond only to the earnings surprise, x_t. Thus,

$$R_t = x_t + y_t. \tag{3.9}$$

These assumptions allow computation of the coefficient b produced by estimating the following regression:

$$R_t = a + bX_t + e_t. \tag{3.10}$$

Recall that $b = \text{Cov}(X_t, R_t)/\sigma^2(X_t)$. Thus $b = \sigma^2/(\sigma^2 + \sigma^2) = 0.5$.[18] The estimated earnings-growth response coefficient is only half of that expected when earnings and returns reflect contemporaneous information. Moreover, earnings would explain only 25 percent of the variation in returns.[19] This example illustrates that stale information in earnings reduces the estimated ERC. This

---

[17] If unexpected earnings deflated by the beginning-of-period price are used, then the ERC is $1 + 1/r$ as in equation (3.5).

[18] $\text{Cov}(X_t, R_t) = \text{Cov}(x_t + y_{t-1}, x_t + y_t) = \text{Cov}(x_t, x_t) = \sigma^2$.

[19] The R^2 would be 0.25 by the following logic: $\sigma^2(R_t) = 2\sigma^2$ and $\sigma^2(R_t) = \sigma^2(a + bX_t + e_t)$. If $b = 0.5$, the explained variation is $0.5^2 2\sigma^2$ or $0.5\sigma^2$, implying the unexplained variation or $\sigma^2(e_t) = 1.5\sigma^2$.

stale information is not value irrelevant. The stale component of earnings is reflected in returns in period t−1.

The regression estimate appropriately measures the relation between returns and earnings *as earnings are computed*. In this sense, estimated ERC is not biased. A doctor administering 500 milligrams of a drug diluted to one-half of its full strength gets a result consistent with the efficacy of a 250mg dose. If the physician does not realize she is administering a diluted drug, she will misunderstand the drug's efficacy. Thus, bias is in the eye of the observer. If the observer unwittingly employs an estimator whose assumptions differ from those the observer holds, he will reach an erroneous conclusion. So too would we reach an erroneous conclusion if, in running this regression, we believed that the ERC obtained represented the expected result in a world where earnings are timely. In this sense, the estimated ERC is a biased measure of the valuation implications of a $1 earnings surprise, because a portion of the earnings growth rate used as an input to the estimation is not a surprise.

To address the uncorrelated omitted variable problem, we can add future earnings to equation (3.10) to incorporate the omitted component of period t returns. That is,

$$R_t = a + bX_t + cX_{t+1} + e_t. \qquad (3.11)$$

A bit of algebra (see Kothari, 2001) shows that $b = 0.5$, $c = 0.5$. The coefficient on X_t remains at 0.5 because X_t contains a component uncorrelated with R_t, y_{t-1}, that has variance equal to its component correlated with R_t, x_t. The R^2 will increase to 50 percent.[20] The explanatory power of the model doubles because the addition of X_{t+1} to the model brings with it the y_t component of returns missing from the single independent variable in equation (3.10). The R^2 remains below 1 because the components of X_t and X_{t+1} that are uncorrelated with R_t compromise the model's explanatory power (i.e., the errors-in-variables problem). Drawing on Kothari and Shanken (1992), Collins et al. (1994) include in equation (3.11) future return (R_{t+1}) to remove the new information error (x_{t+1}) from the future earnings growth variable X_{t+1}. In addition, they include lagged earnings yield and lagged investment growth as

---

[20] The R^2 of 0.5 can be derived as follows: $\sigma^2(R_t) = 2\sigma^2$ and $\sigma^2(R_t) = \sigma^2(a + bX_t + bX_{t+1} + e_t)$. If $b = c = 0.5$, the explained variation is $0.5^2 2\sigma^2 + 0.5^2 2\sigma^2 = \sigma^2$, implying the unexplained variation or $\sigma^2(e_t) = \sigma^2$.

proxies for the anticipated component (y_{t-1}) of current growth X_t.[21] Collins et al. (1994) find that current and future earnings adjusted for expectational errors explain roughly three to six times as much of the annual return variation as current earnings alone.[22]

3.3.1.3.2. Unexpected Earnings

This framework allows us to add rigor to our definition of untimely earnings and the effect of controlling for expected earnings. X_t is untimely in two senses: It contains stale, value-relevant information already impounded in price (this is represented by the y_{t-1} component of X_t), and it lacks information about future shareholder benefits available currently to investors (this is represented by the y_t component of X_{t+1}). If the stale portion of X_t can be viewed as the expected portion of current earnings, the unexpected portion of X_t is x_t. This is the value-relevant information the market learns from the current earnings report. We can now determine the effect of controlling for expected earnings in equation (3.10) by rewriting it as

$$R_t = a + bUX_t + e_t, \tag{3.12}$$

where $UX_t = x_t$ and $b = \mathrm{Cov}(UX_t, R_t)/\sigma^2(UX_t) = \mathrm{Cov}(x_t, R_t)/\sigma^2(x_t) = \mathrm{Cov}(x_t, x_t + y_t)/\sigma^2(x_t) = \sigma^2(x_t)/\sigma^2(x_t) = 1$. Thus, the effect of untimely earnings on the estimated ERC coefficient can be lessened if the researcher identifies the earnings expectations of the marginal investor without error, which is a difficult task. However, the R^2 of the equation (3.12) estimation continues to suffer from the lagged recognition of value-relevant information represented by y_t. Unexpected earnings growth cannot fully explain returns because a source of return variation is not yet contained in earnings.[23]

[21] The variables of interest are (1) the unanticipated component of current earnings growth and (2) the revision in the market's expectations, from the beginning to the end of the period, about the t + 1 period's earnings growth. The controls are (1) the previously (at t−1) anticipated portion of the current period's earnings growth, and (2) the earnings growth in period t + 1 generated by events in period t + 1 that were not anticipated in period t. These controls differ from the value-irrelevant noise or the garbling component of earnings as in Beaver, Lambert, and Morse (1980).

[22] Fama (1990), Schwert (1990), Easton, Harris, and Ohlson (1992), and Warfield and Wild (1992) expand the earnings-return measurement window to mitigate both errors-in-variables and omitted-variable problems. Kothari and Sloan (1992), Warfield and Wild (1992), and Jacobson and Aaker (1993) regress current and past returns on current-period earnings to overcome the errors-in-variables problem.

[23] The R^2 of 0.5 can be derived as follows: $\sigma^2(R_t) = 2\sigma^2$ and $\sigma^2(R_t) = \sigma^2(a + bUX_t + e_t)$. If $b = 1$, the explained variation is $1^2\sigma^2 = \sigma^2$, implying the unexplained variation or $\sigma^2(e_t) = \sigma^2$.

3.3.1.4. Mispricing from Pervasive Investor Biases

Coefficients produced by estimates of equation (3.5) might also differ from $(1/r + 1)$ because prices do not reflect expected payouts to shareholders. The explanation for such price behavior is that many investors have similar information-processing biases, and costly arbitrage constrains any cadre of investors from taking advantage of this mispricing opportunity at an unlimited scale and eliminating it. An example of a processing bias is that investors might overextrapolate and thus overreact to positive information, though they lack a statistical basis for a trend. Alternatively, investors might underreact to less salient information. As noted above, Kormedi and Lipe's (1987) result suggests that stock prices act as if investors incorporate cross-sectional variation in the persistence of the earnings surprise. However, an insight of Sloan (1996) is that prices might not fully reflect this variation. Sloan's empirical tests reject the hypothesis that prices fully reflect the greater persistence of earnings buttressed by cash flows.[24] Research also documents a tendency of prices to drift in the direction of the earnings surprise in the months following the earnings announcement (Ball and Brown, 1968; Foster, Olsen, and Shevlin, 1984; Bernard and Thomas, 1989, 1990). This result suggests that investors underreact to the information related to expected future shareholder payouts. Underreaction would cause the ERC to be less than $1/r + 1$.

3.3.2. Empirical Research Estimating ERC

Given this discussion, we review the empirical estimation of ERC beginning with Beaver, Lambert, and Morse (1980). Beaver, Lambert, and Morse (1980) use an annual return window and annual earnings changes, regressing stock returns on earnings-per-share growth. Their specification mirrors that of equation (3.10). They use earnings before nonrecurring items (presumably because these items are less persistent) to reduce cross-sectional variation in earnings persistence. They find the ERC or coefficient on X_t to be 0.12. They interpret this low coefficient as suggesting that "earnings are not perceived to be well approximated as a random walk when perceived from the perspective

[24] Sloan (1996) uses the Mishkin (1983) test to draw his inferences. Kraft, Leone, and Wasley (2007) show that the accrual anomaly documented in Sloan (1996) vanishes when additional explanatory variables are incorporated into the Mishkin test. See also Lewellen (2010).

of other information reflected in prices" (pp. 13–14). This interpretation aligns with the Kothari framework, where a portion of earnings growth, y_{t-1}, is anticipated and incorporated into price.

Hagerman, Zmijewski, and Shah (1984) use a five-day window surrounding the quarterly earnings announcement to measure returns and use the percentage change in quarterly earnings. They estimate an ERC of 0.0189 and an adjusted R-squared of 2.78 percent. Hagerman, Zmijewski, and Shah (1984, p. 529) note a "puzzling aspect" of their results: earnings seem to play a "small role" in explaining returns around the earnings release. Referring to the framework above, if the short-event window of Hagerman, Zmijewski, and Shah (1984) successfully reduces effects produced by the release of value-relevant information not yet incorporated into earnings (i.e., y_t), the explanation for the low ERC and R-squared is that the percentage change in quarterly earnings is a poor proxy for x_t. That the earnings change is a poor proxy for unexpected earnings seems reasonable, given that information undoubtedly becomes available throughout the quarter that is useful for predicting the quarter's earnings. Research as early as Ball and Brown (1968) provides evidence that information useful for predicting upcoming earnings becomes available throughout the fiscal period.

Using analyst forecasts to proxy for the market's expectation of earnings does not necessarily solve the x_t estimation problem. Research suggests that analyst forecasts are slow to reflect information in current prices (e.g., Lys and Sohn, 1990; Abarbanell, 1991) or are predictably biased (e.g., Frankel and Lee, 1998). Research also suggests that analysts face pressure to deviate from issuing accurate forecasts. For example, they might seek to satisfy managers to gain access to information or investment banking business (Francis and Philbrick, 1993; Dugar and Nathan, 1995; Lin and McNichols, 1998; Lim, 2001). Research finds that analysts tend to be optimistic (e.g., O'Brien, 1988) but reduce their subsequent forecasts (Richardson, Teoh, and Wysocki, 2004), appearing to play an earnings guidance game with managers and investors. Managers also appear to take action to avoid reporting negative earnings surprises (Kasznik and Lev, 1995; Burgstahler and Dichev, 1997; Matsumoto, 2002; Bradshaw and Sloan, 2002). For example, managers might try to shape analyst forecasts or the earnings concept that analysts forecast. Analysts forecast street earnings, a modified form of GAAP earnings, with the stated goal of removing the effects of nonrecurring, noncash items from GAAP earnings. But items excluded from GAAP earnings are associated with future cash flows (Doyle, Lundholm, and Soliman, 2003). The results of Doyle, Jennings, and Soliman (2013) suggest that managers' exclusions from GAAP earnings enable them to meet or beat analyst expectations.[25] Given the vagaries arising from street earnings, the relation between forecast errors and returns might differ from the relation between the GAAP earnings surprise (our x_t) and returns. More accurate forecasts of GAAP earnings need not be more highly correlated with returns (O'Brien, 1988; Bradshaw and Sloan, 2002; Brown and Sivakumar, 2003; Bradshaw et al., 2018).

What seemed a mere valuation exercise, attempting to estimate the valuation properties of earnings, pulls us back to the incentive problems inherent in imperfect and incomplete markets. Our assessment of the valuation properties of unexpected earnings measures is incomplete unless we consider the incentives of the parties that influence our proxies. In this case, investors use earnings and the earnings surprise to gauge firm performance and value. Therefore, earnings and the earnings surprise affect managers' wealth. In anticipation of this wealth effect, managers can alter the earnings surprise through their influence on (1) the GAAP-earnings realization, (2) items excluded to compute street earnings, and (3) analyst forecasts. Investors, in turn, anticipate the incentives of managers and analysts. In response, we might expect investors to alter their measurement techniques and reevaluate these performance measures as incentive effects are brought to light. A massive body of research explores issues related to street earnings, analyst expectations, and manager incentives to meet expectations. Reviewing this research is outside the purview of our ERC discussion, but the issues raised illustrate our essential point. These accounting measures (earnings and earnings surprises) must have efficiency effects if we observe demand for them and production to satisfy this demand.[26] Efficiency effects imply that these measures alter actions, outcomes, and the payoffs of concerned parties. They force us to consider the incentive effects that underlie these measures.

[25] Items excluded by firms in their earnings press release can differ from items excluded by analysts in making their forecasts (Gu and Chen, 2004). Because analysts can reject management's exclusions, the assumption is that management can influence analysts to exclude items from earnings. Regulation G requires the firm to reconcile reported non-GAAP earnings with GAAP earnings, presumably to reduce misleading exclusions.

[26] We discuss this point in Chapter 4.

3.3.3. The Basu (1997) Coefficient and Its Interpretations

The small magnitude of the ERC relative to its predicted value motivated researchers to advance several hypotheses and explanations we discussed earlier. The other prominent phenomenon that sparks a significant interest in the literature is that the incremental slope on negative returns is positive in a piecewise linear regression of earnings on returns. This incremental slope on negative returns is called the Basu (1997) coefficient.[27] While there is little disagreement on the existence of a positive Basu coefficient, its cause and interpretation remain controversial. In this section, we discuss the estimation of the Basu coefficient and the various explanations advanced in the literature. One primary explanation for this empirical regularity is conditional conservatism, that is, accounting rules impose a higher verification threshold for economic gains than for economic losses. Intuitively, conservative accounting rules exist because managers, on average, tend to withhold bad news but voluntarily disclose good news (Kothari, Shu, and Wysocki, 2009). In this reduced-form analysis, we take a firm's accounting practice as given and do not delve into the economic determinants of conditional conservatism.[28] Our focus is on the observed asymmetric earnings-return relation and its explanations. While conditional conservatism can lead to an asymmetric earnings-return relation, it is not the only cause. Economic factors such as a firm's abandonment option, cash-flow asymmetry, and adjustment costs can also lead to an asymmetric earnings-return relation *absent accounting influences*.[29] Thus, the Basu coefficient and the extent of conditional conservatism are not equivalent.

3.3.3.1. The Basu Coefficient and Conditional Conservatism
Basu (1997) runs a reverse regression (Beaver, Lambert, and Ryan, 1987; Collins and Kothari, 1989) of annual earnings on current annual returns. He uses concurrent stock returns to proxy for new information about firm value during the fiscal period. He predicts that earnings are more strongly

---

[27] We choose not to call it the "asymmetric timeliness coefficient" because asymmetric earnings timeliness is not the only cause of the asymmetric earnings-return relation (as elaborated later in this section).

[28] In equilibrium, the extent of conditional conservatism is driven by economic incentives, debt and compensation contracting, governance, GAAP, regulation, and taxes (Watts 2003a, b).

[29] Here we refer to the direct effects of these economic factors on the earnings-return relation, not their indirect effects through their influence on a firm's accounting practice.

associated with concurrent negative returns, which proxy for "bad news," than with positive returns, which proxy for "good news." Specifically, he runs the following regression:

$$X_{it}/P_{it-1} = a_0 + a_1 D(R_{it} < 0) + b_0 R_{it} + b_1 D(R_{it} < 0) \times R_{it} + \varepsilon_{it} \qquad (3.13)$$

where X_{it} is earnings per share of firm i in year t; P_{it-1} is beginning-of-period stock price of firm i; R_{it} is the stock return on firm i from nine months before fiscal year-end t to three months after fiscal year-end t; and D(.) is an indicator function taking the value of 1 when stock returns are negative, and 0 otherwise. Basu predicts and finds a positive coefficient b_1. He interprets this positive coefficient b_1 as evidence of accounting conservatism, that is, earnings reflect bad news more quickly than good news. This definition of conservatism is termed *conditional conservatism* (Ball and Shivakumar, 2005; Beaver and Ryan, 2005) because the timeliness with which earnings incorporate economic shocks depends on their sign. The research objective of the Basu model based on equation (3.13) is to measure how accounting earnings incorporate the information in stock returns rather than to estimate the ERC in a regression of annual stock returns on annual earnings.[30] Basu (1997) also predicts and finds that ERCs are higher for positive earnings changes than for negative earnings changes, consistent with negative earnings changes being less persistent than positive earnings changes.

Initially, the Basu coefficient was *assumed* to be a valid measure of conditional conservatism largely due to its intuitive appeal. Ball, Kothari, and Nikolaev (2013a) build on the literature on prices leading earnings and develop a formal model that derives and analyzes the Basu coefficient in a reduced-form setting. Their model focuses on the effects of accounting rules and practices per se and distinguishes three components of information. The first information component is always contemporaneously incorporated into earnings. This component represents the information verifiable at low cost, such as news about cash receipts and payments and working capital accruals.

The second information component is incorporated into earnings either contemporaneously or with a lag, depending on its sign or magnitude. This

---

[30] Dietrich, Muller, and Riedl (2007) claim that the Basu regression specification is misspecified because (1) earnings cause returns and (2) conditioning on the sign of the returns induces sample truncation bias. Ball, Kothari, and Nikolaev (2013a) point out that both claims are based on the misconception that the objective of a Basu specification is to estimate the ERC in a regression of annual returns on annual earnings.

component represents information that is costly to verify, and it is the source of conditional conservatism (i.e., a lower accounting verification threshold for negative news about future cash flows than for positive news). This type of information leads to revisions of expectations about unrealized future cash flows from long-term fixed assets or purchased intangible assets (e.g., patents and goodwill), the marketability of inventory, or lawsuit settlements. Ball, Kothari, and Nikolaev (2013a) take the extent of the asymmetry as exogenously given because their objective is not to provide an equilibrium model of the extent of conditional conservatism but rather to investigate the validity of the Basu coefficient.

The third information component in the model is always incorporated into earnings with a lag, such as news about "unbooked" rents or growth options. These three components are all reflected in current stock returns, but they differ on when they are incorporated into earnings. In the Ball, Kothari, and Nikolaev (2013a) model, earnings also incorporate "noise" that reverses over time (e.g., due to random errors in counting inventory or in valuing accounts receivable). This model incorporates the salient properties of accounting recognition rules and practices, and it demonstrates that the Basu asymmetric timeliness coefficient is positive in the presence of conditional conservatism and zero in the absence of conditional conservatism, consistent with it being a valid estimator.[31]

An implicit assumption in estimating the Basu (1997) model, as in equation (3.13), is that the expected components of earnings and returns do not vary cross-sectionally and thus are captured in the intercepts. This regression without controls for expected values is well specified when the research objective does not require separating the expected and news components of returns (e.g., in contracting contexts where lenders are indifferent between expected and unexpected changes in firm value). However, failure to control for the expected components of earnings and returns biases Basu estimates of how earnings incorporate the *unexpected* component of returns. Ball, Kothari, and Nikolaev (2013b) recommend several remedies to adjust for

---

[31] The Ball, Kothari, and Nikolaev (2013a) model explains why a negative relation between (beginning-of-period) market-to-book ratios and Basu coefficients is expected, refuting the criticism by Pae, Thornton, and Welker (2005) and Givoly, Hayn, and Natarajan (2007). Ball, Kothari, and Nikolaev (2013a) argue that this negative relation arises because the market-to-book ratio is correlated with the relative amount of total price revision associated with revisions in "unbooked" components, such as growth option expectations. Roychowdhury and Watts (2007) offer a similar argument. Lawrence, Sloan, and Sun (2013) provide a different explanation, arguing that the beginning-of-period book-to-market ratios reflect the likelihood that nondiscretionary write-downs are warranted.

this bias. Ball, Kothari, and Nikolaev (2013b) show that researchers can substantially reduce or eliminate bias by including a simple control for a small number of well-known risk factors that determine expected returns and by employing a relatively crude method of removing the expected components of earnings (e.g., including firm fixed effects).

3.3.3.2. Economic Fundamentals

Economic fundamentals, apart from accounting rules and measurement issues, can also contribute to the observed earnings-return relation. Recall that early research by Kormendi and Lipe (1987), Easton and Zmijewski (1989), and Collins and Kothari (1989) identifies persistence, risk, growth, and interest rate as economic determinants of ERC(s). We discuss next three examples of economic factors (i.e., the abandonment option, cash-flow asymmetry, and adjustment costs) that can lead to an asymmetric earnings-return relation. The implication is that we should not attribute observed earnings-return patterns *exclusively* to accounting effects. While conditional conservatism leads to an incremental positive slope on negative returns in a piecewise linear regression of earnings on returns, this positive Basu coefficient can be driven by economic factors as well. Thus, controlling for those economic factors is essential when using the Basu coefficient as a proxy for conditional conservatism.

3.3.3.2.1. Abandonment Option

Several studies note that the asymmetric earnings-return relation reflects the lower expected loss persistence driven by a firm's curtailment activity. Hayn (1995) points out that firms have an abandonment option to discontinue the loss-making operation; as a result, losses are less persistent than profits, which leads to a lower ERC for losses than for profits (in a regression of annual returns on annual earnings). Mak, Strong, and Walker (2011) extend the standard model of adaptation value to the context of the corporate refocusing activities of UK-listed companies and provide evidence of an increased Basu coefficient in the refocusing announcement year and in the year following the announcement. Lawrence, Sloan, and Sun (2018) provide further evidence that losses lead to curtailments (typically involving the liquidation of working capital), reducing loss persistence and leading to an asymmetric earnings-return relation. Hemmer and Labro (2019) explore the theoretical relation between earnings and returns, assuming that financial reports are also used to facilitate more frequent internal managerial decisions. They show that the optimal managerial decision rule is asymmetric with respect to gains versus losses, leading to the kinked earnings-return relation obtained from the Basu regression.

3.3.3.2.2. Cash Flow Asymmetry

Collins, Hribar, and Tian (2014) provide evidence that the asymmetric earnings-return relation from the Basu regression (i.e., equation (3.13)) holds when researchers use either operating cash flows (CFO) or accruals (i.e., earnings minus operating cash flows) as the dependent variable. They argue that CFO asymmetry does not reflect differential verification thresholds for recognizing economic gains versus economic losses but instead is driven by a firm's life-cycle stage. They reason as follows: The value of a start-up or growth firm depends more on its future growth opportunities than the cash flows generated from its assets in place, and this is particularly true in good economic environments in which it is not uncommon for a growth firm with negative operating cash flows to have positive stock returns. During bad economic environments, however, young growth firms tend to have fewer external financing options and need to rely more on the operating cash flows; thus, CFOs are more closely related to changes in firm value in this environment. Hence, there is a stronger relation between CFO and returns for young growth firms in negative return environments, which leads to significant CFO asymmetry among growth firms. For mature firms, changes in firm value are closely related to changes in the cash flows generated from the assets in place in both good and bad economic environments. Hence, mature firms will exhibit less cash-flow asymmetry or none at all. Consistent with these arguments, Collins, Hribar, and Tian (2014) find stronger evidence of CFO asymmetric timeliness for young growing firms (firms in early life-cycle stages) than for mature, stable firms (firms in late life-cycle stages). Collins, Hribar, and Tian (2014) further show that using accruals as the dependent variable successfully removes many of the biases caused by cash-flow asymmetry, and they recommend using accruals as the dependent variable in studies of conditional conservatism.

3.3.3.2.3. Adjustment Costs

The cost accounting literature documents that costs are sticky in the sense that they rise more for sales increases than they fall for equivalent sales decreases (see, e.g., Anderson, Banker, and Janakiraman, 2003). This asymmetric cost behavior stems from adjustment costs, such as severance payments to dismissed workers and disposal costs for property, plant, and equipment. In the presence of adjustment costs, managers tend to retain slack resources and do not cut costs proportionally when sales decrease. Still, they tend to add required resources and increase costs proportionally when sales increase. These tendencies result in the observed cost stickiness. Banker et al. (2016) note that cost stickiness contributes to the asymmetric earnings-return relation, and they show that controlling for a piecewise linear effect of sales changes in the Basu model decreases significantly the measured Basu coefficient. They argue that future empirical research on conditional conservatism should recognize the effect of sticky costs on the earnings-return relation.

Further, Ball and Shivakumar (2006) and Banker, Basu, and Byzalov (2017) argue that while stock prices efficiently combine information about future cash flows to estimate overall firm value, additional indicators that predict cash flow over shorter time horizons have an incremental effect on current-period earnings. For example, a sales decrease can signal a reduction in the expected short-term cash flow from inventory on hand and trigger an inventory write-down even if the stock return is positive. Banker, Basu, and Byzalov (2017) document that earnings exhibit asymmetric timeliness with respect to multiple indicators, including the stock return, sales change, and operating cash flow change. They also demonstrate an interaction effect between indicators, such that the total impact of several consistent indicators is greater than the sum of their individual impacts.[32]

Breuer and Windisch (2019) propose the standard neoclassical model of investment under uncertainty with short-run adjustment frictions as a benchmark for earnings-return patterns absent accounting influences. They show that their proposed benchmark generates an asymmetric earnings-return relation. The two channels in their model are as follows. First, current-period earnings respond more strongly to negative than to positive persistent profitability shocks because adjustment costs exacerbate the earnings-decreasing effects of negative profitability shocks and reduce the earnings-increasing effects of positive profitability shocks. Second, future earnings respond more strongly to positive than to negative persistent profitability shocks because capital divestments in response to a persistent

---

[32] Relatedly, Byzalov and Basu (2016) build on the microfoundations of conservatism—asset impairment tests—and document that accrual conservatism manifests as a sum of asymmetries for a vector of news indicators, rather than as an asymmetry for a scalar aggregate news proxy.

negative shock in the current period allow firms to minimize the impact of their decreased demand or productivity in the future (i.e., the abandonment option). Since returns capture both current and future earnings responses to shocks, returns react less strongly to negative than to positive shocks, relative to current-period earnings, resulting in the asymmetric earnings-return relation as in Basu (1997).

3.3.3.3. A Modified Basu Measure of Conditional Conservatism

The takeaway from this discussion on the Basu coefficient and its various explanations is that the observed earnings-return relation results from both accounting and economic factors. We should not simply equate the Basu coefficient with the extent of conditional conservatism. Recognizing and carefully controlling for the various nonaccounting factors is necessary when using the Basu coefficient as a proxy for conditional conservatism.[33]

Badia et al. (2021) take an important step in this direction by making four simple modifications to the Basu model. The authors demonstrate that their modified Basu measure captures conditional conservatism and is largely free of the statistical biases and economic confounds identified in existing research. We recommend that researchers follow their procedures to modify the piecewise linear earnings-return model (i.e., equation (3.13)) when using the Basu coefficient to proxy for conditional conservatism. These modifications include (1) using unexpected earnings as the dependent variable and unexpected returns in the interactive explanatory variables, (2) including firm fixed effects, (3) including interactive controls for return variance (i.e., the variance of daily stock returns during the fiscal year), and (4) including interactive controls for the beginning market-to-book ratio of assets.

---

[33] Other nonaccounting factors can also affect the estimated earnings-return relation. For example, Patatoukas and Thomas (2011) demonstrate the existence of scale-related effects on the Basu coefficient. They argue that price, which is used to scale earnings, is inversely related to stock return variance, causing a "variance effect," and also inversely related to the incidence of losses, causing a "loss effect." Patatoukas and Thomas (2016) further note that earnings, accruals, and other measures of performance are often related to second and higher moments of the distribution of returns, which can lead to an asymmetric earnings-return relation absent accounting influences. Dutta and Patatoukas (2017) develop a valuation model and identify expected returns, cash-flow persistence, and asymmetry in the returns distribution as three nonaccounting factors that affect the Basu coefficient.

3.4. ERC and the Role of Financial Accounting

As noted in Chapter 2, Ball and Brown (1968) examine the relation between earnings and returns by dividing firm-year observations of annual
earnings and stock returns into two categories—those with positive unexpected earnings and those with negative unexpected earnings. We describe
their procedure in the framework of our equation (3.1) as follows. They estimate γ_1 for the special case of a binary unexpected-earnings variable and
wish to know whether $\gamma_1 > 0$. They test the theory that unexpected earnings
are positively associated with shareholder value if earnings are "useful."
Webster's Third New International Dictionary defines "useful" as "advan-
tageous . . . producing or having the power to produce good." A useful car
helps the driver and passengers get to their destination. Similarly, useful accounting practices help the firm do *something*; the *something* is not specified
by Ball and Brown. The theory that Ball and Brown cite (e.g., Chambers,
1964; Sterling, 1967) directed its attention to methods for measuring economic income, assuming that accounting practices that produced an income number that better approximates economic income help the firm or
help investors and thereby enhance shareholder value.[34] Ball and Brown seek
to identify earnings properties that might aid in the development of such a
theory. For example, they conclude by suggesting an investigation of the relation between the *magnitude* of the unexpected earnings and the returns,
saying that such results might "furnish insight into the statistical nature of
the income process, a process little understood but of considerable interest to
accounting researchers" (Ball and Brown, 1968, p. 177).

Beaver, Clarke, and Wright (1979) examine the correlation between the
magnitude of the earnings forecast error and returns. They substitute twenty-
five portfolios for Ball and Brown's two. They place firm-year observations
into these twenty-five portfolios based on the relative magnitude of unexpected earnings and compute the rank correlations of portfolio average unexpected earnings and portfolio average unexpected returns. The paper uses
two models of expected earnings. The first model is a martingale model or
random walk with a drift estimated from past earnings changes, and the
second is a market index–based model.

---

[34] Regulatory considerations, such as social welfare and Pareto optimality, were also a concern
(Gonedes and Dopuch, 1974).

Beaver, Clarke, and Wright (1979) give a methodological motive for their refinement of Ball and Brown's test. They note that Ball and Brown's approach was adequate for examining the null of no association between prices and earnings, but "as the research questions asked become more refined, treatment of the earnings forecast error may become critical. This is our motivation for extending one aspect of the Ball and Brown study" (Beaver, Clarke, and Wright, 1979, 317). They offer a sterile interpretation of this correlation and seem unwilling to attach evocative but spongey terms like "meaning," "utility," or "useful" to their finding of a positive rank correlation between portfolio average unexpected earnings and portfolio average unexpected returns. They explain, "The reason a dependency exists appears to rest upon the simple premise that prices and earnings both are the result of mappings from a common underlying set of events" (p. 322).

An application of Beaver, Clarke, and Wright's (1979) method can be found in Biddle and Lindahl's (1982) research on LIFO adoption.[35] One method to understand the role of accounting is to check the effect of unexpected accounting changes on firm value. Using LIFO can increase firm value by reducing the present value of taxes. Biddle and Lindahl use Beaver, Clarke, and Wright's (1979) method in their research design to distinguish earnings performance effects from LIFO-adoption effects per se. Biddle and Lindahl reasoned that the underlying performance of the firm might be related to a manager's decision to adopt LIFO (Sunder, 1973). The tax benefits of LIFO might be more valuable to firms with better performance and higher expected taxes. Therefore, the positive news with respect to the pretax earnings performance that the announcement of LIFO adoption might reveal to investors can confound attempts to isolate the firm-value effect of LIFO adoption per se.

Biddle and Lindahl (1982) estimate the following equation:

$$UR_{it} = g_0 + g_1 TS_{it} + g_2 UX_{it} + e_{it} \qquad (3.14)$$

where TS_{it} is an estimate of the LIFO adoption-year tax savings (i.e., fiscal year t) for firm i. UR_{it} is the cumulative unexpected return over the fifteen

---

[35] LIFO, an acronym for last-in-first-out, is an inventory cost-flow assumption. The LIFO assumption uses the cost of recent purchases to determine cost of goods sold. The Internal Revenue Code ties use of LIFO for tax reporting to use of LIFO for financial reporting. In a period of inflation, recent costs exceed older costs, and use of the LIFO assumption shifts income to latter periods, lowering the present value of taxes.

months before the end of fiscal year t for firm I, and UX_{it} is the change in earnings calculated as if the firm had not made the LIFO change. Unlike Beaver, Clarke, and Wright (1979), Biddle and Lindahl do not use portfolio ranks for UX. Biddle and Lindahl find that the coefficients on γ_1 and γ_2 are positive and statistically significant.

Our purpose in reviewing Biddle and Lindahl (1982) is as follows: First, their paper illustrates how the ERC-research design can be a means to answering economic questions. Biddle and Lindahl's goal is to understand how investors react to the LIFO accounting-method change. If investors focus on the cash-flow effect (arising from tax savings), the coefficient on TS_{it} is expected to be positive. However, if investors fixate on the reduction in reported earnings due to higher reported cost of goods sold (and lower income) caused by the LIFO adoption, the coefficient on TS_{it} is expected to be negative. The word "fixate" is used to describe this behavior because in reacting to the cost of goods sold change, investors seem to react naïvely, revising their valuations based on the reported number while ignoring the underlying cash-flow effects resulting from the tax savings. Evidence of fixation is evidence against market efficiency because market efficiency predicts that prices will reflect Bayesian-updated expectations of cash flows when the market responds to new information.[36] In this case, the information is the news of LIFO adoption and related publicly available information that investors use to estimate the expected reduction in taxes from adoption.[37] Thus, the ERC-based design is used to control for a correlated factor that could affect the interpretation of the main coefficient in this joint test of market efficiency and the cash-flow effects of a particular accounting-method choice.[38]

[36] The term 'functional fixation' is used to describe a market-price reaction to an observed signal that ignores the properties of the information system that generates the signal. Beaver and Dukes (1972) trace this use of the term to Ijiri, Jaedicke, and Knight (1966). In a more famous example, Sloan's (1996) "naïve" earnings-expectation model is based on the idea that investors fixate on current earnings and do not distinguish between the differing predictive implications of the accrual and cash-flow components.

[37] Biddle and Lindhal (1982) measure returns during the fifteen months prior to the fiscal-year-end month, hoping to capture the period during which the LIFO adoption and the tax-savings information are revealed. However, investors might anticipate LIFO adoption prior to this time, and the expected probability of LIFO adoption might differ across firms (Lanen and Thompson, 1988). Jennings, Mest, and Thompson (1992) model the anticipated probability of LIFO adoption at the firm level. They also take steps to limit the return-measurement window to a period when they believe it is likely that information allowing investors to update this probability is released. They find that their measure of the change in this probability is positively correlated with returns.

[38] They further control for the risk changes and still find a positive and significant coefficient of tax savings.

Second, the results illustrate the application of methodological refinements in the ERC-based design. Controlling for the correlated variable of performance in the market-efficiency test requires us to measure unexpected earnings. Biddle and Lindahl (1982), inspired by Beaver, Clarke, and Wright's (1979) finding that the sign and magnitude of unexpected earnings are associated with returns, use a continuous earnings change measure. The need to control for unexpected earnings raises the further issue of how to measure this concept. A noisy measure leaves residual performance effects that continue to confound the interpretation of the market-efficiency test. Early researchers like Ball and Brown (1968), Beaver, Clarke, and Wright (1979), and Biddle and Lindahl (1982) used prior-period earnings, sometimes adjusting this expectation measure for the earnings performance of firms in the industry or prior-year earnings changes. Later researchers used analyst earnings forecasts. For example, a later LIFO-adoption study by Jennings, Mest, and Thompson (1992) uses Value Line earnings expectations as a proxy for expected earnings.

3.5. Concluding Remarks

Perhaps some distaste for ERC research stems from disappointment. Beginning with Ball and Brown (1968), researchers have used the relation between earnings and stock prices as the foundation for understanding earnings. Researchers knew that linking the earnings-return relation to the welfare or shareholder-value effects of financial reporting regulations and choices was problematic because they lacked a formal theory supporting these links. Ball and Brown (1968, p. 177) note that "a mechanism has been provided for an empirical approach to a restricted class of the controversial choices in external reporting." They did not elaborate on the nature of this restricted class or the logic behind the restrictions. ERC research was in its infancy, and much work remained to be done on methodological issues (e.g., measuring unexpected earnings and returns), elaborating the valuation model linking these variables, and testing its empirical validity.

As this work proceeded, and confidence in the methodological and valuation underpinnings of the earnings-return research design grew, researchers began to explore whether specific financial-statement variables (e.g., purchasing power gains/losses under SFAS 33, unrealized gains/losses from cash-flow hedges) are associated with price in order to provide input into the standard-setting process. For example, Alford et al. (1993) compare earnings-return correlations across countries. The paper discusses the debate over listing requirements for foreign firms on US exchanges but contains no statements linking these correlations to this debate. The authors' indirection suggests their awareness that such statements could not be supported. Pownall's (1993, p. 228) discussion of the paper notes,

> This comparison can suggest which set of accounting numbers might be more useful for contracting or monitoring *under some conditions* but *does not directly address* "usefulness" to current or potential shareholders. Therefore, this comparison is *not of direct relevance* to the policy issues motivating the paper. (emphasis added)

The authors' unwillingness to connect their results to issues of concern to regulators (while nonetheless mentioning these issues) and the discussant's choice to include equivocating adjectives and adverbs like "direct" and "directly" suggest that both the authors and the discussant retained lofty aspirations for the implications of returns/earnings correlations, despite their reservations.

Some researchers more explicitly take the primary objective of financial reporting to be "the prediction of future investor cash flows or stock returns" (Lev, 1989, p. 157). For example, Lev (1989, p. 155) states,

> While misspecification of the return/earnings relation or the existence of investor irrationality ("noise trading") may contribute to the weak association between earnings and stock returns, the possibility that the fault lies with the low quality (information content) of reported earnings looms large.

Holthausen and Watts (2001) review the value-relevance literature, highlighting many papers containing statements that link return and earnings estimations to accounting regulation. They say that such statements must be grounded in theory linking the behavior of standard setters to the correlation between accounting numbers and stock prices. According to Holthausen and Watts (2001, p. 4),

> Those authors have to specify the objective of standard setting and how using the association criterion helps standard setters achieve that objective.

If the specified objective and the association criterion do not explain or predict standard setters' actions, it is incumbent on the authors to explain (i) why standard setters do not pursue that objective and (ii) why pursuit of that objective is relevant and feasible.

Holthausen and Watts go on to note that while value-relevance tests can indicate whether accounting earnings have properties consistent with serving as an input to equity valuation, "input to valuation" is just one of the many roles of financial reporting regulators consider.[39] Holthausen and Watts further note that the most highly associated income number is not necessarily the most accurate measure of equity value or its changes.[40] Holthausen and Watts also discuss features of current accounting practice inconsistent with enhancing value relevance (e.g., the tendency of the income statement to delay recognition of gains while anticipating losses and the tendency of the balance sheet to capture the liquidation value of separable net assets), suggesting that other objectives guide managers and regulators. Finally, they argue that information asymmetry and incentive conflicts shape financial reporting, and these issues are absent from the reduced-form models that link earnings to equity value.[41]

When much of the value-relevance research was conducted, the contracting and incomplete market literature was just getting started. While contracting theory suggests that the performance measure should be associated with management effort and actions (see, e.g., Holmstrom, 1979; Lambert and Larcker, 1987), it was not known whether formal links could be established between earnings-return correlations and contracting efficiency or whether research would be able to support unequivocal statements for many firms under most circumstances. Perhaps models could be developed relating higher earnings-return correlations to financial-reporting externalities or the protection of naïve investors, concerns cited by regulators. Our present point is that the rhetorical dance of Alford et al. (1993) and their discussant shows that both understood that they lacked these theoretical

[39] They note the influence of four other factors: stewardship, taxes, litigation, and regulation.

[40] Holthausen and Watts (2001, pp. 15–16) illustrate this point as follows: Assume that net income is intended to measure permanent income (a perpetuity whose value equals the value of equity) and stock price / income regressions are estimated for each alternative net income measure. Then the most accurate measure is the income number whose regression yields an estimated intercept of 0 and an estimated slope coefficient of 1 over the discount rate (see Lambert, 1996, pp. 19–26). The income measure most associated with stock price could be one with an estimated intercept significantly different from 0 and an estimated slope coefficient significantly different from 1 over the discount rate.

[41] We discuss this point in detail in Chapter 4.

links and took care not to say things outside their understanding. Moreover, papers like this pushed researchers to understand better the problems associated with linking value relevance to efficiency. The resulting research gives us the hindsight to denigrate value-relevance research. The disappointment of these once-lofty expectations should not obscure the valuable understanding we can gain by reviewing this research if we can resist the temptation to link value relevance to efficiency or social welfare. Specifically, ERC-related research can enhance our understanding in multiple areas: valuation, earnings characteristics, tests of market efficiency, tests of contracting and disclosure theory, and regression econometrics.

References

Abarbanell, J. S., 1991. Do analysts' earnings forecasts incorporate information in prior stock price changes? *Journal of Accounting and Economics* 14 (2), 147–165.

Alford, A. J., Jones, R., Leftwich, R., Zmijewski, M., 1993. The relative informativeness of accounting disclosures in different countries. *Journal of Accounting Research* 31, 183–223.

Anderson, M. C., Banker, R. D., Janakiraman, S. N., 2003. Are selling, general, and administrative costs "sticky"? *Journal of Accounting Research* 41 (1), 47–63.

Badia, M., Duro, M., Penalva, F., Ryan, S. G., 2021. Debiasing the measurement of conditional conservatism. *Journal of Accounting Research* 59 (4), 1221–1259.

Ball, R., Brown, P. R., 1968. An empirical evaluation of accounting income numbers. *Journal of Accounting Research* 6 (2), 159–178.

Ball, R., Kothari, S. P., Nikolaev, V. V., 2013a. On estimating conditional conservatism. *The Accounting Review* 88 (3), 755–787.

Ball, R., Kothari, S. P., Nikolaev, V. V., 2013b. Econometrics of the Basu asymmetric timeliness coefficient and accounting conservatism. *Journal of Accounting Research* 51 (5), 1070–1097.

Ball, R., Kothari, S. P., Robin, A., 2000. The effect of international institutional factors on properties of accounting earnings. *Journal of Accounting and Economics* 29 (1), 1–51.

Ball, R., Shivakumar, L., 2005. Earnings quality in UK private firms: Comparative loss recognition timeliness. *Journal of Accounting and Economics* 39 (1), 83–128.

Ball, R., Shivakumar, L., 2006. The role of accruals in asymmetrically timely gain and loss recognition. *Journal of Accounting Research* 44 (2), 207–242.

Ball, R., Shivakumar, L., 2008. How much new information is there in earnings? *Journal of Accounting Research* 25 (2), 103–129.

Ball, R., Watts, R., 1972. Some time series properties of accounting income. *Journal of Finance* 27 (3), 663–681.

Banker, R. D., Basu, S., Byzalov, D., 2017. Implications of impairment decisions and assets' cash-flow horizons for conservatism research. *The Accounting Review* 92 (2), 41–67.

Banker, R. D., Basu, S., Byzalov, D., Chen, J. Y., 2016. The confounding effect of cost stickiness on conservatism estimates. *Journal of Accounting and Economics* 61 (1), 203–220.

Basu, S., 1997. The conservatism principle and the asymmetric timeliness of earnings. *Journal of Accounting and Economics* 24 (1), 3–37.

Beaver, B., Dukes, R., 1972. Interperiod tax allocation, earnings expectations, and the behavior of security prices. *The Accounting Review* 47 (2), 320–332.

Beaver, W. H., Clarke, R., Wright, W. F., 1979. The association between unsystematic security returns and the magnitude of earnings forecast errors. *Journal of Accounting Research* 17 (2), 316–340.

Beaver, W. H., Lambert, R. A., Morse, D., 1980. The information content of security prices. *Journal of Accounting and Economics* 2 (1), 3–28.

Beaver, W. H., Lambert, R. A., Ryan, S. G., 1987. The information content of security prices: A second look. *Journal of Accounting and Economics* 9 (2), 139–157.

Beaver, W. H., McAnally, M. L., Stinson, C. H., 1997. The information content of earnings and prices: A simultaneous equations approach. *Journal of Accounting and Economics* 23 (1), 53–81.

Beaver, W. H., Ryan, S. G., 2005. Conditional and unconditional conservatism: Concepts and modeling. *Review of Accounting Studies* 10 (2–3), 269–309.

Bernard, V. L., Thomas, J. K., 1989. Post-earnings-announcement drift: Delayed price response or risk premium? *Journal of Accounting Research* 27, 1–36.

Bernard, V. L., Thomas, J. K., 1990. Evidence that stock prices do not fully reflect the implications of current earnings for future earnings. *Journal of Accounting and Economics* 13 (4), 305–340.

Biddle, G. C., Lindahl, F. W., 1982. Stock price reactions to LIFO adoptions: The association between excess returns and LIFO tax savings. *Journal of Accounting Research* 20 (2), 551–588.

Bradshaw, M. T., 2004. How do analysts use their earnings forecasts in generating stock recommendations? *The Accounting Review* 79 (1), 25–50.

Bradshaw, M. T., Christensen, T. E., Gee, K. H., Whipple, B. C., 2018. Analysts' GAAP earnings forecasts and their implications for accounting research. *Journal of Accounting and Economics* 66 (1), 46–66.

Bradshaw, M. T., Sloan, R. G., 2002. GAAP versus the street: An empirical association of two alternative definitions of earnings. *Journal of Accounting Research* 40 (1), 41–66.

Breuer, M., Windisch, D., 2019. Investment dynamics and earnings-return properties: A structural approach. *Journal of Accounting Research* 57 (3), 639–674.

Brown, L. D., Rozeff, M. S., 1978. The superiority of analyst forecasts as measures of expectations: Evidence from earnings. *Journal of Finance* 33 (1), 1–16.

Brown, L. D., Sivakumar, K., 2003. Comparing the value relevance of two operating income measures. *Review of Accounting Studies* 8 (4), 561–572.

Brown, S., Lo, K., Lys, T., 1999. Use of R^2 in accounting research: Measuring changes in value relevance over the last four decades. *Journal of Accounting and Economics* 28 (2), 83–115.

Burgstahler, D., Dichev, I., 1997. Earnings management to avoid earnings decreases and losses. *Journal of Accounting and Economics* 24 (1), 99–126.

Byzalov, D., Basu, S., 2016. Conditional conservatism and disaggregated bad news indicators in accrual models. *Review of Accounting Studies* 21 (3), 859–897.

Chambers, R., 1964. Measurement and objectivity in accounting. *The Accounting Review* 39 (2), 264–274.

Coase, R. H., 1992. The institutional structure of production. *American Economic Review* 82 (4), 713–719.

Collins, D. W., Hribar, P., Tian, X. S., 2014. Cash flow asymmetry: Causes and implications for conditional conservatism research. *Journal of Accounting and Economics* 58 (2–3), 173–200.

Collins, D. W., Kothari, S. P., 1989. An analysis of intertemporal and cross-sectional determinants of earnings response coefficients. *Journal of Accounting and Economics* 11 (2–3), 143–181.

Collins, D. W., Kothari, S. P., Shanken, J., Sloan, R. G., 1994. Lack of timeliness and noise as explanations for the low contemporaneous return-earnings association. *Journal of Accounting and Economics* 18 (3), 289–324.

Dechow, P. M., Hutton, A. P., Sloan, R. G., 2000. The relation between analysts' forecasts of long-term earnings growth and stock price performance following equity offerings. *Contemporary Accounting Research* 17 (1), 1–32.

Dietrich, J. R., Muller, K. A., Riedl, E. J., 2007. Asymmetric timeliness tests of accounting conservatism. *Review of Accounting Studies* 12 (1), 95–124.

Doyle, J. T., Jennings, J. N., Soliman, M. T., 2013. Do managers define non-GAAP earnings to meet or beat analyst forecasts? *Journal of Accounting and Economics* 56 (1), 40–56.

Doyle, J. T., Lundholm, R J., Soliman, M. T., 2003. The predictive value of expenses excluded from pro forma earnings. *Review of Accounting Studies* 8 (2–3), 145–174.

Dugar, A., Nathan, S., 1995. The effect of investment banking relationships on financial analysts' earnings forecasts and investment recommendations. *Contemporary Accounting Research* 12 (1), 131–160.

Dutta, S., Patatoukas, P. N., 2017. Identifying conditional conservatism in financial accounting data: Theory and evidence. *The Accounting Review* 92 (4), 191–216.

Easton, P. D., Harris, T. S., Ohlson, J. A., 1992. Aggregate accounting earnings can explain most of security returns: The case of long return intervals. *Journal of Accounting and Economics* 15 (2–3), 119–142.

Easton, P. D., Zmijewski, M. E., 1989. Cross-sectional variation in the stock market response to accounting earnings announcements. *Journal of Accounting and Economics* 11 (2–3), 117–141.

Eliot, G., 1871–1872. *Middlemarch, A Study of Provincial Life*. Edinburgh, Scotland, UK: William Blackwood and Sons.

Fama, E. F., 1990. Stock returns, expected returns, and real activity. *Journal of Finance* 45(4), 1089–1108.

Foster, G., Olsen, C., Shevlin, T., 1984. Earnings releases, anomalies, and the behavior of security returns. *The Accounting Review* 59 (4), 574–603.

Francis, J., Philbrick, D., 1993. Analysts' decisions as products of a multi-task environment. *Journal of Accounting Research* 31 (2), 216–230.

Frankel, R., Lee, C. M., 1998. Accounting valuation, market expectation, and cross-sectional stock returns. *Journal of Accounting and Economics* 25 (3), 283–319.

Freeman, R. N., Tse, S. Y., 1992. A nonlinear model of security price responses to unexpected earnings. *Journal of Accounting Research* 30 (2), 185–209.

Garman, M. B., Ohlson, J. A., 1980. Information and the sequential valuation of assets in arbitrage-free economies. *Journal of Accounting Research* 18 (2), 420–440.

Givoly, D., Hayn, C. K., Natarajan, A., 2007. Measuring reporting conservatism. *The Accounting Review* 82 (1), 65–106.

Gonedes, N. J., 1975. Information-production and capital market equilibrium. *Journal of Finance* 30 (3), 841–864.

Gonedes, N. J., Dopuch, N., 1974. Capital market equilibrium, information production, and selecting accounting techniques: Theoretical framework and review of empirical work. *Journal of Accounting Research* 12, 48–129.

Greene, W. H., 2012. *Econometric Analysis* (7th ed.), Prentice Hall, Boston, Massachusetts.

Groysberg, B., Healy, P. M., Maber, D. A., 2011. What drives sell-side analyst compensation at high-status investment banks? *Journal of Accounting Research* 49 (4), 969–1000.

Gu, Z., Chen, T., 2004. Analysts' treatment of nonrecurring items in street earnings. *Journal of Accounting and Economics* 38, 129–170.

Hagerman, R. L., Zmijewski, M. E., Shah, P., 1984. The association between the magnitudes of quarterly earnings forecast errors and risk-adjusted stock returns. *Journal of Accounting Research* 22 (2), 526–540.

Hayek, F. A., 1945. The use of knowledge in society. *American Economic Review* 35 (4), 519–530.

Hayn, C., 1995. The information content of losses. *Journal of Accounting and Economics* 20 (2), 125–153.

Hemmer, T., Labro, E., 2019. Management by the numbers: A formal approach to deriving informational and distribution properties of "unmanaged" earnings. *Journal of Accounting Research* 57 (1), 5–51.

Holmstrom, B., 1979. Moral hazard and observability. *Bell Journal of Economics* 10 (1), 74–91.

Holthausen, R. W., Watts, R. L., 2001. The relevance of the value-relevance literature for financial accounting standard setting. *Journal of Accounting and Economics* 31 (1–3), 3–75.

Ijiri, Y., Jaedicke, R., Knight, K., 1966. The effects of accounting alternatives on management decisions. In: Jaedicke, R., Ijiri, Y., Nielsen, O. (Eds.), *Research in Accounting Measurement*. American Accounting Association, Sarasota, Florida, 186–199.

Jacobson, R., Aaker, D., 1993. Myopic management behavior with efficient, but imperfect, financial markets: A comparison of information asymmetries in the US and Japan. *Journal of Accounting and Economics* 16 (4), 383–405.

Jennings, R., Mest, D. P., Thompson, R. B., 1992. Investor reaction to disclosures of 1974–75 LIFO adoption decisions. *The Accounting Review* 67 (2), 337–354.

Kanodia, C., 1980. Effects of shareholder information on corporate decisions and capital market equilibrium. *Econometrica* 48 (4), 923–953.

Kasznik, R., Lev, B., 1995. To warn or not to warn: Management disclosures in the face of an earnings surprise. *The Accounting Review* 70 (1), 113–134.

Kormendi, R., Lipe, R., 1987. Earnings innovations, earnings persistence, and stock returns. *Journal of Business* 60 (3), 323–345.

Kothari, S. P., 2001. Capital markets research in accounting. *Journal of Accounting and Economics* 31 (1–3), 105–231.

Kothari, S. P., Shanken, J., 1992. Stock return variation and expected dividends: A time-series and cross-sectional analysis. *Journal of Financial Economics* 31 (2), 177–210.

Kothari, S. P., Shu, S., Wysocki, P., 2009. Do managers withhold bad news? *Journal of Accounting Research* 47 (1), 241–276.

Kothari, S. P., Sloan, R. G., 1992. Information in prices about future earnings. *Journal of Accounting and Economics* 15 (2–3), 143–171.

Kraft, A., Leone, A. J., Wasley, C. E., 2007. Regression-based tests of the market pricing of accounting numbers: The Mishkin test and ordinary least squares. *Journal of Accounting Research* 45 (5), 1081–1114.

Lambert, R. A., 1996. Financial reporting research and standard setting. Unpublished manuscript.

Lambert, R. A., Larcker, D. F., 1987. An analysis of the use of accounting and market measures of performance in executive compensation contracts. *Journal of Accounting Research* 25, 85–125.

Lanen, W. N., Thompson, R., 1988. Stock price reactions as surrogates for the new cash flow effects of corporate policy decisions. *Journal of Accounting and Economics* 10 (4), 311–334.

Lawrence, A., Sloan, R., Sun, E., 2018. Why are losses less persistent than profits? Curtailments vs. conservatism. *Management Science* 64 (2), 673–694.

Lawrence, A., Sloan, R., Sun, Y., 2013. Non-discretionary conservatism: Evidence and implications. *Journal of Accounting and Economics* 56 (2–3), 112–133.

Lennox, C., Wu, J. S., 2022. A review of China-related accounting research in the past 25 years. *Journal of Accounting and Economics* 74 (2–3), 101539.

Lev, B., 1989. On the usefulness of earnings and earnings research: Lessons and directions from two decades of empirical research. *Journal of Accounting Research* 27, 153–192.

Lewellen, J., 2010. Accounting anomalies and fundamental analysis: An alternative view. *Journal of Accounting and Economics* 50 (2–3), 455–466.

Lim, T., 2001. Rationality and analysts' forecast bias. *Journal of Finance* 56 (1), 369–385.

Lin, H. W., McNichols, M. F., 1998. Underwriting relations, analysts' earnings forecasts, and investment recommendations. *Journal of Accounting and Economics* 25 (1), 101–127.

Lys, T., Sohn, S., 1990. The association between revisions of financial analysts' earnings forecasts and security-price changes. *Journal of Accounting and Economics* 13 (4), 341–363.

Mak, C. Y., Strong, N., Walker, M., 2011. Conditional earnings conservatism and corporate refocusing activities. *Journal of Accounting Research* 49 (4), 1041–1082.

Matsumoto, D. A., 2002. Management's incentives to avoid negative earnings surprises. *The Accounting Review* 77 (3), 483–514.

McNichols, M., O'Brien, P. C., 1997. Self-selection and analyst coverage. *Journal of Accounting Research* 35, 167–199.

Miller, M. H., Rock, K., 1985. Dividend policy under asymmetric information. *Journal of Finance* 40 (4), 1031–1051.

Mishkin, F. S., 1983. *A Rational Expectations Approach to Macroeconometrics: Testing Policy Ineffectiveness and Efficient-Markets Models*. University of Chicago Press, Chicago, Illinois.

O'Brien, P. C., 1988. Analysts' forecasts as earnings expectations. *Journal of Accounting and Economics* 10 (1), 53–83.

Ou, J. A., Penman, S. H., 1989a. Financial statement analysis and the persistence of stock returns. *Journal of Accounting and Economics* 11 (4), 295–329.

Ou, J. A., Penman, S. H., 1989b. Accounting measurement, price-earnings ratio, and the information content of security prices. *Journal of Accounting Research* 27, 111–144.

Pae, J., Thornton, D. B., Welker, M., 2005. The link between earnings conservatism and the price-to-book ratio. *Contemporary Accounting Research* 22 (3), 693–717.

Patatoukas, P. N., Thomas, J. K., 2011. More evidence of bias in the differential timeliness measure of conditional conservatism. *The Accounting Review* 86 (5), 1765–1793.

Patatoukas, P. N., Thomas, J. K., 2016. Placebo tests of conditional conservatism. *The Accounting Review* 91 (2), 625–648.

Pownall, G., 1993. Discussion of the relative informativeness of accounting disclosures in different countries. *Journal of Accounting Research* 31, 224–229.

Revsine, L., Collins, D. W., Johnson, W. B., Mittelstaedt, H. F., Soffer, L. C., 1999. *Financial Reporting and Analysis*. Prentice Hall, Upper Saddle River, New Jersey.

Richardson, S., Teoh, S. H., Wysocki, P. D., 2004. The walk-down to beatable analyst forecasts: The role of equity issuance and insider trading incentives. *Contemporary Accounting Research* 21 (4), 885–924.

Ross, S., 2005. *Neoclassical Finance*. Princeton University Press, Princeton, New Jersey.

Roychowdhury, S., Watts, R. L., 2007. Asymmetric timeliness of earnings, market-to-book, and conservatism in financial reporting. *Journal of Accounting and Economics* 44 (1–2), 2–31.

Schwert, G. W., 1990. Stock returns and real activity: A century of evidence. *Journal of Finance* 45 (4), 1237–1257.

Sloan, R. G., 1996. Do stock prices fully reflect information in accruals and cash flows about future earnings? *The Accounting Review* 71 (3), 289–315.

Sterling, R., 1967. Elements of pure accounting theory. *The Accounting Review* 42 (1), 62–73.

Sunder, S., 1973. Relationship between accounting changes and stock prices: Problems of measurement and some empirical evidence. *Journal of Accounting Research* 11, 1–45.

Sunder, S., 2017. Statistical studies of financial reports and stock markets. *Journal of Capital Markets Studies* 1, 5–9.

Warfield, T. D., Wild, J. J., 1992. Accounting recognition and the relevance of earnings as an explanatory variable for returns. *The Accounting Review* 67 (4), 821–842.

Watts, R. L., 2003a. Conservatism in accounting, part I: Explanations and implications. *Accounting Horizons* 17 (3), 207–221.

Watts, R. L., 2003b. Conservatism in accounting, part II: Evidence and research opportunities. *Accounting Horizons* 17 (4), 287–301.

Zuo, L., 2016. The informational feedback effect of stock prices on management forecasts. *Journal of Accounting and Economics* 61 (2–3), 391–413.

4
The Economics of Accounting Earnings

4.1. Overview

The importance of accounting earnings as a financial metric is uncontroversial.[1] Managers fret over earnings numbers because they affect managers' compensation and their careers. Investors use price-earnings multiples to assess share values. Bondholders assess a firm's credit risk, in part, based on its earnings performance. Demand for earnings springs from sources like these, and these forces shape earnings' properties.

A measure of the change in the economic value of a firm's net assets matters for valuation as well as assessment of credit risk and firm performance. Yet accounting rules do not yield an earnings number that represents the change in the value of the firm's net assets, nor do they encompass all of the effects of a manager's actions. For example, accountants subtract current-period research and development expenditures to compute current-period earnings. Current-period earnings ignore new contracts signed with customers that create legal obligations for profitable future deliveries, and depreciation formulas seem a caricature of fixed asset value and deterioration. Someone not indoctrinated in the ways of accounting (i.e., a student of finance, economics, or English) might question the sanity of the system and seek refuge in cash flows.

Our thesis is that earnings and other outputs of financial accounting help firms function more efficiently. We take "function" in its broad sense to encompass the firm's operating, investing, and financing activities that involve its use of human, physical, and financial capital. Our thesis amounts to an application of the idea that the quest to enhance shareholder value shapes a firm's behavior, including its financial reporting.[2] An earnings number that

---

[1] We treat "earnings," "profits," "income," and "net income" as synonyms.
[2] See the Appendix, "The Shareholder Value Maximization Principle," for a discussion of the economic consequences of pursuing the objective of value creation and the implications for social welfare.

The Economics of Accounting. Richard M. Frankel, S. P. Kothari, and Luo Zuo, Oxford University Press.
© Oxford University Press 2024. DOI: 10.1093/oso/9780197680766.003.0004

measures the change in value or provides information about value might not serve this purpose in every circumstance or even on average. In short, the earnings computation seeks to enhance firm value rather than just measure the change in that value.

To illustrate this point, the discussion here centers on earnings and proceed in stages. We first discuss imperfect and incomplete markets and relate these market conditions to information asymmetry and incentive conflicts. Next we describe how these conditions create the possibility that firms might perform some activities more efficiently than individuals operating via arm's-length transactions. Finally, we address how earnings aid firms, considering information gathering and processing costs, information asymmetry, and attendant incentive conflicts, which give rise to transaction costs and the formation of firms in the first place.

Markets are imperfect and incomplete when transaction costs exist and certain goods or claims cannot be traded. The notion that earnings somehow enhance the efficiency of firms that exist because of imperfect and incomplete markets yields three implications for the nature of the earnings measure. First, the firm's value differs from the value of its separable assets and liabilities. Imperfect and incomplete markets imply that some aspects of the firm's value are not priced as individual, identifiable assets and that this intangible portion makes the firm a worthwhile endeavor. Otherwise, people would not need to organize themselves as firms and could do all their business via individual arm's-length transactions. This intangible value will be lost if the firm is forced to liquidate. Cultivating this value requires the firm to create long-lived claims, such as long-term debt and equity. Earnings characteristics reflect attempts to aid the pricing and creation of these claims and limit the conflicts of interest they create.[3]

Second, incentive conflicts inherent in imperfect and incomplete markets leave an indelible mark on the earnings report. In part, the value of financial accounting information stems from how it affects the individuals who produce it. When information asymmetry exists, conflicts of interest arise between the producers and users of financial information if that information affects decisions and therefore has value. In short, if financial reports

---

[3] In many cases, earnings reports alone cannot serve this role, and other methods arise to complement earnings reports. For example, venture capitalists require decision rights and access to the firm's internal information. They offer limited, short-term financing with additional financing contingent on realized performance. Banks offer loans tied to collateral. Start-ups must be financed by the entrepreneur's wealth (and credit cards) when information and incentive problems vis-à-vis outside investors cannot be resolved.

have value to the firm, real effects, such as altered actions and attendant conflicts, follow. Earnings are not an exogenous instrument used to measure firm activities the way a counting chamber measures the growth of bacteria. Instead, earnings are endogenous to the ecology of the firm: the nature of the firm's operating, investing, and financing activities influences the properties of its earnings information, but simultaneously the earnings report alters managers' decisions and thus affects firm efficiency and output. Therefore, any discussion of the earnings metric must consider incentive problems and how to confront them. The designer of the accounting system must ponder incentive conflicts and real effects.

Finally, the objective of accounting rules cannot be merely to measure the change in value or provide information to assess value. While financial accounting enhances efficiency by conveying information about the firm, this information might or might not directly concern firm value. This is not simply because the incentive problems would be too costly to resolve or because the number would be relevant but unreliable. A more fundamental objection begins by asking how a change-in-value measure maximizes firm efficiency. To enhance efficiency, earnings must do more than merely provide better information about a firm's equity value, serve as a better measure for debt contracting, *or* promote better contracting with managers. Instead, earnings reflect the trade-offs associated with a measure that attempts to satisfy multiple demands. Consider an analogy. There are over 10,500 bird species in the world. Thus there is not just one combination of feathers, beak, eyes, wings, and feet best suited for nesting, mating, and feeding in all circumstances. Aerial agility matters crucially to a peregrine falcon but not to a penguin.

This analogy allows one to glimpse the burden borne by accounting theorists and standard setters. Standard setters select a few accounting procedures that best suit all public firms' reporting needs.[4] They often cite theory to justify their actions. Regulators' quest for theory presumes that they can reduce firms' circumstances to a few crucial factors that will allow regulators to prescribe efficient reporting rules.[5] Accounting researchers

[4] Since 1934 the Securities and Exchange Commission has regulated financial reporting for publicly listed companies in the United States.
[5] Sims (1996, p. 105) aptly describes theory as "discoveries of ways to compress data concerning the natural world . . . with minimal loss of information." See also Friedman (1953, p. 8): "A hypothesis is important if it explains much by little, that is, if it abstracts the common and crucial elements from the mass of complex and detailed circumstances surrounding the phenomena to be explained and permits valid prediction on the basis of them alone."

produce theories and often motivate their work by referring to regulatory concerns.

To make our discussion more concrete, we describe the income-statement and balance-sheet approaches to computing earnings as a means of organizing and highlighting specific limitations and efficiency considerations that arise in the earnings computation. These approaches represent extremes on a conceptual continuum, and we might expect that earnings amalgamate these approaches. The income-statement approach captures operating flows (revenues and expenses) during the reporting period to measure earnings. The balance-sheet approach, in contrast, seeks beginning and ending values of the assets and liabilities to measure earnings.[6] A little algebra can convert one into the other. However, in imperfect and incomplete markets, information is costly, and the practicalities of implementation lead to decisive differences between these two approaches. An approach that continuously records revenues and expenses as transactions occur produces an earnings number that differs from an approach that records the price changes of assets and liabilities and uses these to infer earnings. These approaches inspire the rules that govern the earnings calculation, constrain the accountant, and influence the earnings report. As currently calculated, earnings mix both approaches, but this jumble can be consistent with user demands.

Our discussion proceeds as follows. Section 4.2 describes imperfect and incomplete markets as a prelude to understanding why firms arise and why the need for an earnings measure follows. Section 4.3 explains two approaches to computing income, describing these features as useful components of an accounting system designed to meet user demands. Section 4.4 offers some concluding remarks.

4.2. Firms and Accounting Earnings in Imperfect and Incomplete Markets

Imperfect and incomplete markets open the gate to a realm where firms can offer value incremental to arm's-length transactions. This incremental value is the difference between the firm's value and the value of its identifiable net

---

[6] The balance-sheet approach is also referred to as the asset-liability approach. Under this approach, the primacy of the balance sheet is a matter of timing, not priority: if one gets the balance sheet right, an accurate income statement will follow.

assets, which is analogous to the difference between the cost of investment and its expected present value. Long-lived claims issued by the firm (equity and long-term debt) encourage managers to nurture this value by forestalling liquidation at the cost of incentive conflicts. Accounting arises to facilitate the realization of the expected present value of the firm's current projects and future contingent projects by providing information for internal decisions and investors and by aligning incentives among parties related by claims and promises to the firm.

4.2.1. From Perfect and Complete Markets to Imperfect and Incomplete Markets

In economics, characteristics that constitute perfect and complete markets are (1) the existence of a quoted price for every state-contingent commodity or claim, (2) price-taking by consumers and firms, and (3) zero transaction costs (Magill and Quinzii, 1996).[7] In this ideal setting, performance measures, such as earnings, are redundant. Information is free and costless to analyze, and earnings cannot enhance the efficiency of the firm's operations; therefore, accounting earnings are unnecessary.

Sterling's (1970) model of a firm, described in his seminal book *Theory of Measurement of Enterprise Income*, illustrates the *uselessness* of earnings in these conditions. He notes the importance of specifying the "firm model" when determining whether an earnings measure captures economic income. The model that provides the basis for his analysis is a wheat trader operating in a perfect (frictionless) market. Sterling's trader is not an organization formed to add value. Its value is simply the value of its initial wheat position. The trader's actions are irrelevant because trading cannot add or reduce value (in expectation). Positive and negative net-present-value projects do not exist. No decision or control demand for the computation of earnings seems present. To borrow a term from Ijiri (1975), there is no "accountability relationship"—no one is accountable to anyone else for activities or their consequences. An unambiguous economic-income concept

---

[7] A state-contingent claim is one whose value depends on the realization of a specified state. For example, a life insurance policy is a state-contingent claim. It pays a specified amount to the beneficiary upon the death of an insured person. The Supplement of this chapter contains a fuller description of perfect and complete markets.

requires complete and perfect markets. However, in this setting, the firm will not incur the expense of producing an earnings report because it serves no purpose.[8]

Markets become imperfect when transaction costs arise. These costs occur because of limited access to information, costs of analysis and enforcement, liquidity constraints, or simply physical limitations—in short, the thorny particularities of real life. For example, before Amazon, sellers of used books had more difficulty finding buyers. Physical locations—used bookstores— helped match sellers with buyers and allowed for assessments of merchandise, price negotiations, and payments. Before Uber, matching willing drivers with people seeking rides was similarly difficult (as anyone knows who has stood on a rainy New York street corner trying to hail a cab). For transactions more complex than the purchase of a book or a ride, like those that entail multiperiod commitments or contingent contracts (say, an auto service warranty), transaction costs include the cost of enforcing the contract and verifying performance.

Incomplete markets mean that many state-contingent claims are not traded. Moral hazard (hidden actions) and adverse selection (hidden information) are two important reasons. For example, insurance against tenure denials for professors does not exist. An insurer cannot observe a professor's effort, so such a contract might induce the professor to shirk (moral hazard). Moreover, an insurer cannot observe the professor's ability, so the contract might appeal more to professors with poor prospects (adverse selection). The existence of information asymmetry (i.e., one party has better information than the other) and incentive conflict between transacting parties (i.e., increasing one party's utility reduces the other's) leads to market incompleteness.

In summary, information asymmetry between parties in an arm's-length transaction leads to imperfect and incomplete markets.[9] Trades do not occur (markets are incomplete), or transaction costs accompany trading (markets are imperfect) because the seller cannot credibly communicate the value of

[8] How perfect and complete markets arise is often unmodeled—it could be the case that these markets result from a very effective accounting system. Thus, perfect and complete markets do not necessarily preclude accounting.

[9] In addition to information asymmetry, physical limits and limited substitutability mean that few markets have an unlimited number of buyers or sellers. If the market is sufficiently small or imperfectly competitive, an individual producer or purchaser might not be a price taker. For example, an individual might be a monopolist, which would allow him to increase price by restricting quantity sold.

a product or service to the buyer, a party cannot credibly commit to actions that cannot be confirmed by the counterparty, or both. These transaction costs include the difference between the buying and selling price, denoted as the bid/ask spread. When trades do occur, the actions of the buyer or seller affect the price. For example, the decision to sell an asset could affect its price if the buyer infers the asset's quality from the seller's willingness to relinquish it. Imperfect markets imply that the sale price, purchase price, and value might differ. There is no single value because the value can depend on the action contemplated by the seller.

Whether value indeterminacy amounts to philosophical quibbling or a substantive problem depends on the circumstance. Consider whether traded-loan prices approximate the value of loans retained. The closeness of this approximation might depend on the difference in quality between the loans a manager decides to retain and those she decides to sell. This difference might depend, in turn, on the information asymmetry between potential buyers and the seller concerning loan quality. If the seller has more knowledge, buyers might infer that only bad loans will be sold, and a variant of Gresham's Law might apply.[10] Bad loans will then drive out good loans, and prices will reflect the value of problem loans. The value of retained loans might be far higher than that of loans held for sale.[11] In this context, traded asset prices differ from held-to-maturity asset prices, even though these assets share similar verifiable characteristics.

4.2.2. Demand for Firms in Imperfect and Incomplete Markets

The existence of imperfect and incomplete markets generates the potential for managers to more efficiently coordinate activities within a firm. Coase (1937, p. 389) notes that "the distinguishing mark of the firm is the supersession of the price mechanism." A hospital nurse does not consider the price of her services for each activity she performs at each hour in choosing where and when to work. Instead, the head of the nursing staff directs her. Though

---

[10] Gresham's Law is the principle that "bad money drives out good." That is, if the same face value is assigned to a new coin containing a lower amount of precious metal ("bad money") than an older coin ("good money"), then only the new coin will be used in circulation, and the old coin will be hoarded.

[11] Dye (2017) discusses this point more fully.

costs and prices pull on the chain of decisions within the firm, the immediate price of every resource employed and every output produced is not available.

What's more, if the firm exists because it can coordinate these activities better than a market exchange, we cannot value this coordination via separable asset prices. The firm's existence suggests that its value exceeds the sum of the priced and separately traded resources. The assumption is that the firm faces competition and would not exist if market transactions alone could provide the firm's services or products more efficiently.

Managers understand that projects in process are tough to value. This is why they issue equity (with an indefinite claim) and long-term debt. They realize that the firm cannot liquidate all its assets and settle all claims in each period without substantial losses due to transaction costs and the destruction of nontransferable assets. For example, Apple is particularly suited to benefit from projects that increase the functionality of its Vision Pro goggles. It cannot sell these incomplete projects to another firm, and one would hope that its production team has unique insight into the potential value of the Vision Pro enhancements. Communicating these insights to outsiders would also erode any competitive advantages from the team's knowledge and experience. These circumstances highlight the paradox inherent in producing a measure of the firm's continuing value by summing the values of its readily saleable assets. If such a measure were possible, the firm could liquidate, and a need for the measure would not arise.

Organizational economics seeks to formalize these nonseparable, intangible benefits and explain the existence of firms (see Gibbons [2005] for an excellent summary). Many of Apple's operating assets, for example, are intangible, such as authority relations between employees, tacit understandings between the firm and suppliers, accepted procedures, firm-specific knowledge, and customer relations. Many of these entail multiperiod relationships. However, markets do not exist for the multiperiod contingent contracts necessary to procure the supplier, customer, employee, and manager relations that sustain these operating assets. In fact, the value created by the operations, investments, and financing that cannot be replicated solely by exchange is the raison d'être of the firm. The idea that firms are a more efficient means of coordination than markets alone implies that the coordinators— the managers—can create or destroy value.

One might object that while the value of critical assets might not be available, stock price reliably and comprehensively reflects the equity value of a publicly traded firm. Therefore, a market-based summary measure exists and suggests an achievable goal for earnings. However, its existence does not imply that an accounting system could replicate the output of the pricing process. Prices contain information beyond the knowledge of a preselected group of individuals (i.e., the firm, its auditors, and experts). Moreover, even if the knowledge of the individuals who guide the firm's accounting system were complete, the attempt to duplicate a freely observable measure (price) would be of doubtful value. Earnings might have uses beyond supplying information for price discovery.

Earnings can tell managers and investors things they do not know. Accounting systems exist in firms without outside investors to help the owner/manager assess consequences and make decisions. Measuring outcomes helps managers understand the world and form expectations. Of course, managers need and use information beyond earnings. These complementary sources of information are perhaps more essential than earnings information. The limited point here is that earnings provide information that helps managers operate firms more efficiently, as economic principles and observed practice suggest.

4.2.3. Demand for Financial Reports in Imperfect and Incomplete Markets

In many cases, the immediate price of every resource employed by a firm and every output produced is not available to measure the opportunity costs of alternative actions, weigh net benefits, and guide operating decisions. Markets for intermediate goods and services are often unavailable, so an internal system of "prices" serves as a substitute. The firm requires a system to track costs and revenues, so managers can summarize and analyze transactions and infer opportunity costs. This information also alerts the managers to profit opportunities. While internal reporting differs from financial reporting, the two systems overlap. Internal information about transactions, collected to aid decision-making, provides a reservoir of information for financial reports. Moreover, though managers have privileged access to critical internal data, earnings and the information in financial reports influence their actions.

Accounting systems provide information not only for internal decision-making and control (e.g., the CEO must control subordinates) but also for external providers of capital. As noted earlier, firms finance operations, in part, with equity and long-term debt. Investors in these securities sacrifice the right to force the firm to liquidate and cash out their claims to allow managers the time to invest without fear of liquidation costs. These investors lack access to internal reports and demand information for at least two reasons: (1) to monitor and control managers and (2) to assess firm value.[12]

Information to monitor and control has ex-post and ex-ante dimensions, which feed back into each other. Ex-ante, shareholders need a means to assess ex-post manager performance to help them determine what to pay the managers and whether to retain them. The ex-ante understanding between the two parties about performance measurement then guides managers' actions. Investors recognize that an incentive conflict can exist: Actions that increase managers' welfare do not necessarily increase investors' welfare. So any measure proposed must resist self-interested distortion by managers.

If the manager's task were well defined (e.g., sell one million Vision Pro goggles) and easily observed by outside owners, the incentive problem could be solved by linking managerial compensation to task completion. However, as seen with Apple, the task shareholders assign to its CEO Tim Cook is multidimensional and dynamic in ways known only to Cook himself. A performance measure based solely on current Vision Pro sales might induce him to forgo other valuable opportunities, like improving Apple's watches or expanding its music-streaming service. These circumstances call for a performance measure that directs him toward the larger goal of value creation, allowing him the freedom to use his skill and knowledge to maximize risk-adjusted shareholder returns. This logic suggests that managers should be compensated based on the current *and* expected consequences of their current actions and that the earnings measure should communicate this information (if distortion can be minimized at a reasonable cost).[13]

Shareholders also need information to determine the value of their stake, and creditors need it to determine default risk. While the information

---

[12] Watts (1977) notes that as early as 1620, the New River Company in London included in its charter a stipulation that limited the payment of dividends to cumulative realized profits as a protection to debtholders. Acheson, Campbell, and Turner (2019) provide evidence that British firms in the late nineteenth century competed with one another for capital by *voluntarily* offering shareholder protections through private contracting, and firms with better protections enjoyed wider share ownership dispersion. See Watts and Zuo (2016) for a discussion of the evolution of Anglo-American accounting and auditing practice. See also Watts and Zimmerman (1978, 1979, 1983, 1986, 1990).

[13] Core (2020) provides an insightful discussion of two real effects of financial reporting on pay and incentives: (1) better earnings leads to better incentives, and (2) if pay is mismeasured, pay can be misused. See Edmans, Gabaix, and Jenter (2017) for a survey of theory and evidence on executive compensation.

necessary to value equity and assess default risk differs, information allowing investors to assess the amount, timing, and uncertainty of future cash flows will be useful as a first approximation. Information that reflects firm value aids both shareholders and creditors. Information on current transactions can help to the extent that it protects the firm's assets from theft and fraud, guides better managerial decisions, and offers investors insight into future cash flows. To the extent that accounting reports reduce information asymmetry among investors, liquidity of investments will be enhanced. In short, both price discovery and management control suggest that earnings should convey information helpful for assessing future performance.

Why do earnings seem shackled to *past* performance, allowing expectations to enter the calculation only in limited ways? The short answer: First, current performance information can help resolve conflicts among the parties that make up the firm, and conflict resolution yields efficiency gains. For example, current performance might determine amounts that can be distributed to managers or investors without impairing ongoing investments or increasing bankruptcy risk. Prearranged reports of current performance might also encourage managers to preemptively disclose difficulties. Second, forward-looking information comes from unverifiable management expectations. Given the incentive conflict between managers and investors and the potential gains available to managers for optimism, the credibility and value of this information are limited, and its addition to the earnings computation can undercut the usefulness of earnings in resolving conflicts. Third, accounting information systems and the audit process have a comparative advantage over other sources in supplying information on past transactions.

4.2.3.1. Financial Accounting as a Means of Using Verifiable Information to Reduce Incentive Conflicts and Value Securities

In constructing the performance measure, shareholders should be aware that the CEO can affect many measures by manipulation or by constructive actions. Unlike a traffic light, which is unmoved by the signal it sends, the earnings report affects its sender: the CEO and other managers. Managers have the incentive and ability to shape the computation in ways that benefit them. Such actions will be optimal despite the threat of shareholders' actions ex-post if managers have limited liability or if enforcement is imperfect and costly. And incentive conflicts between managers and shareholders cannot be brushed aside by saying the audit will solve them. Managers can exploit the conflict because of the unobservability of their efforts and decision-making and the costs of writing contracts that specify all appropriate actions (Holmstrom, 1979). Auditors cannot verify everything, and the verification they do is costly. In some cases, the cost might exceed the value added. If so, requiring audits does not increase efficiency.[14]

The constraint imposed by incentive conflicts on the properties of accounting information produced for outsiders means that verifiability and reliability are preconditions for its usefulness and relevance. In this sense, characterizing the usefulness of earnings as a function of a trade-off between relevance and reliability leaves a false impression. Reliability and relevance are both necessary. Consider the analogy of a used car. In a world where details of the car's history are costlessly available to all, information on use, storage, and maintenance would matter to a buyer. However, absent some means of making a seller's claims about this information reliable (e.g., verifiable service records, a mechanic's inspection, a warranty, the dealer's reputation), it is valueless and does not affect the transaction price. Thus, in practice, mileage serves as an imperfect but verifiable and inexpensive measure of car quality.

Why do we observe financial statement information that seems unreliable at first glance (e.g., asset useful-life assumptions, allowance for doubtful accounts.)? These claims are subject to reasonable verification, and financial reporting is a repeated game. For example, current accounting rules require a firm to anticipate and record an expense for uncollectible customer accounts, such as accounts receivable write-offs. The eventual write-offs of the receivables can be observed. Any predictions involve a short-enough horizon to allow an outside observer to infer the bias of the forecast; verifiable conditions are present when management predicts that receivable write-offs can provide sufficiently strong evidence to dissuade managers from biasing the forecast. This evidence can allow auditors to determine whether managers overlooked important information and let investors infer whether managers are being too optimistic. If the portfolio contains many small accounts and shocks to the collectibility of individual accounts are independent, forecasts should be reasonably accurate.

However, if predictions cannot be assessed for bias, they are unreliable and less relevant for investor decisions. Managers' assertions about the value of a subsidiary fall into this category. More specific statements about the

---

[14] Excess verification from the point of view of the firm and its investors might yield external benefits. For example, investors and managers of Firm B might benefit from finer data about Firm A.

subsidiary's sales, cash flows, or inventory levels have more chance of verification and better reliability. If a firm reports higher income by increasing the useful-life prediction for one of its assets, this income should be ignored or highly discounted for valuation purposes unless the useful-life change can be verified by events visible to investors (e.g., X-rays of airframe stress points indicating that the planes can withstand more takeoffs and landings than expected). Another possibility is that the managers who predicted the useful life of an asset are still with the firm when the investors eventually learn how long the asset lasted. The number of unexpected shocks affecting an asset's life allows investors to evaluate managers' claims (and infer their credibility) and settle up. This likelihood of settling up enhances the reliability and value of the information.

Verifiable claims might be used as inputs to produce an income measure, but the value of this measure might well differ from the change in the firm's market value. Evidentiary standards constrain the calculation. The resulting measure can be used to enforce and settle contracts because the integrity of the calculation can be assessed by third parties such as judges and juries.

4.2.3.2. Effect of Demand for Periodic Performance on Properties of Accounting

The demand for periodic performance stems from at least three sources: (1) managers' liquidity needs, (2) shareholders' management evaluation and retention decisions, and (3) incentive conflicts.

4.2.3.2.1. Managers' Liquidity Needs

Demand for a periodic performance measure arises partly because managers face liquidity constraints. Managers will have difficulty using future performance realizations as collateral for borrowing because a lending relationship gives rise to moral hazard and adverse selection. Information asymmetry implies that the lender will have difficulty assessing the manager's talent, and the manager might shirk after borrowing, which is unobservable and noncontractible. Moreover, the borrower's limited liability, which arises from bankruptcy laws and the prohibition of corporal punishment, prevents the lender from recouping funds if the borrower fails to pay. Yet managers require periodic compensation to pay their bills. A periodic performance measure (computed before all cash flows from the manager's present actions materialize) becomes necessary as a basis for performance-based pay so that managers can have some spending money.[15] Presumably, the firm is less capital constrained than the manager, so gains to trade can be achieved if the firm provides liquidity to the manager. However, outside investors might be concerned about the manager's limited liability. Therefore, the firm might wish to use a performance measure that limits payments in advance of future expected gains that will require future manager effort to achieve (because so-called clawback provisions might not be enforceable).

4.2.3.2.2. Shareholders' Management Retention Decision

Shareholders and directors also require a periodic performance measure to determine whether they should retain managers. This measure helps them preserve value by terminating poor managers and altering the course of the firm before the consequences of any managerial missteps fully manifest. For this purpose, a more forward-looking and verifiable measure is useful. A trade-off can exist between the properties of a measure used to determine interim pay and those of one used to assess management ability.

4.2.3.2.3. Incentive Conflicts

Incentive problems from failure to recognize the expected future payoffs of current efforts are a deficiency of the earnings measure.[16] Managers might seek other means to convey this value. They might describe new products and estimate the size and growth of potential markets. A deficiency does not imply that remediation is feasible or efficient. Many cars are unable to pull trailers, but fixing this deficiency would require modifying a car's transmission and engine in ways that can increase manufacturing costs and make the car less suitable for commuting. Competition in the car market forces manufacturers to consider the costs and benefits before remediating this deficiency. In the same way, firms consider the costs and benefits of alternative income measures.[17]

Information asymmetry and limited corporate liability also create payoff conflicts between shareholders and other parties lending services or resources to the firm. Agreements between debtholders and shareholders

---

[15] Managers' career concerns are a related problem. To enhance their negotiating position with their current employer, managers aim to maximize their market value to other employers. A verifiable performance measure is useful for this purpose.

[16] For example, a measure that incorporates only realized gains and losses may lead managers to focus on the short term.

[17] Financial reporting regulations also affect observed earnings properties. Regulators might consider costs and benefits beyond those relevant to parties transacting with the firm.

have received significant attention because contractual evidence is available, contracts use accounting measures, and researchers believe they understand the payoff functions of the parties. Agreements between shareholders and creditors require reliable measures. The payoffs of these parties also differ as a function of firm value.[18] These differences can lead debtholders to prefer a conservative earnings measure for use in their contracts, where conservatism is defined as requiring a higher burden of proof to recognize gains than losses. Shareholders, for their part, can benefit at the expense of the debtholders by pushing for the adoption of risky projects, even though these projects may reduce the firm's value. The shareholders then may benefit from the upside created by the new project. However, if the firm goes bankrupt, the shareholders do not bear the total downside cost. The creditors share the downside loss but get no upside participation beyond their promised payments. Thus creditors are more risk-averse than shareholders. The riskiness of the creditors' claims also increases when shareholders withdraw less risky assets like cash. Under these conditions, we might expect accounting earnings to limit recognition of riskier unrealized gains and recognize losses (both realized and unrealized) quickly to provide a performance measure that can be used in lending agreements to protect creditors.[19]

In addition, in the event of continued poor performance or bankruptcy, creditors are paid only the liquidation value of the firm's assets; thus, they demand a balance sheet that records the firm's separable and salable assets (net of its economic obligations). Creditors often ignore goodwill—firm value in excess of the value of separable net assets—in their lending decisions because goodwill often vanishes quickly upon liquidation. The practice of immediate expensing of advertising and R&D expenditures is consistent with the balance sheet reflecting only "hard" net assets.

A substantial theoretical literature analyzes the incentive problems associated with information asymmetry in markets and within the firm (e.g., Bolton and Dewatripont, 2004). Here our objective is to highlight the fundamental effects of omnipresent incentive conflicts and liquidity constraints so that the earnings computation seems less alien to a new student. The existence of imperfect and incomplete markets also allows the earnings measure

---

[18] *Firm value* is defined as the sum of equity value and debt value.
[19] Empirical evidence documents that debt market investors reward conservative firms by offering lower borrowing costs (e.g., Zhang, 2008), equity market investors reward them by engaging in less price protection (e.g., Kim et al., 2013), and accounting conservatism reduces potential underinvestment in the presence of information frictions (e.g., Balakrishnan, Watts, and Zuo, 2016).

to influence the efficiency of firm operations, either through reduction of incentive conflicts or relaxation of liquidity constraints, imbuing earnings with
economic significance.

4.2.3.3. The Implications of Competition in the Information-Production Market

Financial accounting information and earnings, in particular, can help a
firm perform better. A firm must decide how much to produce and what the
characteristics of its output should be.[20] Parties transacting with the firm
also seek information, but the existence of demand is only part of the equation. Supply-side considerations also arise. These considerations include the
cost of production. We have noted that verification costs and information-
processing costs are considerations, as are proprietary costs. That is, firms
know that disclosing some information (e.g., trade secrets or market intelli-
gence) might damage their competitive positions.

Another supply-side consideration is the availability of substitute information sources. The firm considers its competitive advantage in producing
and incorporating information into its financial statements. Initially, this
issue might seem trivial because the firm seems to have monopoly access
to information on its own performance. Closer consideration suggests that
outsiders can access a trove of data on variables that affect the firm's value,
such as commodity prices, interest rates, exchange rates, industry competition, and consumer beliefs. Information intermediaries gather and supply
such information. The firm can also reveal information via channels outside
financial statements, like press releases.

But the firm does have unique access to every one of its own transactions.
The firm requires reliable systems to accumulate and track such data for
internal decision-making, control, and taxes. Transactions often produce evidence that an auditor can use for verification. Transactions
can be grouped, and totals can be reported to mask competitively dam-
aging detail while preserving useful performance measures. In short, financial reporting based on transaction details offers many supply-side
advantages. First, the information is already collected for another purpose so that incremental production costs would be low. Second, the firms
have monopoly access to much of the information (but not all—obviously,
counterparties can also report their transactions with the firm). Third,

---

[20] As noted, regulation shapes this decision. For the present, we omit this force.

reports are grounded in reliable information—which is useful given underlying incentive conflicts. Fourth, aggregation provides a means of tailoring reports to minimize their usefulness to competitors. Fifth, litigation concerns and class-action lawsuits lead firms to abstain from disclosures unsupported by tangible evidence. This logic leads us to expect financial reports to focus on aggregating and reporting information related to past transactions.

One drawback of these reports is their lack of timeliness. Financial reports focus on realizations rather than expectations and "soft" information that leads to revised expectations. However, regular periodic disclosure of transaction category totals can encourage managers to reveal private information they have not yet recorded in the accounting system via other means (such as press releases). Pressure for timely disclosure will arise (1) if managers benefit from a reputation of transparency or face legal liability for withholding information and (2) if, after the fact, outside parties can verify that managers were aware of information but failed to disclose it.

The key takeaway of this supply-side discussion is that firms will not meet all the information needs of outsiders, and a firm's financial reporting practices will tend toward the efficient alternative. No business seeks to supply everything its customers need; rather, it seeks to identify the right combination of appealing product characteristics and acceptable costs. Given imperfect and incomplete markets, solving this problem is costly. Businesses determine what they can and cannot do better than competitors by testing their products or services in the marketplace. Sometimes, they fail. In sum, we can view financial reporting choices like managers' other value-maximizing decisions.

4.3. Two Approaches to the Computation of Accounting Earnings

The literature offers two approaches to defining and computing earnings: the income-statement and balance-sheet approaches. The economic underpinnings of this duo differ, even though they are mathematically equivalent. The balance-sheet approach seeks to calculate economic income as the idealized measure (Demsetz, 1969; Ball and Brown, 2014), while the income-statement approach attempts to measure the firm's output (performance) for a period (e.g., Dichev, 2017).

The income-statement approach begins with revenues as the primitive and defines earnings as the difference between revenues and expenses. It has historical precedent and corresponds to the method used in practice to compute operating income. The balance-sheet approach defines earnings as the change in the value of net assets (adjusted for net dividends). At first glance, it has intuitive appeal, as it generates income consonant with principles from economics and finance. As the conceptual framework's definitions of assets and liabilities suggest, regulators support a balance-sheet approach (Storey and Storey, 1998).

The two approaches represent two distinct views of the conceptual foundations of income measurement and, thus, financial reporting. In reviewing them, we aim to build an understanding of earnings through the intricacies of their computations in the imperfect and incomplete markets in which the demand for accounting arises. Impediments relegated to the status of "frictions" in a neoclassical world thus rise to primary importance in formulating and answering questions related to financial accounting.[21] We hope that focusing on two specific income-computation methods can illustrate the costs and benefits of various income-measurement methods, as many methods combine these approaches.

4.3.1. The Income-Statement Approach

Early accounting researchers struggled to define and compute accounting income—a struggle that continues to this day. In their influential monograph, Paton and Littleton (1940) view the business enterprise "as an organization designed to produce income" (p. 23) and state that "the principal concern of accounting is the periodic matching of costs and revenues" (p. 7). This approach, now called the *income-statement approach to earnings computation*, begins by determining revenues and then estimating the costs incurred to generate these revenues. The approach does not refer to "value" or link income to any "change in value." Revenue recognition is limited to amounts that are earned and collectible.[22] Next, the *matching principle*

---

[21] An analogous situation in finance is financial intermediation. Intermediaries create value when frictions limit the applicability of Modigliani and Miller (1958)'s results on the irrelevance of capital structure. In a larger sense, the debate about the appropriate share of the economy taken by financial institutions is a debate about the importance of frictions (Greenwood and Scharfstein, 2013; Cochrane, 2013).

[22] Specifically, the revenue recognition principle limits the recording of revenue to amounts that are (1) earned (either goods delivered or services performed) and (2) realized or realizable (either

requires that expenses be recorded when the corresponding revenue is recorded in the accounting system.[23] These two steps result in a performance measure (i.e., earnings) whose conceptual goal is to match accomplishments (revenues) with efforts (expenses) during a given period rather than measuring the change in value.

Under the income-statement approach, the balance sheet is secondary. It is a consequence of the income computation. Assets are recognized because cash payments have not yet been matched against yet-to-be-recognized revenues.[24] Such assets reside in a holding account to delay the reduction in future income and, therefore, shareholders' equity. These assets represent "unexpired costs"—a concept that seems obscure compared to the more straightforward notion that assets should represent value or future economic benefits. Other assets (e.g., receivables) arise because the revenue recognition principle determines when income is recognized, and the resulting increase in shareholders' equity must be offset by creating an asset. Receivables seem more congruent with the notion that assets are future benefits. Nondebt liabilities materialize by similar logic. They are placed on the balance sheet not because they represent the value of future economic sacrifices but because they allow assets to equal liabilities plus shareholders' equity (when recognition of revenue is delayed, even though cash has been received or the expenses are matched and deemed incurred before payments are made).

The goal of matching current-period accomplishments with efforts seems ad hoc and cramped—arbitrarily constraining the quest for change in value. The revenue recognition rules limit the set of "accomplishments" included in income to those that are earned and collectible. The rules thus limit recognition of growth before its harvest and sale. For example, we might argue that a manufacturer adds value by assembling an automobile, but the value added

cash received or collection of cash reasonably assured). See Chapter 1 for a detailed discussion of the double-entry bookkeeping system and a related discussion of the role of accruals (i.e., the difference between earnings and cash flows).

[23] Product cost, which is well-matched to the generation of some revenue, is recognized in the same period the revenue is recognized. Period expense, which is not directly related to any revenue, is recognized in the period it is consumed.

[24] The need to recognize an asset increase, liability decrease, or share-equity decrease when recording a cash payment is a consequence of maintaining the equality of the balance-sheet equation and double-entry bookkeeping. Double-entry forces the accountant to attribute causality to each cash payment (or receipt) as it occurs. In this way, double-entry accounting accumulates the effects of individual transactions, assigning these effects on an ongoing basis throughout the period. This approach to income computation—by accumulation rather than reference to end points—is consistent with the income-statement approach.

will not be recognized until the automobile is sold. The strained logic relating assets to "unexpired costs" only reinforces the image of the accountant as a priest following ancient rites when she should instead be an economic actor producing an information factor of production. Perhaps we can alleviate some discomfort by noting that terms such as "asset," "liability," and "income" are imperfect labels that summarize complex concepts. The firm's goal is *not* to make the financial-accounting measure correspond more closely to the economic connotation of the label. Instead, the firm seeks to enhance the net benefits of the measure. We will see that the income-statement approach aims to measure the net benefits of arm's-length transactions rather than the change in value.[25]

4.3.2. The Balance-Sheet Approach

Income computation is straightforward if the firm is seen as a portfolio of net assets akin to a portfolio of stocks. Just as one computes the income on a portfolio of stocks by aggregating price changes and dividends across holdings, one can do likewise with the firm's asset holdings. Applying portfolio logic to the computation of accounting earnings leads to the balance-sheet approach. First, determine the beginning and ending asset and liability values.[26] Second, take the difference in these changes and add (subtract) any payments to (additional investment from) equity investors. The result is earnings.

The logic of the balance-sheet approach rests on the economic-income concept. *Economic income* refers to the income generated from the ownership of an asset or a collection of assets—think of this collection of assets as a firm. It is the change in the present value of expected future cash flows accruing to shareholders after adjustments for investments (deposits) or distributions (withdrawals) (Edwards, 1938; Hicks, 1946). Mathematically, it is the difference in the value of the ownership between the end and the beginning of the period, adjusted for investments and distributions. Thus,

---

[25] In a survey of US chief financial officers, Dichev et al. (2013) find that a large majority of CFOs believe that the FASB's neglect of matching and emphasis on fair value adversely affects earnings quality.

[26] The valuation basis (e.g., fair value, historical cost, or present value of cash flows) is distinct from the income-computation approach. However, fair value is a natural implication of the balance-sheet approach. Depreciated-historical-cost asset values imply use of the income-statement approach.

the amount of economic income hinges on the determination of value of the ownership (net assets) at the beginning and the end of the period.

Early accounting researchers commonly adopted the economic-income standard when assessing accounting standards—advocating measures that more closely approximate economic income (e.g., Paton, 1922; Canning, 1929; Alexander, 1950). The economic-income standard also motivates proposals for uniformly applying current cost or fair-value accounting to all assets and liabilities (e.g., Edwards and Bell, 1961; Chambers, 1966; Sterling, 1970; Barth, 2014).[27] *Fair value* is "the price that would be received to sell an asset or paid to transfer a liability in an orderly transaction between market participants at the measurement date" (Financial Accounting Standards Board, 2011; International Accounting Standards Board, 2011, 2011). Barth (2006, p. 98) notes, "In almost every standard-setting project of the FASB and IASB, the boards consider fair value as a possible measurement attribute." However, the fair-value approach to earnings measurement still faces the challenge of capturing synergies, as Barth (2014, p. 350) candidly acknowledges: "The aggregate of fair values does have meaning, but it does not capture the effects of synergies among the assets." Hence, even if firms were perfectly symmetric in recognizing upward and downward changes in the values of individual assets (whether in timing or thresholds of evidence), the balance-sheet approach would still impose a form of conservatism by delaying the recognition of synergies.[28]

4.3.3. Comparison of the Two Approaches

To compare these approaches, we begin by noting the mathematical equivalence of their income equations. Mathematical equivalence does not imply actual equivalence in a world of imperfect and incomplete markets. Each

[27] There is considerable agreement about using fair values based on observable prices in liquid markets (e.g., marketable securities), but expanding fair values to settings where we need to rely on unverifiable managerial estimates is more controversial. Ball, Kothari, and Robin (2000, p. 6, emphasis added) concisely summarize a necessary condition for numbers reported by self-interested managers to be useful: "While timeliness per se is desirable, information asymmetry between managers and users creates a demand for an income variable that *is observable independently of managers.*" Similarly, Botosan and Huffman (2015) and Botosan (2019) argue that fair value is the relevant measurement attribute for in-exchange assets (e.g., the platinum held for sale) while historical cost accounting is the relevant measurement attribute for in-use assets (e.g., the platinum held for use in catalytic converter manufacturing).

[28] Synergies are recognized as goodwill only when a firm is purchased by another.

approach has merit in certain circumstances. The income-statement approach seems better suited for measuring operating income, where realized flows can be quantified. In contrast, operating assets' beginning and ending values are ill-defined and must be approached by estimating projected flows. Still, the forward-looking nature of the valuation-based balance-sheet approach influences the measurement of these flows, leading to the capitalization of some expenditures and incorporation of expected losses. In the case of financial assets, the balance-sheet approach seems more appropriate. The markets for these assets are more liquid than those for operating assets, so direct, reliable measures of beginning and ending values can be obtained. However, the balance-sheet approach does not capture any synergies among financial assets.

4.3.3.1. Mathematical Equality of the Two Approaches

Articulation between the balance sheet and the income statement implies mathematical equality between the incomes derived from the two approaches. For the income statement approach, we begin with the definition of income:

$$\text{Income}_t = \text{Cash Flows}_t + \text{Accruals}_t. \quad (4.1)$$

The income-statement approach requires the insertion of "accruals" into the earnings calculation because Cash Flows$_t$ does not generally equal revenues earned net of the cost necessary to generate these revenues during the period. Cash Flows$_t$ fails to capture operating performance because of timing and matching problems. Timing problems result when the firm earns revenues in a different period from the cash receipt. Matching problems occur when the cash payments necessary to generate revenues occur in a different period from when the revenue is earned.[29] These timing and matching problems fall into four categories: (1) cash paid but not yet recognized as a shareholders' equity reduction (i.e., an expense), (2) expenses recognized in anticipation of cash sacrifices, (3) cash received but not yet recognized as revenue, and (4) revenues recognized in anticipation of cash receipts. Under the

---

[29] See Dechow (1994), Dechow, Kothari, and Watts (1998), and Larson, Sloan, and Giedt (2018) for elaboration. For more recent evidence on the relation between accruals and future earnings or cash flows, see Bushman, Lerman, and Zhang (2016), Lewellen and Resutek (2019), Nallareddy, Sethuraman, and Venkatachalam (2020), and Ball and Nikolaev (2022).

income-statement approach, accrual recognition results from applying the revenue recognition and matching concepts we have discussed.

This abbreviated discussion of the intuition behind accrual recognition seems to leave an awful lot to the reader's imagination. The topic is deep and fundamental. Financial reporting issues involve the causes and effects of firms' accrual recognition decisions. Assuming that firms have limited scope to affect income measurement by altering Cash Flows$_t$, the desired income properties can be achieved only by altering accrual recognition. Determining appropriate accrual recognition is the heart of the income-computation problem. If we take cash flows as given, accounting amounts to determining accruals. Because earnings are the sum of cash flows and accruals, we can view accruals as the means used to obtain an earnings measure with the desired properties. Expectations enter the income computation because accrual measurement necessitates using expectations (e.g., the percentage of receivables expected to be collected). In general, accounting rules limit the use of expectations to short-horizon predictions that can be supported by verifiable evidence. Empirical evidence generally shows that earnings are a better performance measure than cash flows (e.g., Dechow, 1994; Ball and Nikolaev, 2022).

Under the balance-sheet approach, we base our income definition on the notion that income equals the change in net assets:

$$\text{Income}_t = \Delta \text{Net Assets}_t + \text{Net Dividends}_t \qquad (4.2)$$

Net Assets$_t$ denotes assets minus liabilities, and Net Dividends$_t$ denotes net cash paid to shareholders (i.e., dividends plus share repurchases minus share issuances). The articulation between the income statement and the balance sheet ensures that equations (4.1) and (4.2) yield the same income. However, in practice, an accounting system tuned to measure accruals produces a different income number than one designed to measure net asset price (or fair value) changes. Conceptually, we might consider the problem in terms of the practical difficulties in measuring stocks versus flows. In some situations, stocks (e.g., assets and liabilities) are more easily measurable than flows (e.g., revenues and expenses), while in other situations, the converse is true (Bromwich, Macve, and Sunder, 2010). For example, it might be easier to count the number of bags of rice in a warehouse at two points in time than to track the flow of bags into and out of the warehouse. In contrast, precise measures of the flow of oil or gas from an underground deposit might be easier to estimate than changes in the subterranean stock of oil and gas.

4.3.3.2. Complementarity of the Two Approaches

While often deemed to be opposing views, these two approaches can be complementary. Depending on a firm's business activities, each can offer a useful perspective. Perhaps this is why the question of which is better produces unending debate. The superiority of one view over the other depends on the facts and circumstances. When both stocks and flows are measurable with reasonable precision, both sets of numbers become inputs into an accounting system, and the articulation between the stock (balance sheet) and flow (income) statements provides an opportunity to gain insight by reconciling the respective signals.

An example is a perpetual inventory system that tracks flows supplemented by periodic inventory counts. When the magnitude of one (stock or flow) variable can be measured much more reliably than the other, an intuitive and reasonable approach is to measure the former and compute the corresponding value of the latter as a plug figure produced by the accounting identity. Longstanding accounting conventions reflect this hybrid approach.

4.3.3.2.1. Operating Income

Consider the computation of operating income. Implementation of the balance-sheet approach requires measures of beginning and ending operating net asset values. How might such values be obtained? Imperfect and incomplete markets suggest that values are not readily available and are likely to be ill-defined.

The operating process of the firm is typically defined as comprising the assets that give the firm its efficiency advantage over arm's-length transactions. However, this process is not separable from the firm's identifiable assets and, therefore, cannot be traded and priced. In addition, some identifiable assets are not traded in liquid markets with many buyers and sellers (e.g., specially modified equipment installed on an assembly line), so their purchase, sale, and in-use values might differ. Because these values differ, we must clarify which one we seek before we can compute the change in value. The need to choose implies that we should specify some criteria for deciding when to implement a balance-sheet approach. This complication undermines what at first glance appeared to be the tautological superiority of the balance-sheet approach—what seemed an "is" problem turns out to be an "ought" problem.[30] We must then resort to evaluating measures by assessing which value produces a measure most consonant with efficiency considerations.[31]

Assuming that no market exists to provide prices of important operating assets, estimates are necessary. Estimating requires discounting predicted net cash flows from operations. Current flows and past flows will generally be useful inputs to these predictions. The income-statement approach provides an estimate of these current and past flows. Thus implementing a balance-sheet approach requires first estimating income using an income-statement approach and then adjusting this estimate for expectations/predictions. Previously, we noted that incorporating management expectations in the income measure can undermine its usefulness as a performance measure. Incentive conflicts exist between managers and investors (who use the measure to evaluate managers), and paying managers for expected performance might undermine incentives to deliver said performance. If we strip out the use of expectations from our implementation of the balance-sheet approach and use current and past flows to estimate the beginning and ending values, then the values used in the balance-sheet approach are a transformation of income from the income-statement approach. In short, though we set out to use the balance-sheet approach to measure operating income, we arrive at the income-statement approach.

However, a pure income statement–based approach might lead managers to direct all their efforts to maximizing current flow.[32] To produce an earnings measure that encourages managers to invest in the generation of future flows, accounting rules allow them to record as assets (rather than expenses) expenditures on assets that will benefit future periods. Examples include purchases of plant, property, and equipment; investments securities; and other companies (e.g., acquisitions and mergers). Allowing the recognition of these assets provides two qualities that are potentially useful for performance assessment. First, current income is not penalized for these investments. Second, future income is reduced as these investments are depreciated, and the value of past investments is available on the balance sheet to provide a

[30] Hume (1740) argues that normative claims cannot be supported by positive premises.

[31] The recognition of this issue led to the "information perspective" (e.g., Beaver, 1973, 1998)—the idea that financial accounting should shift from attempting to measure value and change in value and instead provide information useful for decisions.

[32] This potential short-termism is offset by managers' expectations that they will be employed with the company in the future and thus will benefit from future income. Changing the organizational form to one less dependent on financial reporting, directors, and dispersed ownership can also reduce short-termism. Private equity and venture-capital financing represent alternative organization forms (Zimmerman, 2016).

means of computing return on investment in future periods. In this way, managers remain subject to the consequences of their past investments via measures of future income and future rate of return.

Conservative accounting provides another way to incorporate expectations in the current flow–oriented income-statement approach. By requiring a lower evidentiary standard for the recognition of anticipated losses than for the recognition of anticipated gains, conservative accounting can press managers to promptly recognize the effects of poorly performing projects. Conservative accounting facilitates the recognition of unrealized losses in the current period. Thus, it might encourage managers to try to mitigate these losses, even though their actions may result in realized losses in the current period. The idea is that managers will not be discouraged from realizing losses if the losses are incorporated into income, regardless of whether they are realized.

4.3.3.2.2. Accounting for Changes in the Value of Claims on Assets

Another set of conceptual valuation problems arises with respect to the claims of the firm. In particular, the value of these claims does not move independently of the value of the firm's assets. Therefore, we must consider accompanying changes in asset value, along with changes in the value of the particular claim, to compute economic income. For example, assume that a firm has assets valued at $100 and debt near maturity with a promised payment of $70. In this example, debt would have a value of $70, and equity would be valued at $30. Assume that the value of assets declines by $40. In this case, equity value declines to zero, and the value of debt declines from $70 to $60.[33] Economic income is -$30. Under these circumstances, adding the $10 gain from the decline in debt value to income makes sense only if the income computation reflects the $40 loss in asset value (not just the $30 loss in equity value). The same logic applies to other claims, including convertible debt, preferred stock, and stock options. Changes in the value of these claims are all positively correlated with the change in asset value. Incorporating

---

[33] For computational simplicity, assume that debt is near maturity, so equity has little value when the value of assets is less than the promised payment on debt. That is, the value of equity is equal to min(0, asset value—promised debt payment). If we consider equity to be an option to acquire the assets of the firm for the promised payment on debt, then equity has some value, even if this option is out of the money. The value of debt is determined by deducting the value of equity from the value of assets. Equity is valued as a call option on the assets of the firm with an exercise price equal to the promised payment on the debt and an expiration date equal to the maturity of the debt. See Galai and Masulis (1976) for further discussion.

changes in the value of the firm's claims into income will move income away from the economic-income concept, unless income also incorporates the change in the value of substantially all assets. Incorporating the changes in the value of nonequity asset claims in income thus requires a balance sheet–based approach.

4.3.3.2.3. *Nonoperating Income*

The firm might also hold some generic assets, such as securities or real estate held for sale that the firm does not intend to develop. These are not uniquely useful to the firm, have no synergy, and can be separated from the firm without losing value. For these assets, market values are available, and if markets are liquid, that value is more clearly defined than in the case of operating assets. The firm's sale of such an asset will not affect its price, so the sales value approximates the purchase value, and both approximate value-in-use by the firm. Realizing unrealized gains requires little effort, so shareholders need not withhold pay to encourage managers to deliver performance. Appreciation in asset value can be incorporated into income without fear that it will induce shirking by managers. Because prices are available, there is no need to estimate flows to value these assets, and the process does not reduce to an application of the income-statement approach, as it does in the case of operating assets. This discussion suggests that the balance-sheet approach should be used to measure income from financial assets; it also supports the use of mark-to-market accounting for such assets.

4.3.3.3. Summary of Discussion on Income-Statement and Balance-Sheet Approaches

Our analysis suggests that the appropriateness of the balance-sheet approach versus the income-statement approach rests on the significance of a firm's operating assets and the distinction between its operating and financial assets. Our analysis offers no bright line. Instead, we offer an approach to apply to the facts and circumstances, using intuition and prudence. To see the complexity, consider a firm whose only product is an exchange-traded fund seeking to track the S&P 500. If the concept of imperfect and incomplete markets did not apply in any circumstance, this would seem to be the one. The firm's predominant assets are highly liquid publicly traded shares of the largest US companies. The application of the balance-sheet approach to compute income seems appropriate. Yet imperfect and incomplete markets remain a significant factor even here. Somehow, the cost and inconvenience of holding individual shares creates an opportunity for a firm to earn fees by managing an exchange-traded fund that, at first glance, appears to be a negative net present value investment. Yet the founders and managers of these funds created billions of dollars of value for company owners.[34] Applying a balance sheet–based approach to income misses the yearly flow that produces this value. Determining the significance of operating value in a dynamic world is an overwhelming task, even for an accountant.

Finally, a case can be made that income from financial assets should be distinguished from operating income. For example, this income might affect shareholders' equity but could be reported in other comprehensive income rather than on the income statement. This income does not result from the skill of managers. To the extent that markets are liquid and efficient, abnormal income is random, and normal rates of return are simply payment for risk. Perhaps it is not a coincidence that the ascendency of the market-efficiency paradigm has led to recognition of these items (as it argues for their reliable measurement), as well as their exclusion from income and their inclusion in comprehensive income.[35]

4.4. Concluding Remarks

Our analysis suggests that the same conditions that give rise to firms foil attempts to define earnings as a change in value and lead parties who contribute resources to the firm to demand a performance measure. Imperfect and incomplete markets allow firms to perform some functions better than market transactions. These conditions also imply that summing the available market prices of a firm's saleable assets will not yield a complete tally of the firm's value. "Value" itself becomes a slippery concept because it can depend on the actions of the firm and the liquidity of markets. For example, a

---

[34] As of December 31, 2017, State Street Corporation held approximately $644 billion of assets under management in exchange-traded funds. These assets and their holdings of $33 trillion in assets under custody were not included in State Street Corporation's balance sheet because they were not owned by State Street's shareholders. The $238 billion of assets shown on State Street's balance sheet were those employed in investment management and investment servicing. The company's shareholder value derives, in part, from its ability to reduce transaction costs on the assets it holds for its customers.

[35] Current accounting standards (ASC 320, ASC 321) require holding gains/losses to be included in net income for debt securities classified as trading and for all equity securities, and they require holding gains/losses to be included in other comprehensive income for debt securities classified as available for sale.

positive NPV project means that the total cost of assets acquired differs from the present value of the project's expected future cash flows. This implies the project has at least two values. Furthermore, information asymmetry that engenders imperfect and incomplete markets gives rise to the demand for performance measurement. Parties need to assess the likelihood that they will be paid for resources provided to the firm, and they need accounting measures to control incentive conflicts.

This analysis leads to the conclusion that measuring the change in value is unlikely to be the overriding characteristic of the earnings measure the firm supplies. But the fact that firms seek to increase value makes their financial-reporting choices consistent with this purpose. This leads to a discussion of how performance measures ease transactions between investors and the firm and how earnings might reduce incentive conflicts. We reach the following conclusions.

First, shareholders demand a periodic measure to evaluate and reward managers. The demand for a reliable, output-based measure underlies the revenue recognition principle. Second, because managers produce performance measures, shareholders and creditors demand verifiable information, given the incentive conflicts between management and shareholders, and between shareholders and creditors. Third, shareholders and creditors demand conservative financial reporting because managers (with respect to shareholders) and shareholders (with respect to creditors) are reluctant to recognize bad news and might take actions to their detriment (e.g., excessive risk taking). Fourth, creditors are particularly interested in a firm's liquidation value in case of continued poor performance. The balance sheet thus focuses on separate and saleable assets and excludes internal goodwill or other intangibles. Fifth, users demand audited financial statements that increase the credibility of management-produced performance measures. Sixth, managers want information for decision-making and internal control.

The goal of our discussion is to provide an economic framework for understanding the demand for and supply of accounting earnings. Research on the relation between earnings and returns might consider returns to be a proxy for economic income and the degree of correlation of returns with earnings to be a proxy for so-called earnings quality. However, our discussion implies that higher-quality earnings help the firm run more efficiently. Viewed this way, returns are a flashlight, illuminating earnings' properties consistent with equity valuation, while other forces, such as demand for accounting measures in management compensation, remain in the shadows. These other forces are not necessarily malign or misguided but might be revealed by a light tuned to wavelengths that illuminate efficiency considerations.

Supplement: Perfect and Complete Markets

This supplement discusses the concept of perfect and complete markets. The discussion serves as a contrast and supportive backdrop to the more realistic setting of imperfect and incomplete markets. The latter setting is foundational to the ideas in our discussion: why do firms exist, and what is the demand for accounting earnings? In contrast, an implication of perfect, complete markets is that firms are redundant, the concept of economic income is well-defined, and the demand for accounting earnings is absent.

S1. Definition of Perfect and Complete Markets

From the time of Adam Smith, economists have studied the role of markets in coordinating diverse activities pursued by many individuals, all acting in their own self-interest. Markets for goods and services—including metals, grains, automobiles, and financial assets, to name a few—seem omnipresent, encompassing a wide array of goods and services,.[36] Smith (1776) describes a *market* as an invisible hand that matches the demand and supply of a good or service via the price system. A positive externality of markets is that self-interested individuals' voluntary trades produce social benefits. This economic thought was formally modeled by Kenneth Arrow, Gérard Debreu, and Lionel McKenzie in the 1950s as the general equilibrium theory of markets.[37] This theory explains the determination of equilibrium prices and quantities in perfectly (i.e., frictionless) competitive markets. It focuses on markets with the following three characteristics: (1) the existence of a quoted price for every commodity, (2) price-taking by consumers and firms, and

[36] In economic terms, a commodity is a good or service available for purchase in the market. A contingent commodity is a promise to deliver a unit of good or service at a specified date, if a certain state occurs. An asset is a title to receive either commodities or dollars at specified future dates in amounts that depend on which state occurs; the payoffs of an asset are thus a vector whose number of elements equals the number of states.

[37] It is also referred to as the *Walrasian theory of markets* (Walras, 1874). See Arrow (1951), Debreu (1952, 1959), Arrow and Debreu (1954), and McKenzie (1954, 1955, 1959).

(3) zero transaction costs. Markets with these characteristics are termed perfect and complete markets.[38]

The traditional general equilibrium model focuses on the certainty setting. Arrow (1953, Chapter 1) and Debreu (1959) extend the analysis to a setting with uncertainty by introducing the concepts of event trees and state-contingent commodities. We explain both settings in this supplement. We describe the concept of economic income in these settings and the implications of perfect and complete markets for demand for accounting. Our discussion draws heavily from Fama and Miller (1972), Mas-Colell, Whinston, and Green (1995), Magill and Quinzii (1996), and Beaver (1998). Our goal is to help readers better understand the intuition behind the technical definitions of these market settings.

S2. Certainty

In a perfect and complete market, investors can costlessly trade any multiple or fraction of claims to future cash flows. Consider a simple two-period economy as an example: $t = 0$ (now), $t = 1$ (one period from now), and $t = 2$ (two periods from now). The completeness of the market with respect to intertemporal claims enables investors to (1) invest at $t = 0$ and receive \$1 at $t = 1$, (2) invest at $t = 0$ and receive \$1 at $t = 2$, (3) contract at $t = 0$ to invest at $t = 1$ and receive \$1 at $t = 2$ (in a futures market), (4) wait to invest at $t = 1$ and receive \$1 at $t = 2$ (in a future spot market), and (5) conduct any combination of these four types of trades.

In a certainty setting, all expectations are realized, and the prices of intertemporal claims must satisfy the no-arbitrage condition. That is, anyone merely repackaging the claims into different bundles cannot earn any profit. In our example, the price to invest at $t = 0$ and receive \$1 each at $t = 1$ and $t = 2$ must equal the sum of (1) the price to invest at $t = 0$ and receive \$1 at $t = 1$ and (2) the price to invest at $t = 0$ and receive \$1 at $t = 2$.[39] More generally,

---

[38] Perfect markets imply the absence of transaction costs. For example, in trading stocks, investors buy at the bid price and sell at the ask price and thus incur a transaction cost of the bid-ask spread. As a result of the spread, stock markets are not perfect. Fama and Miller (1972, p. 277) state the following formal conditions for perfect markets: "All goods and assets are infinitely divisible; any information is costless and available to everybody; there are no transactions costs or taxes; all individuals pay the same prices for any given commodity or asset; no individual is wealthy enough to affect the market price of any asset; and no firm is large enough to affect the opportunity set facing consumers."

[39] The same condition applies to prices of commodities. For example, assuming that the market for gasoline and chocolate bars is perfect and complete, the price of different combinations of gallons of gasoline and numbers of chocolate bars must equal the total price of buying the same quantities of the two commodities individually.

any compound claim to future cash flows can be characterized as a bundle of simple claims, and the price of the compound claim is the sum of the prices of the simple claims that form the bundle. Equivalently, the price of a compound claim to future cash flows can be computed as the present value of those cash flows.

This present-value characterization allows us to convert a stream of cash flows in different periods into a single number, and this single number (i.e., present value) can be used to compare different streams of cash flows. In perfect and complete markets, any cash flow stream can be expressed as an infinite number of other cash flow streams with the same present value. This property ensures that in comparing two cash flow streams, the cash flow stream with a higher present value can be expressed as an equivalent cash flow stream that strictly dominates the cash flow stream with a lower present value. Investors unanimously prefer the cash flow stream with a higher present value. The implication is that corporate managers can use the present-value rule in project selection, and increasing shareholder value makes each shareholder better off, regardless of individual taste or preference.

S3. Uncertainty

Under uncertainty, the future state (or event) drawn from a set of states (or events) is unpredictable. In a complete market, prices exist for each state-contingent claim or commodity. For example, consumers value an umbrella or UBER ride on a rainy day differently than they would on a sunny day, and market completeness implies that an ex-ante price exists for the ex-post delivery of an umbrella or UBER ride after the realization of the state of the world (e.g., rainy versus sunny).

Arrow (1953, Chapter 1) and Debreu (1959) pioneered the general equilibrium analysis of pricing in complete markets under uncertainty. In the classical Arrow-Debreu model, a comprehensive collection of contingent contracts (for each state-contingent commodity) is traded at the initial date; no trade happens afterward, and agents simply receive or deliver the state-contingent commodity based on their contractual obligations. Arrow (1953, Chapter 1) demonstrates that any Arrow-Debreu equilibrium can be achieved with a more realistic sequential system of markets comprising Arrow securities and spot markets at each date-event. An Arrow security at date t is a primitive claim to \$1 at date $t + 1$ if a certain event occurs.

A complete set of Arrow securities permits agents to trade, at each date-event, spot contracts for current delivery of each commodity, and Arrow securities for delivery of income at the following date-event. This sequential trade model demonstrates the fundamental role of financial securities in achieving an efficient resource allocation.

The Arrow-Debreu model follows two strands of economic literature: the Ramsey (1926), von Neumann-Morgenstern (1944), and Savage (1954) theory of choice under uncertainty and the traditional model of general equilibrium. The Arrow-Debreu model combines (1) a state space (or event tree) to model possible outcomes, (2) expected utility to represent preferences, and (3) the standard general equilibrium framework. More importantly, Arrow's work explicitly recognizes the problem of optimal risk sharing and the role of financial markets in achieving an optimal risk allocation. A theory of risk sharing is absent in the previous two hundred years of classical economics literature.

Under uncertainty, the price of an Arrow security (i.e., a primitive claim to $1 at date $t + 1$ if a certain state occurs) reflects investors' preferences for the cash flow in that state and their beliefs about the probability of that state occurring. A complex claim to future contingent cash flows can be viewed as a bundle of primitive claims (i.e., Arrow securities), and the price of this complex claim is the sum of the prices of the primitive claims that form the bundle. To compute the price or present value of a complex claim, expected cash flows are discounted at expected rates of return.[40]

In the uncertainty setting, managers can continue to use the present value to rank projects only if individual investors' expected rates of return can somehow be aggregated into a consensus belief across investors. The Sharpe-Lintner capital asset pricing model (CAPM)[41] dispenses with this problem by assuming that investors have homogeneous beliefs and preferences. More generally, managers seek to maximize market value. Shareholders still prefer market-value maximization, as in the certainty setting, because prices are rich and reflect shareholder preferences and the implications of managerial decisions.

[40] A key assumption for this computation to be feasible is the independence between the ex-post rates of return and the future expected rates of return at any point in time (Beaver, 1998, p. 61).

[41] The mean-standard deviation of the asset pricing model was developed by Sharpe (1964), Lintner (1965a, b), and Mossin (1966).

S4. Economic Income in Perfect and Complete Markets

Economic income refers to the income generated from the ownership of an individual asset or a collection of assets (firm). It is defined as the change in the present value of expected future cash flows, after adjustments for investments (deposits) or distributions (withdrawals) (Edwards, 1938; Hicks, 1946). Mathematically, economic income is the difference in the value of the ownership between the end of the period and its beginning, adjusted for investments and distributions. Thus, the amount of economic income hinges on the determination of the value of the ownership (assets) at the beginning and end of the period.

In perfect and complete markets under certainty, a firm's economic income is well defined and can be measured by tallying observable market prices of its individual assets and liabilities. Moreover, economic income equals permanent income, computed as the value at the beginning of the period times the interest rate. Economic income has several desirable properties: (1) More of it is preferred to less in any given year, (2) it reflects multiperiod effects of managerial actions, and (3) shareholders unanimously prefer projects that generate more. However, economic income is a byproduct of a valuation and does not provide additional information beyond the present values.

The introduction of uncertainty changes these conclusions in some respects. Economic income can still be defined, but complications arise. First, an asset-pricing model is needed to define risk and incorporate it into the computation of the present value of risky cash flows (e.g., the CAPM). Second, risk implies that realizations differ from expectations. Thus, expected economic income and realized economic income differ. Expected economic income depends on the (unobservable) expected rate of return derived from the asset-pricing model. If individual investors' beliefs and preferences for a given firm's net assets can be characterized by a market-wide risky discount rate, this rate provides the basis for determining expected economic income.[42] Expected economic income equals the value of initial net assets times this risky rate, and the value of initial net assets equals expected net cash flows discounted at this risky rate. Expected economic income is permanent income. Realized economic income equals the difference between the initial value of net assets and the (realized) value of net assets at the end of the period, adjusted for net shareholder investments. Unexpected

---

[42] See Fama and Miller (1972) and Ingersoll (1987) for rigorous technical analyses.

income—the difference between realized income and expected income—is transitory. Both measures of economic income are a byproduct of the valuation. Thus their economic role, if valuation is known, is tenuous.

S5. Implications of Perfect and Complete Markets for the Demand for Accounting

In a world of perfect and complete markets, asset values are readily observable; thus, income, defined as the change in net asset value, is an unambiguous measure of performance. In such a world, financial reporting is unnecessary: asset values can be observed, even without financial information. The critical insight here is that deviations from perfect and complete markets give rise to a demand for financial accounting as a source of information that helps determine asset values. Once we recognize that the nature of accounting information will influence the estimated values of the assets, it is easy to imagine the following: (1) the information itself might be used in making operating decisions that, in turn, affect asset values; and (2) the producers of accounting information might have a vested interest in shading the information to influence asset values that are set by investors/traders in the market. Imperfect and incomplete markets thus lead to ambiguity in the concept of value and simultaneously suggest a role for financial accounting in that accounting methods can affect outcomes, and individuals can have accounting-method preferences. Moving away from perfect and complete markets breaks the mathematical correspondence between income and change in value. The intuition that these concepts must correspond, which is derived from a perfect and complete market setting, can be misleading. Our discussions are devoted to developing an understanding of the properties of accounting earnings in imperfect and incomplete markets.

We close this supplement with a parallel between the economics of accounting earnings and the theory of capital structure in corporate finance (Modigliani and Miller, 1958, 1963). The capital structure–irrelevance theorem states that if a manager's operating decisions (i.e., investment policy) are transparent knowledge to all (i.e., there is no information asymmetry), and if frictions, especially taxes and financial distress costs, are zero, then the firm's value does not vary with its financing decisions. The theorem is insightful precisely because it shows that capital structure matters when one or more of the underlying assumptions are violated. Thus, the situation of accountants resembles that of bankers trying to understand their role in a

Modigliani and Miller world, where information asymmetry and other frictions are absent, and capital structure has no effect on value. Modigliani and Miller's theorem offers valuable insights because managers can make operating decisions in light of the range of economic forces that affect a firm. Similarly, the value of accounting relates to forces that require us to consider the value implications of income beyond its correspondence to an economic concept (change in value) whose definition is evident only in the absence of these forces.

References

Acheson, G. G., Campbell, G., Turner, J. D., 2019. Private contracting, law and finance. *Review of Financial Studies* 32 (11), 4156–4195.

Alexander, S. S., 1950. Income measurement in a dynamic economy. In: *Five Monographs on Business Income*, Alexander, S.S., M. Bronfenbrenner, S. Fabricant and C. Warburton (Eds.). American Institute of Accountants, New York City, New York.

Arrow, K. J., 1951. *Social Choice and Individual Values*. John Wiley & Sons, New York City, New York.

Arrow, K. J., 1953. Le rôle des valeurs boursières pour la répartition la meilleure des risques. *Colloques Internationaux du Centre National de la Recherche Scientifique* 11, 41–47. [Translated as Arrow, K. J., 1964. The role of securities in the optimal allocation of risk-bearing. *Review of Economic Studies* 31 (2), 91–96.]

Arrow, K. J., Debreu, G., 1954. Existence of an equilibrium for a competitive economy. *Econometrica* 22 (3), 265–290.

Balakrishnan, K., Watts, R. L., Zuo, L., 2016. The effect of accounting conservatism on corporate investment during the global financial crisis. *Journal of Business Finance and Accounting* 43, 513–542.

Ball, R., Brown, P. R., 2014. Ball and Brown (1968): A retrospective. *The Accounting Review* 89 (1), 1–26.

Ball, R., Kothari, S., Robin, A., 2000. The effect of international institutional factors on properties of accounting earnings. *Journal of Accounting and Economics* 29 (1), 1–51.

Ball, R., Nikolaev, V. V., 2022. On earnings and cash flows as predictors of future cash flows. *Journal of Accounting and Economics* 73 (1), 101430.

Barth, M. E., 2006. Including estimates of the future in today's financial statements. *Accounting Horizons* 20 (3), 271–285.

Barth, M. E., 2014. Measurement in financial reporting: The need for new concepts. *Accounting Horizons* 28 (2), 331–352.

Beaver, W. H., 1973. What should be the FASB's objectives? *Journal of Accountancy* 136 (2), 49–56.

Beaver, W. H., 1998. *Financial Reporting: An Accounting Revolution*. Prentice Hall, Upper Saddle River, New Jersey.

Bolton, P., Dewatripont, M., 2004. *Contract Theory*. MIT Press, Cambridge, Massachusetts.

Botosan, C., 2019. Pathway to an integrated conceptual framework for financial reporting. *The Accounting Review* 94 (4), 421–436.

Botosan, C., Huffman, A., 2015. Decision-useful asset measurement from a business valuation perspective. *Accounting Horizons* 29 (4), 757–776.

Bromwich, M., Macve, R., Sunder, S., 2010. Hicksian income in the conceptual framework. *Abacus* 46 (3), 348–376.

Bushman, R., Lerman, A., Zhang, F., 2016. The changing landscape of accrual accounting. *Journal of Accounting Research* 54 (1), 41–78.

Canning, J. B., 1929. *The Economics of Accountancy: A Critical Analysis of Accounting Theory.* Ronald Press Company, New York City, New York.

Chambers, R. J., 1966. *Accounting Evaluation and Economic Behavior.* Prentice Hall, Upper Saddle River, New Jersey.

Coase, R. H., 1937. The nature of the firm. *Economica* 4 (16), 386–405.

Cochrane, J. H., 2013. Finance: Function matters, not size. *Journal of Economic Perspectives*, 27 (2), 29–50.

Core, J. E., 2020. The real effects of financial reporting on pay and incentives. *Accounting and Business Research* 50 (5), 448–469.

Debreu, G., 1952. A social equilibrium existence theorem. *Proceedings of the National Academy of Science* 38 (10), 886–893.

Debreu, G., 1959. *Theory of Value: An Axiomatic Analysis of Economic Equilibrium.* Wiley, New York City, New York.

Dechow, P. M., 1994. Accounting earnings and cash flows as measures of firm performance: The role of accounting accruals. *Journal of Accounting and Economics* 18 (1), 3–42.

Dechow, P. M., Kothari, S. P., Watts, R. L., 1998. The relation between earnings and cash flows. *Journal of Accounting and Economics* 25 (2), 133–168.

Demsetz, H., 1969. Information and efficiency: Another viewpoint. *Journal of Law and Economics* 12 (1), 1–22.

Dichev, I. D., 2017. On the conceptual foundations of financial reporting. *Accounting and Business Research* 47 (6), 617–632.

Dichev, I. D., Harvey, G., Graham, J., Rajgopal, S., 2013. Earnings quality: Evidence from the field. *Journal of Accounting and Economics* 56 (2–3), 1–33.

Dye, R. A., 2017. Optimal disclosure decisions when there are penalties for nondisclosure. *RAND Journal of Economics* 48 (3), 704–732.

Edmans, A., Gabaix, X., Jenter, D., 2017. Executive compensation: A survey of theory and evidence. In: *The Handbook of the Economics of Corporate Governance*, B. Hermalin and M. Weisbach (Eds.) vol.1, 383–522. Amsterdam, the Netherlands, Elsevier.

Edwards, E. O., Bell, P., 1961. *The Theory and Management of Business Income.* University of California Press, Berkeley, California.

Edwards, R. S., 1938. The nature and measurement of income. *The Accountant* 99, 22–26.

Fama, E. F., Miller, M. H., 1972. *The Theory of Finance.* Dryden Press, Hinsdale, Illinois.

Financial Accounting Standards Board (FASB), 2011. *Fair Value Measurement (Topic 820): Amendments to Achieve Common Fair Value Measurement and Disclosure Requirements in U.S. GAAP and IFRSs.* Update No. 2011–04. FASB, Norwalk, Connecticut.

Friedman, M., 1953. *The Methodology of Positive Economics: Essays in Positive Economics.* University of Chicago Press, Chicago, Illinois.

Galai, D., Masulis, R. W., 1976. The option pricing model and the risk factor of stock. *Journal of Financial Economics* 3 (1–2), 53–81.

Gibbons, R., 2005. Four formal(izable) theories of the firm? *Journal of Economic Behavior & Organization* 58 (2), 200–245.

Greenwood, R., Scharfstein, D., 2013. The growth of finance. *Journal of Economic Perspectives* 27 (2), 3–28.

Hicks, J. R., 1946. *Value and Capital: An Inquiry into Some Fundamental Principles of Economic Theory.* Clarendon Press, Oxford, United Kingdom.

Hölmstrom, B., 1979. Moral hazard and observability. *Bell Journal of Economics* 10 (1), 74–91.

Hume, D., 1740. *A Treatise of Human Nature, Book III: Morals.* Retrieved from https://www.earlymoderntexts.com/.

Ijiri, Y., 1975, *Studies in Accounting Research #10: Theory of Accounting Measurement.* Lakewood Ranch, Florida: American Accounting Association.

Ingersoll, J. E, 1987. *Theory of Financial Decision Making.* Rowman and Littlefield, Totowa, New Jersey.

International Accounting Standards Board (IASB), 2011. *Fair Value Measurement.* International Financial Reporting Standard 13. IASB, London, United Kingdom.

Kim, Y., Li, S., Pan, C., Zuo, L., 2013. The role of accounting conservatism in the equity market: Evidence from seasoned equity offerings. *The Accounting Review* 88 (4), 1327–1356.

Larson, C. R., Sloan, R., Giedt, J. Z., 2018. Defining, measuring, and modeling accruals: A guide for researchers. *Review of Accounting Studies* 23 (3), 827–871.

Lewellen, J., Resutek, R. J., 2019. Why do accruals predict earnings? *Journal of Accounting and Economics* 67 (2–3), 336–356.

Lintner, J., 1965a. Security prices, risk, and maximal gains from diversification. *Journal of Finance* 20 (4): 587–615.

Lintner, J., 1965b. The valuation of risk assets and the selection of risky investments in stock portfolios and capital budgets. *Review of Economics and Statistics* 47 (1), 13–37.

Magill, M., Quinzii, M., 1996. *Theory of Incomplete Markets.* MIT Press, Cambridge, Massachusetts.

Mas-Colell, A., Whinston, M. D., Green, J. R., 1995. *Microeconomic Theory.* Oxford University Press, New York City, New York.

McKenzie, L. W., 1954. On equilibrium in Graham's model of world trade and other competitive systems. *Econometrica* 22 (2), 147–161.

McKenzie, L. W., 1955. Equality of factor prices in world trade. *Econometrica* 23 (3): 239–257.

McKenzie, L. W., 1959. On the existence of general equilibrium for a competitive market. *Econometrica* 27 (1), 54–71.

Modigliani, F., Miller, M. H., 1958. The cost of capital, corporation finance and the theory of investment. *American Economic Review* 48 (3), 261–297.

Modigliani, F., Miller, M. H., 1963. Corporate income taxes and the cost of capital: A correction. *American Economic Review* 53 (3), 433–443.

Mossin, J., 1966. Equilibrium in a capital asset market. *Econometrica* 34 (4), 768–783.

Nallareddy, S., Sethuraman, M., Venkatachalam, M., 2020. Changes in accrual properties and operating environment: Implications for cash flow predictability. *Journal of Accounting and Economics* 69 (2–3), 101313.

Paton, W. A., 1922. *Accounting Theory with Special Reference to the Corporate Enterprise.* Ronald Press Company, New York City, New York.

Paton, W. A., Littleton, A. C., 1940. *An Introduction to Corporate Accounting Standards: Monograph No. 3.* Lakewood Ranch, Florida: American Accounting Association.

Ramsey, R. P., 1926. The foundations of mathematics. *Proceedings of the London Mathematical Society* 2 (1), 338–384.

Savage, L. J., 1954. *The Foundations of Statistics.* John Wiley and Sons, Hoboken, New Jersey.

Sharpe, W. F., 1964. Capital asset prices: A theory of market equilibrium under conditions of risk. *Journal of Finance* 19 (3), 425–442.

Sims, C., 1996. Macroeconomics and methodology. *Journal of Economic Perspectives* 10 (1), 105–120.

Smith, A., 1776. *An Inquiry into the Nature and Causes of the Wealth of Nations.* W. Strahan and T. Cadell, London, United Kingdom.

Sterling, R. R., 1970. *Theory of the Measurement of Enterprise Income.* University Press of Kansas, Lawrence, Kansas.

Storey, R. K., Storey, S., 1998. *The Framework of Financial Accounting Concepts and Standards.* Norwalk, Connecticut: Financial Accounting Standards Board.

von Neumann, J., Morgenstern, O., 1944. *Theory of Games and Economic Behavior.* Princeton University Press, Princeton, New Jersey.

Walras, L., 1874. *Éléments d'économie Politique Pure.* F. Rouge, Lausanne, Switzerland.

Watts, R. L., 1977. Corporate financial statements, a product of the market and political processes. *Australian Journal of Management* 2 (1), 53–75.

Watts, R. L., Zimmerman, J., 1978. Towards a positive theory of the determination of accounting standards. *The Accounting Review* 53 (1), 112–134.

Watts, R. L., Zimmerman, J., 1979. The demand for and supply of accounting theories: The market for excuses. *The Accounting Review* 54 (2), 273–305.

Watts, R. L., Zimmerman, J., 1983. Agency problems, auditing, and the theory of the firm: Some evidence. *Journal of Law and Economics* 26 (3), 613–633.

Watts, R. L., Zimmerman, J., 1986. *Positive Accounting Theory.* Prentice-Hall, Englewood Cliffs, New Jersey.

Watts, R. L., Zimmerman, J., 1990. Positive accounting theory: A ten-year perspective. *The Accounting Review* 65 (1), 131–156.

Watts, R. L., Zuo, L., 2016. Understanding practice and institutions: A historical perspective. *Accounting Horizons* 30 (3), 409–423.

Zhang, J., 2008. The contracting benefits of accounting conservatism to lenders and borrowers. *Journal of Accounting and Economics* 45 (1), 27–54.

Zimmerman, J., 2016. Private equity, the rise of unicorns, and the reincarnation of control-based accounting. *Journal of Applied Corporate Finance* 28 (3), 56–67.

APPENDIX

The Shareholder Value
Maximization Principle

A.1. Overview

The view that firms (managers) behave as if their goal is to increase shareholder value is the *shareholder value maximization principle*.[1] While many agree that this principle governs managerial behavior, it continues to incite debate.[2] Many authors have articulated the shareholder value maximization principle, including, most influentially, Friedman (1970) and Jensen (2001). Friedman (1970) implores managers, as shareholders' agents, to "conduct the business in accordance with their desires, which will generally be to make as much money as possible while conforming to the basic rules of the society, both those embodied in law and those embodied in ethical custom." This Appendix expands the normative arguments for shareholder value maximization by examining the arguments against it. Our presentation is positive (i.e., descriptive) in the sense that we reason based on the equilibrium behavior of economic actors.

The argument that managers should seek to increase shareholder value begins with the premise that society's resources are scarce. Judicious use of scarce resources implies that resources should be directed toward higher net-value activities. If prices measure opportunity costs and benefits, the net value of an activity can be determined by subtracting the price of resources devoted to an activity from the revenues generated by it. Because an activity might endure for multiple periods and employ long-lasting resources (e.g., plant, property, and equipment), a net present value (NPV) calculation is often necessary to compare cash inflows and outflows occurring in different periods. This NPV corresponds to the project's effect on its owner's wealth. These arguments yield the following proposition: Judicious use of society's resources implies that each project's owners maximize the NPV of their projects.

Many individuals with wealth do not have attractive projects of their own. They will seek projects that promise high returns, placing their wealth in the hands of project managers. The owner must then compensate the project managers for their effort and expertise, which are also scarce resources. Separating the ownership of wealth from its management does not alter our conclusion that judicious use of resources requires owners to

---

[1] *Shareholder value* here refers to the value of the shareholders' investment in a company, i.e., the present value of all future cash flows. For most discussions, we focus on the owner-manager setting for simplicity. The role of agency conflicts between shareholders and managers is discussed in section A.5.

[2] For a series of articles on the shareholder-stakeholder debate, see ProMarket (2020).

seek higher-value projects. Our logic implies that firm managers judiciously employ a society's resources when they seek to increase shareholder value.

Even so, the shareholder value maximization principle has been the subject of criticism from many economists, activists, politicians, and even business executives. We divide these criticisms into four more specific objections.

1. **Shareholders might prefer objectives other than or in addition to value maximization, such as concern for the environment.** This is a two-part criticism: (a) Managers may be reluctant to pursue other objectives because those contravene value maximization, and (b) pursuit of these other objectives is a means to increase shareholder value, but managers do not fully appreciate this. We explain that the political realm might be a better path by which to pursue objectives contrary to value maximization, because competition undermines firms seeking other unrelated objectives, and managers face an intractable problem when trying to consolidate competing objectives into a distinct target. As for the objectives consistent with maximization of shareholder value (e.g., sensitivity to worker happiness), managers would and should[3] gladly embrace these, subject to the constraints of competition, law, and ethics.

2. **Firms might plunder other stakeholders.**[4] We explain that competition and constraints imposed by law and ethical standards minimize, if not eliminate, the exploitation of (or theft from) other stakeholders as a means to increase shareholder value. Competitive product, labor, and capital markets counter the pull of incentives to maximize shareholder value at the expense of other stakeholders.

3. **Managers are shareholders' agents, but they will pursue their own objectives.** This well-known incentive (agency) conflict is hardly unique to organizations that maximize shareholder value. Any organization, regardless of the objective one wishes its managers to pursue, encounters incentive conflicts. Incentive problems also exist in nonprofits and governments.

4. **Managers and shareholders might suffer from behavioral biases.** We explain that such biases would also hamper organizations seeking alternative goals.

Before we delve into each of these criticisms, we begin by assuming that investors in corporate organizations seek to maximize the value of their investment. Therefore, we expect firms and their managers to strive to maximize shareholder value and compete to devise the most efficient means of doing so. We describe the economic consequences of

[3] The word "should" is not meant to be normative but to recognize that managers are duty bound to act to maximize shareholder value when shareholders seek that objective.

[4] Due to this concern, the Business Roundtable recently changed its statement of "the purpose of a corporation" and stated that corporate leaders should take into account "all stakeholders"—that is, employees, customers, and society writ large (Benoit, 2019). BlackRock also stated publicly that companies in its portfolio should have at least two female directors (Krouse, 2018) and "benefit all of their stakeholders" (Fink, 2018; Pozen, 2018). Priya Mathur, the president of the California Public Employees' Retirement System (CalPERS), advocated environmental, social, and governance investing, but she was criticized for this focus and unseated by government workers (Atkins, 2018). The UK Financial Reporting Council asks asset owners and managers to consider environmental, social, and governance factors at companies in which they are investing (Trentmann, 2019). The Walt Disney Company threatened to boycott Georgia over its new abortion law (Victor, 2019). In contrast, Warren Buffett explicitly stated that Berkshire Hathaway would not consider diversity when hiring board members (Sorkin, 2019), and CalPERS's directors recently opposed proposals to sell stocks in private prisons, gun retailers, and companies tied to Turkey (Gillers, 2019).

pursuing the objective of value creation and implications for social welfare under a set of assumptions (a "positive" approach).[5]

The merit of pursuing other objectives is a normative question.[6] Suspicion regarding the pursuit of wealth dates back at least to Aristotle, who was suspicious of wealth seeking because it had no natural limit. For example, one might question the sanity of an individual with one million spoons trying to acquire one million more. However, the irrationality of an individual with $10 million seeking $10 million more is less clear. Negative views can also be found in the Bible: "Again I tell you, it is easier for a camel to go through the eye of a needle than for someone who is rich to enter the kingdom of God" (Matthew 19:24).[7]

All we can argue is that societies are (predicted to be) poorer when corporations that are chartered to be governed in the best interest of shareholders pursue other objectives, and that such corporations tend to pursue shareholder value maximization. This conclusion is positive rather than normative. We draw it by assuming the following:

1. Competition exists.
2. Prices approximate opportunity costs.
3. Resources lack prices due to the absence of property rights that allow them to be bought and sold.
4. Absent property rights, the ever-changing opportunity cost of unowned resources cannot be determined and will be one factor among many (e.g., interests of parties and their political influence, culture) that determine the cost to use the unowned resource.
5. Neither people in the private sector nor those in the public sector are angels.

Given these assumptions, limits on shareholder value maximization are constraints that can lead to a shareholder value below the unconstrained maximization. Thus, our position amounts to arguing that constraints are costly. This position is subject to falsification by empirical testing. Some constraints might not bite.

This conclusion is also a narrow one. It is consistent with the view that wealth does not bring happiness. That is, we do not take a position on whether the constrained optimum is more desirable than the unconstrained optimum. For example, people might prefer a society where CEOs make no more than twenty times as much as any employee at their firms after seeing the effect of the constraint on outcomes. Folks in the Soviet Union thought that imposing restrictions on property rights and freedom of exchange would lead to desirable results, but they revised their beliefs. Some regimes place constraints on shareholder value maximization that do not exist in others (e.g., Norway, France, Belgium, and Italy have quotas requiring corporate boards to contain women; Britain does not). Given that these quotas have not been repealed, the populations of these countries seem

---

[5] Gould and Ferguson (1980, p. 3) note, "The business of an economist is a positive, not a normative, one. That is, given a social objective, the economist can analyze the problem and suggest the most efficient means by which to attain the desired end."

[6] Of course, history offers many examples of societies that embrace other objectives. The motives of a society, if the concept can be coherently defined, are difficult to fathom. Rousseau wrestles with the definition of "general will" because he requires the concept to establish legitimate political authority and argues that education can create public-minded citizens (Sreenivasan, 2000). Thucydides offers a short list of motives for war: honor, fear, and interest (wealth).

[7] An excellent discussion of these views and their historical evolution can be found in Muller (2002).

to think the current outcome is preferable to the pre-quota outcome. Our conclusion is also consistent with the existence of charities and not-for-profit corporations chartered to pursue goals consistent with reducing their donors' wealth. It is consistent with for-profit corporations yielding to prevalent ideologies and customs. Thus, the existence of forces that push corporations to pursue other goals by ostracism or by imposing ESG (environmental, social, governance) reporting requirements that facilitate ostracism is consistent with our conclusion. We note the inherent problems with these other goals given assumptions 3 and 4.

It is a positive conclusion in the sense that, given these assumptions, corporations chartered to maximize shareholder value tend to act to do so. If they deviate from shareholder value maximization, they will face costs not borne by their competitors. These costs will reduce shareholder returns, and their shareholders will seek other opportunities. The remainder of this appendix elaborates on this logic.

How can society incorporate the alternative objectives that are the passions of many individuals, who might also be shareholders? Forming a consensus might be impossible (Arrow, 1951; Gibbard, 1973; Satterthwaite, 1975). Still, competing objectives espoused by shareholders and members of society are, in our opinion, the purview of politics. We recognize that politics and law are imperfect avenues to convert these competing shareholder objectives into restraints on firm actions. Politics is fraught with challenges encountered in motivating the electorate, acting either directly or through elected representatives, and bringing about change that reflects the collective (majority) will. However, we argue here that the political route dominates the alternative of expecting managers to understand and pursue a multiplicity of objectives.

While we champion shareholder value maximization, our position is *not* that society's only goal should be the unconstrained pursuit of wealth. Hyman Roth is one Hollywood avatar of this position. When discussing the murder of Moe Green with Michael Corleone, he says, "This is the business we've chosen. I didn't ask who gave the order, because it had *nothing to do with business*" (Coppola, 1974). The rule of law is necessary to prevent coercion and fraud. Laws, ethics, and custom, as well as competition, constrain the actions of a corporation. Examples of legal constraints include prohibitions of bribery, child labor, and forced labor. Ethical principles, such as honesty, keeping one's word, and the sanctity of human life, constrain individual behavior in situations ill-suited for state interference. Still, shareholder value maximization remains the objective, *subject to these constraints and future constraints, as the society's objectives evolve into new laws and ethical customs.*

In section A.2, we expand on the economic consequences of the shareholder value maximization principle and address the issues of monopoly and externalities. In section A.3, we describe the problems corporate managers face if they seek to pursue goals other than shareholder value maximization, including the difficulty of weighing competing shareholder preferences and the incompatibility of other goals with the forces of competition in input, output, and capital markets. We discuss exploitation of other stakeholders, management incentive conflicts, and behavioral biases in sections A.4, A.5, and A.6, respectively. Section A.7 offers concluding remarks.

A.2. Economic Rationale for the Shareholder Value Maximization Principle

The idea that firms should act to increase firm value (and thereby increase social welfare) is longstanding and fundamental to economics. It was, perhaps, most famously championed by Friedman (1962, 1970). The notion is premised on the belief that incentives influence individuals' actions and the recognition that resources are scarce. From scarcity follows the inescapable conclusion that the firm lacks the means to fully satisfy the demands of all its stakeholders (e.g., customers, workers, suppliers, capital providers, and the local community). Therefore, any method used to decide who gets what will result in unmet needs and dissatisfaction. Conceding the inevitability of trade-offs forces the line of inquiry toward favoring a method that will create incentives for individuals to maximize the size of the pie, rather than seeking some utopian solution that will meet all unmet needs. In this light, shareholder value maximization seems better than any alternative means of guiding decisions.

Friedman (1970) and Jensen (2001) reason that value maximization leads to social welfare maximization absent externalities and monopoly rents, though Jensen points out that the idea is at least two hundred years old (Smith, 1776). Their logic proceeds along the following lines: Prices of inputs/outputs reflect opportunity costs. Value maximization implies that the value of output sold exceeds the opportunity cost of inputs used. The point is better seen in the case of a sole proprietorship, whose owner seeks to maximize the present value of long-term profits. The social benefit of this organization can be measured by the difference between the price she can sell products for and what it costs her to produce them. In maximizing the present value of her expected future profits, the sole proprietor maximizes social welfare. Each sole proprietor making the best use of her resources, including the possibility of combining resources with others, makes the best use of the society's resources.

The welfare implications of shareholder value maximization hinge on the existence of competition. In addition, law enforcement is presumed, which is another way of saying that managers are expected to adhere to laws and ethics. Below we summarize the issues that arise from monopolies and externalities, as they relate to shareholder value maximization. The criticisms that remain even after we address monopolies and externalities are the subject of sections A.3 to A.6.

A.2.1. Monopolies

Monopoly implies that the firm faces a downward sloping demand curve that allows it to select a price by choosing a quantity. Firms with monopoly power select prices that maximize profits. Equilibrium unit prices thus exceed the marginal production cost, and consumers who value the product above the marginal production cost but below the price do not purchase the product. At first glance, a welfare loss results. This leads to the conclusion that shareholder value maximization should be curtailed by regulation to prevent the welfare loss and allow consumers the opportunity to purchase the product at marginal cost plus an allowance for capital costs. However, further consideration reveals that the net welfare loss has not been demonstrated, because this ex-post analysis fails to consider ex-ante incentives. Moreover, intervention to curtail monopoly requires self-interested parties to make this intractable calculation and to implement the policy. In this way, intervention itself creates the potential for welfare loss.

To expand on these issues, first note that the consequences of monopoly are not prima facie negative. Entrepreneurs discover new ways to combine resources and earn returns that exceed those that can be earned by alternative uses of these resources. These "economic rents" exist because the entrepreneur initially has a monopoly. Rents created in this way reflect value added, and the potential for these rents stimulates innovation.

Intellectual property protections (e.g., patent protection, copyright protection, and trade-secret protection) are examples of laws designed to reward investments in innovation. The laws recognize that if entry by competitors cannot be blocked, these rents will dissipate and risk-taking will be discouraged. In short, ex-post monopoly profits are the prize that encourages innovation and an investment that improves social welfare.[8] If individuals expect this prize to be taken away when their efforts yield success, they will reconsider expending efforts in the first place. To justify intervention and removal of rents, the regulator must be able to show that there is too much investment in innovation. That is, the prizes are too big because they stimulate too much effort. Obviously, this case is tough to make when the efforts focus on drugs that cure cancer (or prevent hair loss).[9] Alternatively, the regulator might argue that those engaging in this effort had no idea the potential payoff would be so large and therefore they have no right to the rewards. In either case, we suggest that such assertions rest on shaky ground. We cannot anticipate all circumstances, and one might imagine that such claims can be supported in limited cases—but in conceding this point, we hope that we have moved the reader away from the initial conclusion that monopolies indicate a loss in social welfare.[10]

Second, "rent creation" differs from "rent seeking." In the latter case, an individual generates monopoly rents by, for example, lobbying for laws that block entrants. Of course, potential entrants will also lobby to reverse the legislation. Monopolies and the lobbying surrounding them destroy value, rather than generating it (Buchanan, 1999). Granting the government indefinite power to interfere in markets spawns rent seeking by market participants eager to use this authority to maintain rents. Moreover, politicians tend to favor the many who might benefit in the short run by forcing the reduction of drug prices. In contrast, the drugs lost by reduced innovation are unseen and receive little consideration in the political realm. Thus, even if one could demonstrate that ex-post payoffs are too large and we can imagine circumstances where curtailing shareholder value maximization in monopoly increases social welfare, the expected benefit of these cases must be weighed against the expected costs of rent-seeking regulation that would arise.

A.2.2. Externalities

Externalities are costs and benefits that are not borne or reaped by the parties in the transaction. The classic example is pollution. A's factory emits smoke that harms B. In seeking to increase shareholder value, A need not consider potential costs to B. Unless

---

[8] Nobel laureate William Nordhaus estimated that "only a minuscule fraction of the social returns from technological advances over the 1948–2001 period was captured by producers, indicating that most of the benefits of technological change are passed on to consumers" (Nordhaus, 2004). See also Kessler (2020).

[9] A related issue is whether rents net of efforts in some markets are positive in expectation. If so, individuals expect to receive more compensation than necessary to encourage innovation. Whether such situations persist in competitive markets is controversial. Competition implies that more resources will be devoted in these situations to innovation, reducing expected rents. The controversy is difficult to resolve because measuring excess compensation in expectation is difficult. An example of this controversy can be seen in the debate surrounding stock market efficiency.

[10] For example, regulators might stop firms from merging to gain monopoly rents, arguing that such mergers do not enhance welfare but merely serve as a means to gain pricing power. Similarly, natural monopolies are thought to exist. These allow a single firm to gain pricing power that more than compensates it for its efforts.

A internalizes these costs, its decisions will not reflect the net social-welfare effect. The issue of externalities requires further elaboration, because it initially appears an insuperable obstacle to linking shareholder value maximization to social welfare.

Many externalities are checked by assigning property rights or by accepted custom in a society. But some externalities remain unaddressed because property rights cannot be assigned, coordination problems make it too costly to meaningfully account for the externalities, or both. These are discussed in section A.3.

A.2.2.1. Assigning Property Rights to Resolve the Problem of Externalities

We argue that externalities do not imply a prima facie case against the social-welfare benefits of shareholder value maximization.[11] We make the following points: (1) externalities are ubiquitous, (2) their net effect on social welfare is difficult to assess, (3) their existence suggests either that it is impossible to assign property rights or that the costs of assigning and enforcing these rights exceed the social benefit, and (4) regulatory intervention does not necessarily reduce the costs of assigning and enforcing these rights. The unaddressed externalities are the subject of the next section.

To expand on the first and second points, note that granting or allowing individuals to acquire rights leads to a profusion of externalities. The exercise of a right by one person tends to affect others. Returning to our example, imagine that A acquires a bundle of rights related to building and operating a factory, such as the right to obstruct B's view and the right of factory employees to drive by B's property. These might be negative externalities to B, but the factory can also create positive externalities. Another property owner C might find her property values enhanced as factory employees move into town. The family members of the business owner might use their wealth to build an art museum and park (e.g., Crystal Bridges Museum of American Art, Bentonville, Arkansas, funded by the heirs to the Walmart fortune), which might generate a positive externality for the local residents. Isolating a single externality is easy. Evaluating the net effect of all externalities arising from A's action is complex. Thus, the dominance of negative externalities is not an inevitable consequence of firms pursuing shareholder value maximization. Still, the negative effects of some externalities might dominate. These are the subject of discussion below.

To take the third point, some externalities can be addressed through the creation of transferable property rights. In our example, if the cost to B from air pollution is less than A's cost of reducing that pollution, A would retain the right to pollute by compensating B for B's costs. Thus, A's operating decisions account for the costs of the externality. Social welfare losses arising from negative externalities would be resolved. This, however, may not always be feasible. According to Coase, transaction costs thwart internalization of externalities via assignment of property rights. In this example, practicalities might prevent A and B from settling the pollution problem through an enforceable contract accompanied by payments. These costs include coordinating the parties who might wish to trade, establishing legally enforceable property rights, drawing up contracts, negotiating terms, and monitoring and enforcing contracts. Many of these costs arise from inadequate information regarding costs and benefits.

---

[11] This discussion relies on Coase (1988).

A.2.2.2. Challenges in Assigning Property Rights

The pollution example (expanded to include many factories like A's and the world population of Bs from hundreds of nations) seems to cry out for a nonmarket resolution. Many parties are damaged by the pollution from A's factory, but they cannot easily coordinate their response. Measuring the damage caused to them is costly, and the costs of mitigation are unclear. These circumstances seem ripe for a regulatory remedy. However, we caution that the social welfare effects of nonmarket methods of investigation and administration are unclear. The key issue is whether a method of determining social welfare effects, allocating rights, and administering and enforcing the arrangement are more efficient. For example, simply preventing A from building a factory without collecting data on relative benefits would involve little transaction cost, but the net effect on all parties would be unclear. Local government might offer a means to aggregate preferences and thus estimate the net externalities imposed on the community by the operation of the factory. However, granting power to politicians to justify taxes and regulations, based on abstract grounds like social welfare, can lead to abuse of power.[12]

The impossibility of assigning all existing rights to individuals in a way that allows for trading and pricing of these rights and the internalization of externalities stems from a more fundamental underlying issue that is central to objections to shareholder value maximization. Markets are incomplete and imperfect (e.g., the global market for pollution caused by fossil fuels, cows in the dairy industry, and other sources). Incomplete and imperfect markets are characterized by transaction costs; information asymmetries between buyers and sellers; liquidity constraints that prevent individuals from executing trades; noncompetitive markets for all assets, securities, and claims; or a combination of these.[13] In markets that are not sufficiently rich, a decision that increases shareholder value might not be Pareto optimal. Some shareholder preferences cannot be priced, and some shareholders might be harmed; their losses cannot be remedied by compensating transactions with shareholders who benefit.

Still, we acknowledge that the unaddressed negative externalities warrant a solution that would entail constraints on shareholder value maximization. The next section expands on this idea and explains why politics is the proper venue for imposing these constraints.

A.3. Why Shareholder Value Maximization Despite Other Objectives

An important objection to shareholder value maximization is that shareholders have preferences aside from increasing the present value of future cash flows and that the value maximization mandate ignores these objectives. For example, shareholders' altruism and desire for social or self-esteem can lead to prosocial behavior (Bénabou and Tirole, 2010; Authers, 2015; Fink, 2018; Pozen, 2018). We describe and critique three avenues of incorporating shareholders' other preferences. First, managers can attempt to gather

---

[12] Alternative solutions might also include a market for emission credits that allows firms with high costs of reducing emissions to trade with low-cost firms and common law adjudication that makes A liable for damages to B.

[13] More precise definitions can be found in Fama and Miller (1972), Mas-Colell, Whinston, and Green (1995), Magill and Quinzii (1996), and Beaver (1998).

information on shareholder preferences, aggregate them, and seek a goal produced by the weights assigned to these preferences (e.g., Hart and Zingales, 2017). We are skeptical of these kinds of solutions but are mindful that these nonfinancial preferences are real and deserve to be addressed. Second, in some cases, shareholders can incorporate other preferences by choosing an organizational form suitable to engaging in activities likely to generate significant nontradable benefits (e.g., sports franchises or charitable work). Finally, we argue that the political realm is a more appropriate venue for addressing other shareholder preferences.

To develop these points, we start with a simple example in which the other preferences are separable from the value maximization. We then describe settings in which the preferences are not separable from the value maximization principle, which tempts many to suggest that managers (or corporations) should pursue other objectives (e.g., a socially conscious corporation).

In our discussion of separability, we do not address the possibility that managers, because of personal malice or bounded rationality, might fail to adopt policies consistent with shareholder value maximization. These issues are addressed in sections A.5 and A.6. For example, one might argue that treating workers with dignity increases profits.[14] We argue that if managers mistreat workers out of malice, thereby destroying shareholder value, competition can limit this behavior inasmuch as it punishes managers who prefer more costly production techniques and thus helps change practices.[15] This mistreatment is an incentive alignment problem—managers' incentives are not aligned with shareholders'—an issue we address in section A.5.

Managers might also mistreat workers because of bounded rationality. Perhaps managers do not recognize the negative shareholder value effects of worker mistreatment because they mistakenly overweight short-term performance or because the governance system (e.g., quarterly earnings targets) encourages them to do so. In this case, behavioral biases might inhibit the competitive process that rewards firms that appropriately weight both the short and long term. Overemphasis on the short run is one of many potential behavioral biases, and we address the possibility that learning does not occur because of behavioral biases in section A.6.

A.3.1. Shareholders' Other Preferences Separable from Value Maximization

Consider an economy in which managers must take into account individual shareholders' preferences for cars as compared to trucks when determining the firm's production mixture of cars and trucks. The counterargument to this proposition is that the firm can maximize profits, and the shareholder can use these profits toward the purchase of a car or truck. This argument assumes that shareholders' preferences are separable from value maximization because markets exist for cars and trucks, independent of the manager's

---

[14] Jim Sinegal, Costco's president and chief executive, said, "The last thing I want people to believe is that I don't care about the shareholder. . . . But I happen to believe that in order to reward the shareholder in the long term, you have to please your customers and workers" (Zimmerman, 2004).

[15] Of course, regulatory barriers can inhibit this process, despite the preferences of private firms (e.g., Carmody, 1968). Here we betray a suspicion of the value of advice offered by those with no skin in the game who believe that they know better than the manager does.

decision. The more general economic proposition is that complete and perfect markets permit a separation between the firm's production decisions and shareholder tastes (Fisher, 1930). In perfect capital markets, maximizing the value of the resources available to the shareholders is generally equivalent to maximizing the utility of the shareholders (Fama and Miller, 1972). Given that a management choice increases the value of the firm, shareholders can be compensated by side payments (taken from the increase in value) for any loss they might suffer, with a residual remaining to make at least one shareholder better off. This separation (or decentralization) property allows managers to avoid the difficult task of aggregating shareholders' preferences.[16]

A.3.2. Shareholders' Other Preferences Inseparable from Value Maximization

Another argument against shareholder value maximization, given diverse shareholder preferences, is that markets are imperfect.[17] Therefore individual shareholders may not wish managers to maximize value, and markets may not be rich enough to accommodate this preference. The importance of the divergence between what each shareholder would want and what he or she would receive, given that managers pursue value maximization, then becomes the point of contention. For example, in the case where making money conflicts with externalities of concern to shareholders (e.g., pollution), shareholder value maximization does not lead to shareholder welfare maximization (Hart and Zingales, 2017). Hart and Zingales propose using shareholder votes to aggregate individual preferences. While this solution might appeal theoretically, it is unlikely to guide managers in day-to-day operations for reasons we discuss in section A.3.4. Moreover, legal scholars have long noted that "few retail investors vote their stock, and the mechanics of the voting process rarely make it rational for them to do so" (Fisch, 2017, p. 60).

A.3.3. Choice of Organization Form to Incorporate Other Preferences

The importance of the divergence in shareholders' preferences depends on the circumstances. In situations where operations create large, nontradable assets that can be controlled by certain shareholders, conflicts arise. For example, assume a firm is a professional sports franchise, and the controlling owners enjoy benefits incidental to their management responsibilities (e.g., socializing with famous athletes, attending sporting events, or garnering publicity and fame). In such a firm, the controlling shareholders might resist management decisions that increase firm value but reduce their own benefits (e.g., trading

---

[16] Milgrom and Roberts (1992) note that total value maximization achieves efficiency in the absence of "wealth effects" (i.e., when individuals' payoffs are fully transferable). Hart (1979) demonstrates that the essential condition for shareholders' unanimous preference for firm value maximization is perfect competition (rather than market completeness). DeAngelo (1981, p. 26) notes that "unanimity theorems which establish strict preference rather than unanimous indifference must rely on a partial-equilibrium concept of competition."

[17] The addition of uncertainty creates further difficulties (e.g., Fama, 1971; Sandmo, 1971), suggesting that shareholder value maximization and social welfare maximization are not coextensive.

a famous but underperforming player or moving to a more profitable but less glamorous market). The organizational form that emerges is a firm with a small group of owners (or just one individual owner). The cost of pursuing objectives other than value maximization is then internalized by the owners with those preferences.

Another example of how the choice of organization can internalize shareholder preferences and reduce disagreement can be seen in the supplier of the abortion drug Mifeprex for use in the United States. The drug's distributor is a private company supported by private foundations. Thus, at the outset, its purpose was not shareholder value maximization. The firm's medical director says, "A lot of what we're about is not driven by the profit motive." According to an individual familiar with the company, "It's extremely unusual. Only people who are truly dedicated to 'the cause' would have stuck with it. The unique thing here is how everybody [involved] has a shared vision" (O'Harrow, 2000).

In short, different organization forms can be used to accommodate disagreement with regard to the value maximization criterion that can exist between potential investors. Shareholders seeking to maximize the value of their investment invest in publicly traded corporations with diffuse ownership. These firms might confine their operations to realms where significant nontradable assets and significant shareholder disagreements are less likely to arise. In this way, corporations with distributed ownership might arise only when the nontradable asset problem is minor. Such organizations would then behave as if shareholders' other preferences do not affect corporate decisions.

Still, the choice of the organizational form might not fully address the challenge of conflicting shareholder preferences. If so, managers might be prodded to pursue another objective or multiple objectives simultaneously. We next discuss the drawbacks of this approach.

A.3.4. Intractability of Managers Pursuing Other Objectives

If shareholders were willing to sacrifice wealth to achieve other objectives, pursuit of other objectives seems the logical solution. However, any other proposed objective will also be subject to the problem of diverse preferences. Thus, the impossibility of achieving shareholder consensus with regard to any choice of management action applies to any decision criterion.

The following example illustrates the intractable conflicts that arise when a corporate manager attempts to pursue specific goals in addition to value maximization. Assume that some or all of the shareholders of an electric company dislike their company's use of coal-powered electricity and are willing to forgo value (i.e., shareholder value) to install wind power. Assume that this investment is a negative NPV investment—not to belittle wind power but to create a conflict between shareholder preferences and the NPV-maximization objective.[18]

The wind-power investment raises three issues. First, the firm's managers have no means of knowing how much they should invest in the negative NPV alternative. Managers do not know how much wealth shareholders wish to forgo to avoid coal power.

[18] One might object that firms overemphasize short-term targets to the detriment of shareholder value. This might occur if the firm operates in an environment where it does not compete for shareholder investment or because behavioral biases prevent stock prices from fully incorporating cash flows beyond a given horizon. We discuss the implications of competition and behavioral biases in section A.6.

Some shareholders might have relatives living in coal-rich places. Some investors might flinch at harm to birds caused by wind turbines. We might ask managers to collect these preferences from shareholders, but aggregating all non-wealth-increasing preferences across investors (including future investors) would be a refractory problem. To add to the complication, shareholder ownership changes daily for most corporations, and mutual funds, which account for much of the ownership for many large firms, represent millions of indirect owners.

Second, the firm resides in a competitive market for inputs, outputs, and financing. If wind power is costlier, either the firm passes the extra cost to customers in the form of higher prices, or shareholders might accept lower returns. However, unless customers too are enthusiastic about wind power, they might, in a competitive industry, gravitate to firms that offer cheaper power. And even if shareholders would accept a lower rate of return, managers must also consider the possibility that the firm will need additional financing. In a competitive environment, managers cannot pass the cost of non-wealth-increasing decisions on to shareholders or other stakeholders. At some point, the burden of non-wealth-increasing decisions crushes the firm. The inability of managers and boards to convert non-wealth-increasing shareholder preferences into a measure that can guide decisions, amid competitive pressures, suggests that increasing shareholder value will be the managers' primary goal.

Third, managers themselves are motivated to maximize profitability to maximize their own compensation and advance their careers. In competitive product and labor markets, nudging or hectoring individual managers might not induce them to pursue nonfinancial objectives. This challenge, in principle, can be tempered by tying management compensation to multiple factors, which could include financial and nonfinancial metrics.

These problems suggest that the imposition of non-wealth-maximizing constraints on managers' choices might be best left under the purview of politics.[19] While aggregating preferences remains a problem even in political systems (Arrow, 1951; Gibbard, 1973; Satterthwaite, 1975), by requiring all firms to use wind power, the political system can alleviate the competitive disadvantage facing wind-power users—at least in the country imposing the constraint.[20] Legal limits on managers' choices do not contradict the view that existing firms should act to increase owner wealth. Instead, these limits act as constraints on the actions available to achieve this increase. For example, many states prohibit direct sales from automobile manufacturers to consumers (Crane, 2016). We predict that manufacturers will act to increase shareholder value, subject to this constraint. The efficiency of a manufacturer-dealer operation, relative to a vertically integrated manufacturer, is irrelevant to our prediction, because vertical integration is prohibited.

---

[19] Friedman (1970) does not place ethical constraints in the political realm in that he argues for shareholder value maximization, subject to ethical constraints and law. It seems unlikely that the only way or the most efficient way to ensure good behavior by managers is government penalties. Culture, community norms, and religion are other means.

[20] Hart and Zingales (2017) argue that shareholder votes substitute for political votes and avoid losses that occur when government actions cannot erase corporate harm. The relative efficiency and consistency achieved by citizen voting, compared to ownership-weighted corporate voting, is unclear. Yet the unsustainability of non-wealth-maximizing constraints on individual corporations in a competitive environment seems an obstacle to shareholder-imposed constraints.

We acknowledge that diffuse voters with their limited resources have difficulty in coalescing to enact laws that would codify their objectives in the form of a law that would constrain corporate behavior (Hart and Zingales, 2017).[21] To make matters worse, firms and industries are well organized and well resourced to lobby against the passage of such laws (i.e., constraints).[22] Our limited point is that if the electorate has difficulty enacting laws that reflect its preferences, it is even less likely that a diffuse and changing group of shareholders could meaningfully elicit value-reducing corporate conduct in a competitive industry.[23]

A.4. Exploitation of Other Stakeholders

Another objection to shareholder value maximization is that firms might transfer wealth from other stakeholders to shareholders. The combination of price-protection and competitive markets for inputs, customers, and capital limits these transfers. For example, airlines might reduce seat sizes to increase plane capacity and reduce per-passenger costs, passing the increased profits on to shareholders. But if air travel is competitive, either (1) passengers will react to these changes by demanding lower ticket prices or increased seat sizes or making other travel plans, or (2) other airlines will follow suit but lower their prices to lure customers. Similar reasoning applies if the airline tries to cut pilot pay and pass the savings onto shareholders if the market for pilot services is competitive.

Price protection implies that the residual claimant (shareholder) bears the cost for losses arising from expected wealth transfers. Price protection means that other stakeholders anticipate the potential for shareholders to seek wealth transfers after contracting and build these transfers into the price. If so, shareholders will bond themselves or otherwise prevent themselves from taking actions whose sole purpose is to transfer wealth after contracting, because shareholders will not gain from retaining the freedom to make transfers and will absorb any damage to firm value caused by executing the transfer. For example, assume that shareholders can transfer wealth from bondholders by paying liquidating dividends. Bondholders will anticipate these transfers and add their expected effects to the debt's interest rate or refuse to lend. Thus, the expected gain from these transfers is zero. Moreover, if the anticipated transfers entail liquidation of profitable investments, shareholders would lose this value.

[21] The desirability of greater ease in enacting laws is not clear. Federalist No. 10 (Madison, 1787) notes that "the violence of the majority faction" is a drawback of direct democracy and discusses the use of competing factions as a way to control powerful interests. Hayek (1944) says that intellectuals might believe they achieve their ends by supporting tyrants, but tyrants, once in power, might not obey intellectuals. See, for example, the support of Ezra Pound, widely regarded as one of the most influential poets of the twentieth century, for Mussolini (Rainey, 1999).

[22] This is a variation of the regulatory capture argument. See Peltzman (1976), Becker (1983), and Dal Bó (2006).

[23] Rajan (2020) makes a similar observation: "Some corporations have taken things even further, such as by developing sustainability guidelines for themselves and their suppliers in the absence of state regulations. Collective acts of corporate *noblesse oblige* are worrisome: guidelines that large players can easily meet may keep out smaller market entrants, and nobly intentioned buyers may form 'cartels' to squeeze suppliers. As such, it would be better if corporations pressed elected governments to regulate, rather than acting on their own."

These arguments focus on the forces countervailing shareholder attempts to exploit other stakeholders. One might still wonder whether it would be socially desirable for shareholders to transfer wealth to other stakeholders, such as workers or customers, if such transfers were somehow feasible.[24] If prices from competitive markets capture opportunity costs and benefits, these transfers would waste society's resources. For example, assume the firm pays employees a higher-than-market rate at the sacrifice of shareholder value. This profligacy acts as a subsidy that retains the scarce resource of employee labor in a less attractive project, squandering a valuable resource that might be better used elsewhere. Similarly, lower prices to customers at the expense of shareholders (if possible) would lead customers to consume too much of the firm's product. Customers would fail to internalize the cost of producing the firm's products or services.

A.5. Incentive Conflicts between Shareholders and Managers

Separation of ownership (shareholders) and control (managers) is a fundamental characteristic of large public firms (Jensen and Meckling, 1976). The challenge, as a result of this separation, is that managers may not act in the best interests of the shareholders. We summarize this well-known agency problem and quickly move to the more important question of the implication of this agency relationship for the shareholder value maximization principle.

In a corporation, shareholders are principals and hire managers as their agents to run the company. In this framework, the goal of the principal (i.e., shareholders) is to maximize shareholder value. The agent (manager) is expected to maximize her own objective function. That the agent maximizes her own utility can affect equilibrium outcomes, but it would not alter the principal's objective function. The principal therefore offers an employment contract to the manager that induces her to act in the best interests of the shareholders. This alignment of interests is formalized in a large literature in contract theory. (See Bolton and Dewatripont [2005] for an excellent summary.) In a typical setting, with rational behavior and perfect contract enforcement, the principal and agent agree to an employment contract that maximizes shareholder value because it takes into consideration two conditions: (1) individual rationality, i.e., the manager earns her reservation utility (compensation that matches the best outside option or opportunity cost),[25] and (2) incentive compatibility, that is, the manager either selects only the contract that is designed to her type (under hidden information) or supplies the efficient level of effort given the cost of effort and risk aversion of the agent (under hidden actions). The solution to this constrained optimization problem produces an optimal contract that maximizes shareholder value, despite the agency conflict between shareholders and managers. The shareholder value achieved in this

---

[24] Zingales (2019) argues that such wealth transfers from shareholders to other stakeholders constitute a form of taxation without representation. Bebchuk and Tallarita (2021) note that "stakeholderism" would increase the insulation of corporate leaders from shareholders, reduce their accountability, and hurt economic performance. Berle (1932, p. 1367) famously noted that "you can not abandon emphasis on 'the view that business corporations exist for the sole purpose of making profits for their stockholders' until such time as you are prepared to offer a clear and reasonably enforceable scheme of responsibilities to someone else."

[25] This statement assumes that the firm has all the bargaining power in a competitive labor market.

optimization problem is second best, in that it is lower than the maximized shareholder value in the absence of agency problems.[26]

There are two takeaways from this discussion. First, managers, despite agency problems, would advance the objective of shareholder value maximization, albeit imperfectly. Second—and more important—these problems are not a unique feature of the shareholder value maximization objective. They would exist no matter what objectives the principals (i.e., shareholders or voters) want their agents (i.e., managers, elected officials, or bureaucrats) to pursue.

A.6. Behavioral Biases

Psychology suggests that individuals making decisions are subject to systematic errors, reflecting limits to their cognitive ability (e.g., Kahneman, 2011; Hanlon, Yeung, and Zuo, 2022). These errors or biases raise two concerns with regard to the social welfare implications of the shareholder value maximization principle. First, they might cause individual managers' decisions to deviate from the path of value maximization, even if value maximization is their intended goal. Rigorous competition in the managerial labor market can limit these errors by stifling the careers of managers more prone to judgment errors. Competition among firms can alert managers to their misjudgments. Learning and expertise can limit these mistakes (Bronnenberg et al., 2015; Caplin and Dean, 2015). Ultimately, the explanatory power of these biases for managers' decisions in a given context is an empirical question. To the extent that such biases apply, they are equally applicable to any objective that shareholders or society impose on managers. For example, a halo bias could affect a superior evaluating a good-looking subordinate's effectiveness, whether that subordinate was charged with increasing profits or increasing community outreach. Likewise, the claim that managers have a bias toward short-term performance has a long history (e.g., Keynes, 1935), though the existence and economic impact of this bias remain debatable (see Roe, 2018). However, even if managers were to suffer from short-termism, it would manifest in their decisions aimed at furthering other goals in life in addition to shareholder value maximization. For example, managers assigned to produce electric cars might overweight immediate benefits for local pollution and underweight the long-term environmental consequences of battery production and disposal.

A second concern is that biases are pervasive, and competition in labor, product, and capital markets is thus constrained, so that prices no longer accurately indicate value or opportunity cost. The inadequacy of prices undermines the link between shareholder value maximization and welfare maximization. However, regardless of one's assessment of whether prices reflect opportunity costs, the inability of markets to provide an adequate indicator of costs and benefits challenges a manager, regardless of her objectives. If the manager believes that shareholders prefer clean energy and wants to decide whether to put solar panels on the corporate headquarters or install windmills, she cannot rely on stock prices or relative equipment costs to inform her of the shareholder welfare implications of her decision. For example, she cannot know whether she is responding

---

[26] This economic analysis explains why, in practice, we might observe outcomes consistent with managers placing their interests above those of shareholders. For example, managers might misuse company aircraft (Yermack, 2006). The cost to shareholders of preventing all misuse can exceed the cost of allowing some misuse.

to shareholder preferences driven by affect bias, which might therefore be mistaken.[27] In short, implementing other objectives does not stamp out behavioral biases. It simply suggests that managers must be prudent and circumspect, regardless of their objective.

A.7. Concluding Remarks

Criticism of shareholder value maximization may arise because of a distaste for the concept as a normative proposition, despite the fact that the proposition predicts firm behavior. That is, we face a disagreement about values disguised as a disagreement about facts. Shareholder value maximization is an efficient means to maximize societal wealth. That doesn't mean society's sole or principal goal should be to maximize wealth. A kinder, freer, more just and peaceful society is unlikely to be reached solely by increasing wealth. Advocates of those objectives have worthy arguments.[28]

But we maintain that managers seeking to increase shareholder value are not acting immorally per se. Therefore, we take issue with demonizing managers for taking steps to increase shareholder value while staying within law. A competitive economy reduces the chances that the firm will flourish if it pursues other objectives. In addition, managers do not have the means to distill the varied preferences of present and future shareholders into an objective function that could feasibly serve as a guide for decision-making. Other objectives then become the purview of the political, cultural, and ethical realms. Advocates of other objectives must persuade other citizens to embrace their opinions and passions. Of course, demonizing managers, companies, and industries solely because they pursue shareholder value maximization might be an effective (though groundless) means of persuasion.

The possibility that CEOs might engage in mercenary behavior is real, and therefore checks and balances are essential to ensure competition in markets and legal (and ethical) behavior on the part of managers. Adam Smith's dim view of businessmen suggests that one must distinguish between defending capitalism and apologizing for capitalists: "People of the same trade seldom meet together, even for merriment and diversion, but the conversation ends in a conspiracy against the public, or in some contrivance to raise prices" (Smith, 1776, p. 105). Likewise, we recognize the necessity of a moral code and laws to set bounds on permissible shareholder value–increasing actions. However, the necessity of moral boundaries is not a shortcoming of shareholder value

---

[27] "Affect" refers to emotions (such as fear and anger) and moods (such as happiness and sadness) and can lead to biased cognition (Forgas, 1995).

[28] Rousseau (1750) argues that civilization decreases human happiness, even if it increases wealth, because it engenders vain appetites and inequality: "So long as government and law provide for the security and well-being of men in their common life, the arts, literature and the sciences, less despotic though perhaps more powerful, fling garlands of flowers over the chains which weigh them down. They stifle in men's breasts that sense of original liberty, for which they seem to have been born; cause them to love their own slavery, and so make of them what is called a civilised people." Obviously, such arguments raise moral issues beyond the scope of this Appendix. Our discussion is limited to practical and Pareto considerations. We note these points because we suspect that many object to shareholder value maximization because of the more basic reasons that Rousseau voiced. The interested reader can find a defense of commercial society and the pursuit of wealth in Hobbes (1651, Chapters 6 and 16), Voltaire (1736), and Smith (1776). They are suspicious of man's nature and the consequences of societies impelled by "higher" moral ends. Wilson (1995) argues that organizing production primarily through privately owned firms and voluntary exchanges provides a protected place for people desirous of making controversial proposals.

maximization. Any alternative goal is similarly incomplete without ethical constraints. Moreover, we are all tempted to give our needs the patina of "morality" to forestall consideration of trade-offs necessary to meet them. After all, the prohibition against the murder of an innocent man is not subject to a cost-benefit analysis. Moral arguments must be countered with moral arguments. They cannot be refuted by efficiency (or even practical) arguments. Stakeholders will be inclined to make moral claims to stymie discussion.

Moreover, shareholder value maximization is not incompatible with strategies that, for example, take into account sustainability, the firm's local community, or customer and employee satisfaction (Bhagat and Hubbard, 2020; Edmans, 2020). If paying attention to sustainability increases firm value, that is what managers will (and should) do. Shareholder value maximization would be the criterion managers apply in deciding how much to invest in "socially responsible activities," similar to any other corporate investment decision they make.

References

Arrow, K. J., 1951. *Social Choice and Individual Values*. John Wiley & Sons, New York City, New York.

Atkins, P. S., 2018. California public employees vote against pension-fund activism. *Wall Street Journal*. October 18.

Authers, J., 2015. Responsible investment: Vice versus nice. *Financial Times*. June 25.

Beaver, W. H., 1998. *Financial Reporting: An Accounting Revolution*. Prentice Hall, Upper Saddle River, New Jersey.

Bebchuk, L. A., Tallarita, R., 2021. The illusory promise of stakeholder governance. *Cornell Law Review* 106 (1), 91–178.

Becker, G. S., 1983. A theory of competition among pressure groups for political influence. *Quarterly Journal of Economics* 98 (3), 371–400.

Bénabou, R., Tirole, J., 2010. Individual and corporate social responsibility. *Economica* 77, 1–19.

Benoit, D., 2019. Move over, shareholders: Top CEOs say companies have obligations to society. *Wall Street Journal*. August 19.

Berle, A. A., 1932. For whom corporate managers are trustees: A note. *Harvard Law Review* 45 (7), 1365–1372.

Bhagat, S., Hubbard, R. G., 2020. Should the modern corporation maximize shareholder value? *AEI Economic Perspectives*. September 10.

Bolton, P., Dewatripont, M., 2005. *Contract Theory*. MIT Press, Cambridge, Massachusetts.

Bronnenberg, B. J., Dubé, J.-P., Gentzkow, M., Shapiro, J. M., 2015. Do pharmacists buy Bayer? Informed shoppers and the brand premium. *Quarterly Journal of Economics* 130 (4), 1669–1726.

Buchanan, J., 1999. *The Logical Foundations of Constitutional Liberty*. Liberty Fund, Indianapolis, Indiana.

Caplin, A., Dean, M., 2015. Revealed preference, rational inattention, and costly information acquisition. *American Economic Review* 105 (7), 2183–2203.

Carmody, D., 1968. Negro group is ordered to halt bus service here. *New York Times*. January 3.

Coase, R. H., 1988. The nature of the firm: Origin. *Journal of Law, Economics, & Organization* 4 (1), 3–17.

Coppola, F. F., 1974. *The Godfather Part II*. Paramount Pictures, Los Angeles, California.

Crane, D., 2016. Tesla, dealer franchise laws, and the politics of crony capitalism. *Iowa Law Review* 101 (2), 573–607.

Dal Bó, E., 2006. Regulatory capture: A review. *Oxford Review of Economic Policy* 22 (2), 203–225.

DeAngelo, H., 1981. Competition and unanimity. *American Economic Review* 71 (1), 18–27.

Edmans, A., 2020. *Grow the Pie: How Great Companies Deliver Both Purpose and Profit*. Cambridge University Press, Cambridge, United Kingdom.

Fama, E. F., 1971. Risk, return, and equilibrium. *Journal of Political Economy* 79 (1), 30–55.

Fama, E. F., Miller, M. H., 1972. *The Theory of Finance*. Dryden Press, Hinsdale, Illinois.

Fink, L., 2018. Larry Fink's annual letter to CEOs. A sense of purpose. Retrieved from https://www.blackrock.com/corporate/investor-relations/larry-fink-ceo-letter.

Fisch, J. E., 2017. Standing voting instructions: Empowering the excluded retail investor. *Minnesota Law Review* 102, 11–60.

Fisher, I., 1930. *The Theory of Interest*. Macmillan, New York City, New York.

Forgas, J. P., 1995. Mood and judgment: The affect infusion model (AIM). *Psychological Bulletin* 117 (1), 39–66.

Friedman, M., 1962. *Capitalism and Freedom*. University of Chicago Press, Chicago, Illinois.

Friedman, M., 1970. The social responsibility of business is to increase its profits. *New York Times Magazine*. September 13.

Gibbard, A., 1973. Manipulation of voting schemes: A general result. *Econometrica* 41, 587–601.

Gillers, H., 2019. Calpers' dilemma: Save the world or make money? *Wall Street Journal*. June 16.

Gould, J. P., Ferguson, C. E., 1980. *Microeconomic Theory*. R. D. Irwin, Homewood, Illinois.

Hanlon, M., Yeung, K., Zuo, L., 2022. Behavioral economics of accounting: A review of archival research on individual decision makers. *Contemporary Accounting Research* 39 (2), 1150–1214.

Hart, O., 1979. On shareholder unanimity in large stock market economies. *Econometrica* 47 (5), 1057–1083.

Hart, O., Zingales, L., 2017. Companies should maximize shareholder welfare not market value. *Journal of Law, Finance, and Accounting* 2 (2), 247–274.

Hayek, F. A., 1944. *The Road to Serfdom*. University of Chicago Press, Chicago, Illinois.

Hobbes, T., 1651. *Leviathan*. Andrew Crooke, London, United Kingdom. Retrieved from https://socialsciences.mcmaster.ca/econ/ugcm/3ll3/hobbes/Leviathan.pdf.

Jensen, M. C., 2001. Value maximization, stakeholder theory, and the corporate objective function. *Journal of Applied Corporate Finance* 14 (3), 8–21.

Jensen, M. C., Meckling, W. H., 1976. Theory of the firm: Managerial behavior, agency costs and ownership structure. *Journal of Financial Economics* 3 (4), 305–360.

Kahneman, D., 2011. *Thinking, Fast and Slow*. Farrar, Straus and Giroux, New York City, New York.

Kessler, A., 2020. To serve the public, seek profits. *Wall Street Journal*. October 11.

Keynes, J. M., 1935. *The General Theory of Employment, Interest, and Money*. Harcourt, Brace and Company, New York City, New York.

Krouse, S., 2018. BlackRock: Companies should have at least two female directors. *Wall Street Journal*. February 2.

Madison, J., 1787. The same subject continued: The union as a safeguard against domestic faction and insurrection. *New York Daily Advertiser*. November 22.

Magill, M., Quinzii, M., 1996. *Theory of Incomplete Markets*. MIT Press, Cambridge, Massachusetts.

Mas-Colell, A., Whinston, M. D., Green, J. R., 1995. *Microeconomic Theory*. Oxford University Press, New York City, New York.

Milgrom, P. R., Roberts, J., 1992. *Economics, Organization, and Management*. Prentice Hall, Englewood Cliffs, New Jersey.

Muller, J., 2002. *The Mind and the Market: Capitalism in Western Thought*. Anchor Books, New York City, New York.

Nordhaus, W. D., 2004. Schumpeterian profits in the American economy: Theory and measurement. Working Paper, National Bureau of Economic Research.

O'Harrow Jr., R., 2000. Drug's U.S. marketer remains elusive. *Washington Post*. October 12.

Peltzman, S., 1976. Toward a more general theory of regulation. *Journal of Law and Economics* 19 (2), 211–240.

Pozen, R. C., 2018. Commentary: The BlackRock letter sets ambitious goals. Here's how CEOs can meet them. *Fortune*. February 9.

ProMarket, 2020. Milton Friedman 50 Years Later. Retrieved from https://www. promarket.org/wp-content/uploads/2020/11/Milton-Friedman-50-years-later-ebook. pdf.

Rainey, L., 1999. Between Mussolini and me. *London Review of Books* 21 (6), 22–25.

Rajan, R. G., 2020. What should corporations do? *The Asset*. October 7.

Roe, M. J., 2018. Stock market short-termism's impact. *University of Pennsylvania Law Review* 167 (1), 71–122.

Rousseau, J.-J., 1750. *Discourse on the Arts and Sciences*. Geneva, Barillot & Fils, Paris, France.

Sandmo, A., 1971. On the theory of the competitive firm under price uncertainty. *American Economic Review* 61 (1), 65–73.

Satterthwaite, M. A., 1975. Strategy-proofness and Arrow's conditions: Existence and correspondence theorems for voting procedures and social welfare functions. *Journal of Economic Theory* 10 (2), 187–217.

Smith, A., 1776. *An Inquiry into the Nature and Causes of the Wealth of Nations*. W. Strahan and T. Cadell, London, United Kingdom.

Sorkin, A. R., 2019. Warren Buffett's case for capitalism. *New York Times*. May 5.

Sreenivasan, G., 2000. What is the general will? *The Philosophical Review* 109 (4), 545–581.

Trentmann, N., 2019. U.K. regulator asks asset owners, managers to consider ESG. *Wall Street Journal*. October 23.

Victor, D., 2019. Disney C.E.O. warns Georgia abortion law would make it 'very difficult' to film in the state. *New York Times*. May 30.

Voltaire, 1736. The worldling. Retrieved from https://mrworldling.com/voltaire-the-worldling-le-mondain/.

Wilson, J. Q., 1995. Capitalism and morality. *The Public Interest* 121, 42–60.

Yermack, D., 2006. Flights of fancy: Corporate jets, CEO perquisites, and inferior shareholder returns. *Journal of Financial Economics* 80 (1), 211–242.

Zimmerman, A., 2004. Costco's dilemma: Be kind to its workers, or Wall Street? *Wall Street Journal*. March 26.

Zingales, L., 2019. Don't trust CEOs who say they don't care about shareholder value anymore. *Washington Post*. August 20.

Index

For the benefit of digital users, indexed terms that span two pages (e.g., 52–53) may, on occasion, appear on only one of those pages.